W9-DCH-081

Revival Power

A Study of Revival in the Book of Acts

By
Ronald J. Fowler

Warner Press, Inc.
Anderson, Indiana

Published by
Warner Press, Inc.
Anderson, Indiana

All scripture passages, unless otherwise indicated, are from the King James Version ©1972 by Thomas Nelson or the Revised Standard Version ©1972 by Thomas Nelson.

Arlo F. Newell, Editor-in-Chief
Dan Harman, Book Editor

Contents

Introduction

The purpose of this book is to explore the Acts of the Apostles for insights into church renewal. Again and again, the body of Christ has experienced periods of spiritual awakening. What began as a small flame of joy behind closed doors as the risen Jesus imparted peace to his disciples has steadily advanced in scope and appreciation. In spite of theological disputes, adverse political opposition, climates of philosophical repudiation, social insensitivities to human worth, and moral and spiritual laxity among believers— Christians have experienced moments of a great empowering of the Spirit, resulting in a revitalized witness and an improved social order.

That is what happened in the awakenings of the sixteenth and seventeenth centuries (1588-1758) through the Protestant and Catholic reformations in Europe. Driven by (1) a hunger for inner assurance; (2) a deep desire to ground the faith in biblical, not human, authority, thus cleansing the Church of abuses and error; and (3) a concern for the total well-being of persons, these principal leaders of the reformation saw themselves not as architects of a new church as much as reformers within the Church.

How indebted the Church is to their vigilant pursuit of truth and righteousness. Their legacy is our strength. Their efforts resulted in the unshackling of the Word of God from its bondage to the Latin language and a heightened awareness of the ministry of the Spirit as teacher and guide.

Later generations would build upon this reformation. With the dawning of the eighteenth century, often referred to as the Age of Reason, the Church experienced a revival as ardent church apologists defended biblical truth against deists and rationalists with their attacks upon miracles.

The Great Awakening of the eighteenth century was characterized by doctrinal clarity, experiential holiness, and evangelistic zeal. This awakening was led by such persons as Jonathan Edwards (1703-1758), John Wesley (1703-1791) who stood with both feet in two continents—England and Colonies of America—Charles Wesley (1707-1788), George Whitefield (1714-1770), John Newton (1725-1807), William Wilberforce (1759-1833), Francis Asbury (1745-1816), and John Woolman (1720-1772), to name a few.

What needs to be remembered is that this renewal which they experienced was widespread. Virtually every aspect of the body of Christ was influenced by it. While each group emphasized different distinctives and differed strongly on several theological fronts, most were consistent in their emphasis upon repentance: the necessity for inward transformation as a precondition for salvation.

The masses were confronted by the claims of the gospel with amazing results. All across America and Europe, the unconverted were reached and reconciled to the body of Christ. The missionary zeal was reborn! The Church was again alive and advancing into all the world!

Dare we to believe that this can happen in our churches, in our land, in our world? Is it possible that what appears in the Acts of the Apostles is really what God invites his body to experience anew: a divine empowerment that results in faith and obedience to his Great Commission? Those who answer that question in the affirmative will want to explore with the author what the Acts of the Apostles may teach us concerning the road to revival.

Acts
Chapter 1:
The Power of a Caring Community

"The highest reward for a person's toil is not what
they get for it, but what they become by it."
—John Ruskin

Caring is the benchmark of the gospel. It was
clearly a distinguishing quality in the life and teaching
of Jesus. As you read the Gospels, you cannot help
but be impressed with Jesus' sensitivity to the needs
of others. No one was outside his discerning eye and
loving concern. All were important to him. Friends,
family, neighbors, children, widows, foreigners,
strangers, sinners, antagonists, enemies, diseased,
demonaic, physically impaired, thieves, seekers of
truth—all found a welcome extended to them by him.

The Gospels could rightly be called "God's Acts of
Compassion." That is what God has done for all. He
has bestowed his love upon us in the person of Jesus
Christ. Everything he did in Christ was "for us." His
coming. His teaching. His serving. His life-style of
servanthood. His humiliation and dying. His pronouncement of forgiveness. His rising from the dead.
His appearings. His impartation of peace. His ascen-

sion. His enthronement. His descent as Paraclete. These were all motivated by a commitment to love.

No one should be surprised to open the Book of Acts and discover that its author, Luke, is motivated by what possessed Jesus—the need for caring. This need is within every person. It is a vital part of our *imago dei*. It is a given. Everyone possesses it. It is a major part of what adds distinction to our being. For we are made in the image of God, and "God is love" (1 John 4:8). Yet, everyone finds it much easier to express this need in relationship to the outer person than they do in relationship to the inner person. Everyone, that is, except those who understand the clear teachings of Scripture: "For what will it profit a man, if he gains the whole world and forfeits his life?" (Matthew 16:26).

Something more important than survival is implied by this. Human responsibility and destiny are at stake. These needs are not antithetical to other needs. The need for bread is as important to the body as the need for the Word is to the spirit of a person. As a physician, Luke was committed to both. But in Acts 1:1, Luke was obviously caught up in meeting the needs of Theophilus for (1) a complete factual and chronological account of all "Jesus began to do and teach" from the moment of Gabriel's glad tidings (Luke 1:26) to the moment of the disciples' joyful gaze upon the ascension of Jesus (Acts 1:2); and (2) for an intellectual basis for his faith.

There are two observations worth noting. First, the motive behind God's dealings with us was a genuine concern for our total wellbeing. As noted earlier, this is what prompted Jesus to "go about doing good." He cared for people—especially their need for faith.

2

Luke was following in his steps. He rightly understood that until a person is inwardly committed to meeting another's need, the circle of God's love would remain incomplete. Completing that circle is the task of every Christian. A passion for reaching people for Christ can be born and sustained only in a caring heart. Yet, history declares with amazing consistency that caring is the most effective route to conviction. For whatever the means by which one seeks to make a witness known, if it is void of caring it becomes what Paul called "sounding brass and tinkling cymbal." It profits nothing! (1 Corinthians 13:1-2). Believers are not called to be performers. They are called to be witnesses. More will be said about this later. As the body of Christ gives itself to the ministry of intercession and intervention, God has always honored its labor.

Second, throughout the history of spiritual awakenings, God has provided the Church with persons capable of translating its convictions into the language of the people. No movement can endure without intellectual credibility. Luke's sensible, caring ministry, and that of all Christian scholars, writers, and teachers, is what gives depth and duration to the Christian witness. Revivals cannot be sustained by dynamic worship experiences alone. Revivals are fanned by learning experiences that allow persons to grapple with the meanings and implications of faith. Only through such a process are we likely to find a place where we can stand with integrity and contagion. A heart-warming experience must eventually rely on a clear head!

This is precisely what you see in the history of revivals and in the Book of Acts. A zeal for missions, a passion for truth, and a celebrative response were all indispensible aspects of the ministry of the Spirit in the Church. Any separation of these coordinates is tantamount to lessening the impact of the others. Each is interdependent on the other. None represents a human orchestration, but a genuine experience of God as the living Word and indwelling Spirit.

Such an experience of God is truly a "lived moment"—a time in which human consciousness is able to lay hold, to grasp, to see with discernment some aspect of God's self-disclosure which was previously veiled to the mind. These "moments" occur in worship, in study, in service, in comtemplation. They are essential for enabling a person to be renewed at all levels—mind and heart, physical and spiritual. Efforts must be resisted to create an imbalance between knowing God with the mind and knowing God with the heart. It is obvious from Luke's writing that he emphasized neither to the exclusion of the other. He exhorts Theophilius to exercise his privilege of knowing his faith as both fact and feeling.

What are some of those "factual" foundations upon which the faith rests? Luke cites several.

First, the Christian faith rests on the assurance that in Jesus of Nazareth God has fulfilled his promise to Israel of the coming Messiah.

He is the "author and finisher of our faith" (Hebrews 12:2). Jesus is our authority for interpreting the mission and ministry of God. Luke stresses this point by stating from the onset that what he is passing on is nothing more than what Jesus did and taught (Acts 1:1). He is the locus of God's activity. In him and through him all that God set out to do and say to his vessels of clay was accomplished. Jesus

4

stands as "first and last." There does not exist apart from him any significant revelation of God or a way by which one can approach God. Jesus is it. No further revelation for substantiating the truth about God's dealings with humankind and humankind's response to God are necessary. Jesus did not fail to reveal or declare anything essential to salvation and service. He is our way to truth. On this you can rely.

Next, Luke suggests that the Christian faith rests on the assurance that Jesus is Lord.

If you should ask, What qualified Jesus to give instructions to the Apostles just prior to his ascension? the answer lies in verse 3: "He presented himself alive." That is God's answer to those who doubt what the Bible declares concerning Jesus. The conquest of his suffering was no human achievement. No amount of misinformation by the Sanhedrin could nullify for Luke the truthfulness of what the apostles saw outside of Bethany (Luke 24:50). What they saw going up on a cloud, they had touched and handled and looked upon. It was Jesus, alive!

Though other biblical writers will present more evidence, Luke was convinced that Jesus' conquest of sin and death, time and space was sufficient for substantiating the claim of his lordship. The subsequent rending of the veil from top to bottom in the Temple upon his death providing access to God, was more than coincidental. His emancipation from the tomb could not have been effected by his followers. They were too afraid and filled with remorse to do so. His appearances to Mary Magdalene at the tomb, to two men on the road to Emmaus, to Peter in Jerusalem, to the ten disciples in the Upper Room, and finally to the eleven disciples at Bethany could not have been concocted. Besides, no lie can endure forever. All evidence points in the direction of corroboration of all biblical witnesses. Jesus is alive because Jesus is Lord!

Also, Luke asserts that the assurance of the Christian faith rests on the conviction that the kingdom of God has come.

If Jesus is Lord, as the Church staunchly affirms, then the kingdom of God has come to all. At least, this is Luke's contention. He takes pain to stress to Theophilus that Jesus, during the forty days prior to his ascension, confined himself exclusively to one topic: the kingdom of God. The exact content of what he shared is not mentioned. What is alluded to is (1) the chief principles of the Kingdom, (2) the chief promise of the Kingdom, (3) the chief preoccupation of the Kingdom, and (4) the chief purpose of the Kingdom, and (5) the chief priority of the Kingdom.

The Chief Principles

Let's examine each. The chief principles of the kingdom of God are obedience and anticipation. A believer derives his or her success from faithfulness, not charisma or coersion. Luke passes on an injunction Jesus issued before his departure—wait (Acts 1:4). Our power comes not from impulsive leaping as the Devil invited Jesus to do (Luke 4:9-10), but from a diligent waiting for divine directions. How much more effective would the church be if her activities were the out growth of a prayer convocation or scriptural commandment rather than a "band wagon" phenomenon. There can be no neutrality when God speaks to his church. All are called to comply. It was this principle of unity that would enable the Holy Spirit to use ordinary people to overcome seemingly impossible odds.

Anticipation was also a key principle of the Kingdom. The disciples were not instructed to expect failure. In light of Jesus' victory, he sought to ready their minds to receive what God wanted to bestow upon them. God is a rewarder of those who seek him. Believers can anticipate God's doing what he has promised to do. Even when many abuse this principle and seek to turn God into a Santa Claus who dispenses whatever is requested, care must be taken not to create an opposite mistake of nurturing low expectations.

In all too many quarters of the Church, believers are suffering from under-confidence in God's power to do what he has promised. How we need to recapture a vision of what Paul wrote to the Thessalonians: "Faithful is he that calleth you, who also will do it." Underscore that last phrase: "who also will do it." Those words inspire confidence to anticipate God doing what he has promised.

Abraham is a prime example of someone who lived with high expectations. He was "fully persuaded that, what he had promised, he was able also to perform" (Rom. 4:21). Is it too much to anticipate revival? Is it too much to anticipate what God is wanting to do if we are willing to obey? Here is a proper focus for the Church—the promises of God. With this vision, the Church has pulled down strongholds and advanced the kingdom of God.

The Chief Promise

The chief promise of the Kingdom is for believers to be "baptized with the Holy Spirit" (Acts 1:5). God's mission in the world depends primarily on his empowerment. This is a basic teaching of Scripture. God is depicted by Isaiah as a zealous lover who is wholly committed to bring to pass the promised Messiah and his attendant kingdom of justice and righteousness (Isaiah 9:7).

Underscore these words in that text: "The zeal of the Lord will perform this." God is the Christian's enabler. This metaphor of baptism is employed to stress commitment, belonging, submission, a kind of singularity of focus that results in the pursuit of newness of life. The Christian experience is not a divine absorption of what is human, thus annihilating human freedom and personality. Baptism points the believer to a new source of dependency in which all that is human is yielded to God. Thus, all that is divine is made available to the believer.

Baptism symbolizes a two-fold blessing: a gift of love in response to a greater gift of love. This greater gift is God's indwelling presence without which the human experience of God is limited to effects, not empowerment. What characterizes the kingdom of God, according to the Apostle Paul, is not the "spirit of timidity but a spirit of power and love and self-control" (2 Timothy 1:7). This gives added significance to God's exhortation to "be strong" throughout Scripture. The real question is not what makes a person strong, but who.

This precious truth, the baptism of the Spirit, is not an option. It is God's gift of adequacy for spiritual growth and ministry. Those who are serious about their commitment will, to borrow a Pauline expression, "stir-up," or "fan" God's ministry gifts through study and deployment (verse 6). Believers are endowed by God. Inferiority, fear, and low self-esteem are symptoms of an inadequate understanding of the redeemed self. Kingdom people ae not invincible primates. They are armed with the best life can offer—the gift of Christ. That, my friend, is the "hope of glory" (Colossians 1:27).

The Chief Preoccupation

The chief preoccupation of the Kingdom is not with the time or date of God's dealings with the world. This kind of concern leads too easily to a religion of signism. John the Baptist took note of the effects this had on the religious leaders of his day. They were more concern with loving themselves than with loving God (Matthew 3:7-10). Avoiding God's wrath was more important than advancing his righteousness. They lacked spiritual depth because they lacked spiritual sincerity.

This is the danger of a religion of signism. It focuses not on what is central to God (behavior and ministry), but what is or is not expedient for the moment. Nothing has hindered the cause of Christ more than this monstrous temptation of succumbing to expediency. God's will is the believer's authority, not signs that depend so heavily upon subjective appraisals. The kingdom of God is a kingdom ruled by God's Word and Spirit. Anything less is too capricious to serve as a guide to faith.

The Chief Purpose

The chief purpose of the Kingdom is to restore power to persons. The disciples had been thinking politically. Like many, they assumed from their early religious training that the Messiah would re-establish a kingdom patterned after David's regime. This Kingdom would be militarily strong, economically independent, socially stable, culturally rich, religiously devout, and morally responsible.

In actuality, the disciples were victims of idealism—glorification of the past. In contrast to other nations, Israel under David was a mini-paradise. Things were better than in the surrounding nations. Israel's problems in later centuries only served to deepen the hunger for a return of the "good old days." But God's mission was not just to make people better, but to make a better people through a transformation of the heart.

Here is the key to a better environment. Turn people away from their sins and you bring to a halt the primal cause of personal debilitation and relational alienation, and social deterioration. In effect, you recreate the community when the person is reborn and renewed in mind.

Evangelicals have long emphasized the former to the exclusion of the latter. This they did while largely ignorant of their roots. For history documents well the "activism" of such persons as John Wesley. He could not conceive of any holiness that did not result in a transformation of social behavior. Nevertheless, many nonevangelicals have erred in equating social improvements with spiritual authenticity.

How skilled the Devil was to suggest to Jesus that the way to become revered is to give people what they hunger for most—bread. Jesus avoided this deceptive trap, and so must the body of Christ. Bread without obedience does not lead to the empowerment of the inner self. Obedience without bread does not lead to the empowerment of others. Holiness and social concerns are wedded to each other. To paraphrase a popular statement: And what God has joined together, the body of Christ dare not put asunder!

Power is what characterizes the kingdom of God. A new adequacy for living and serving is made available for all believers to draw upon. In Christ, a person is rescued from a state of powerlessness. New options are possible. New opportunities are achieveable. Kingdom people can now "walk," pursue a lifestyle of "peace on earth, and good will among men." This is surely an indication that the kingdom of God is present in power, even though its glory is not wholly present at any one time. This is God's promise for the future. The experience of this future glory is the desire of every believer.

The Chief Priority

The chief priority of the Kingdom of God is prayer. Cultivating an inner relationship with God is essential to the total life of a person. Unity of heart can be achieved only through a process of communication in which a person opens the self for dialogue with God.

God uses a variety of ways to make himself known. Meditation and prayer are powerful means for developing a consciousness of the Lord's presence. It is out of this heightened awareness that understanding flows. That is the key—understanding, meaning. For if the contemplative life led only to a sensation, it would leave the core of the self unchanged. Prayer is God's way of adjusting the aperture of heart and mind to a common dimension so that what flows into one flows into the other. Both aspects of the self grip and hold something in common.

Perhaps we can better understand why prayer results in unity of being. It brings about an honest flow of feelings and thoughts for God's examination and clarification. A search for light! Yet, those who wait in prayer have reported a heightened sense of awareness, a fluidity of insights, a creativity that resembles a geyser of truths rushing upward into the mind.

Prayer is not passivity. Speaking the truth is only one aspect of prayer. Discerning the truth requires the subduing of distractions, the enlarging of what is really important. The disciples of Jesus were in danger of enlarging what was good—beholding the ascending Jesus—out of proportion to what was God's will: witnessing.

The Church faces this constant menace in the priority she gives to her activities. What is really important often goes lacking because so many in God's work force are preoccupied with lesser things. A kind of tyranny of the lesser is draining resources, both human and economical, from a rightful investment into more critical and demanding tasks. There will always be a need for God to send messengers to the body of Christ whose sole task is to refocus the commitment of believers.

Luke also attests to the fact that the assurance of the Christian faith rests on the conviction that the reign of evil cannot prevail in general or persist unexposed in the Church. Evil is the archenemy of God's people. No one needs to explain its origin to comprehend its reality. Who among the disciples of Jesus understood the deceptive nature of evil more than Peter? He knew from experience the inability of a person to control nature's pull toward transgression alone.

His standing in Acts 1:15 is significant. It points to the obvious stature he has achieved in the eyes of this young fellowship. It also implies that the disciples were compassionate in their dealings with one another. For the greatest evil a church can experience is a failure to forgive. Simon is now doing what Jesus had commanded him to do—feed his sheep (John 21:15-17). But for one who previously placed an inordinate confidence in his understanding, Simon Peter demonstrates tremendous growth in maturity. He is not perfect, but he learned to accept the authority of God's *Word*.

Simon Peter cites two references in the Psalms that described the tragic circumstances that evolved upon Judas. This raises an interesting question. Was Judas unable not to do what he did—betray Jesus? Hardly! Scripture is truth, and truth implies a divine necessity; what it declares must come to pass. But Scripture does not selectively impose a particular role on any. It forecasts events because its author is omniscience. It rightly describes the kind of person who will become an agent of evil or instrument of good. But it does not push either role upon anyone. Scripture announces the kind of call many will hear, but few choose to answer whether the call be to do good, or to do evil. Judas, so to speak, got aboard a train that transported him to a region of darkness he was unprepared to cope with. That is the nature of evil. It baits one to do something for which the doer will be doomed for doing. Evil knows no mercy.

C. S. Lewis, in his book *Till We Have Faces*, describes a dialogue between the King and his counselor, Fox. In order to advert a calamity that was to fall upon the nation, it was decided that a Great Offering, a human sacrifice, would need to made to appease the gods. Fox proceeds to share with the king that in his homeland a similar incident had taken place, but with disastrous results:

> "Master," said the Fox, "I had not finished telling you. It is very true that a Greek king sacrificed his own daughter. But afterwards his wife murdered him, and his son murdered the wife, and Those Below drove the son mad." At this the King scratched his head and looked very blank. "That's just like the gods," he muttered. "Drive you to do a thing and then punish you for doing it"(*Till We Have Faces*, Harvest Books, N.Y., 1956, p. 58).

Judas was also deceived by "Those Below." Evil by its very nature deprives one of peace, and denies one the enjoyment of what is gained by evil means. Consider the lesson of history. Ahab possessed Naboth's vineyard, but he never got to enjoy the grapes that grew there. David possessed a child through adultery, but he likewise never got to enjoy his childhood. Judas purchased a field with blood money. No act was more heinous. But he never got to enjoy what he obtained through evil means. Truth may be mocked. But in the end, truth will be vindicated.

There is one more thing needing to be set forth regarding evil. Sin is essentially harmful. It leaves scars upon the spirits of those most affected by a person's fall. But a preoccupation with our wounds only limits our vision of God's resourcefulness.

Judas was a gifted manager of money. He understood well the miracle of multiplication. That was his specialty—getting the most with the least. Judas' greed, however, led him to cease practicing the discipline of denial. He saw before any of the other disciples that Jesus was going to die. He failed to comprehend the Master's word concerning his resurrection. He saw an end without a beginning.

He threw away eternal life for momentary pleasure. Judas in the end would fail to practice good economics. His investment policy was doomed to fail.

There was obvious hurt, disappointment, and perhaps anger concerning what Judas did. What you do not see is a "camp out" on Judas. These believers turned the corner and directed their energies toward something constructive. Everyone is important. No one is indispensible, except Jesus.

In order to carry out the Master's commission to the Jews, the disciples knew that their claim to be the new Israel would lack credibility if their leadership composition was less than twelve. There was nothing sacred about twelve. But in the minds of the Jews in Jerusalem, there was something very special about that number. Twelve tribes constituted the nation. Twelve Apostles would constitute the true people of God. Had not even Jesus declared that his disciples would "sit on thrones judging the twelve tribes of Israel" (Luke 22:30)? Of course. These disciples

15

believed in honoring those traditions that gave meaning to the lives of those they served.

One has to be impressed with God's bullpen. One leader falls. Another is prepared to assume his place. That will always be. God is not without his "relief" specialists. Israel did not have a ready supply of gapmen. But God has always raised up a servant to fulfill his will. Matthias was chosen. His qualifications were evaluated closely. His commitment was proven. His calling was accepted. His appointment was ratified. That's not bad for a young church in its first attempt to fill a leadership position. Can the body of Christ learn something from this procedure?

Acts
Chapter 2:
The Power of an Anointed Community

"Important as thinking is, the deepest truth
appears not in ideas but in events."
—Elton Trueblood

There were few events in the life of Israel more important than Pentecost. This national celebration had become international in scope due to centuries of dispersions and migrations. Pentecost was a harvest festival originally instituted to celebrate God's blessings upon the nation's barley and wheat crops. This tradition is well detailed in Exodus 23:16; Leviticus 23:17-22; and Numbers 28:26-31.

Later Judaism would shift the focus of this tradition to the instituting of the Law at Mount Sinai. This was a way of remembering and reaffirming the nation's commitment to the covenant of law. Israel's dark night of bondage convinced her leaders of the necessity of a national pledge of obedience to God's Word as contained in the Torah.

The early Christian community looked upon what happened at Pentecost as a divine anointing characteristic of the Spirit's coming upon certain called persons in Israel's past (1 Samuel 10:6ff.) And, perhaps more importantly, this anointing of the personal and corporate life of God's people represented the continued ministry of Jesus. He was no longer just "with" them. He was now "in" them as he had promised (John 14:17). Jesus was manifesting himself through his new body, the Church, as God had tabernacled in the person of Jesus.

The Spirit is what gives the body of Christ its dynamism and contagion. No one in the Upper Room was surprised by what the Spirit enabled them to do. The surprise was found in those outsiders for whom the news about Jesus' resurrection-ascension was largely unknown. Those who were in the Upper Room were anticipating the promised anointing of the Spirit. Everything depended upon it. They knew themselves as being weak clay apart from the potter's hands. But with God's presence came God's power and glory. This was their need and joy. Thus, they waited for God's enabling moment.

In Acts 2:1, Luke states, "They were all with one accord in one place." Togetherness is not necessarily a phenomenon of the Spirit. Koinonia or fellowship is. But not togetherness. Nothing has demonstrated more unity than the forces of evil. Those who conspired against Jesus were together.

This verse does reveal a togetherness that goes beyond a common purpose or lineage. Their togetherness came as a result of a kindred experience that profoundly affected a change in their identity and reason for being. Each was lit from within by the experience of truth. They found in Jesus the long-awaited Christ, the Savior of the world.

Here lies one of the distinctives of this community.

18

Unlike its Jewish counterpart, from which their earliest experiences of God were derived, these believers knew themselves as belonging to one another. They function more like a family than a organization. Mutuality is what characterizes their interaction. All are concerned about all. Did not Jesus instruct the disciples that such love would have power to convince others of identification with him (John 13:34)? Could this account for the remarkable impact this community had upon their environment? Undoubtedly! Mutuality gives a community strength and authority.

It must be kept in mind that these disciples were under orders. Jesus had commanded them to wait. That order was nonnegotiable. By giving themselves unreservedly to what Jesus said, they found a common place to stand. What good is a community without a center. If there is no center, there is no circumference. In such a *normless* community, there can be no fire to inspire a life of selfless devotion.

Such a community will not produce any fanatics, persons who are prepared to die for what they believe. Without a transcendant reference to which all become subordinate, no decisive progress is possible. But here were believers who knew why they were in Jerusalem. They knew what their immediate and long range assignments were. They had a "big picture" perspective to guide them. They shared a common experience of God. They were prepared for a life of sacrifice. They lived for something bigger than personal happiness. They were living for the One who died for them. It is little wonder that they experienced an abundant life.

Having a sense of belonging and common commitment seem to be a precondition for a revival of the Spirit in the life of the Church. This is the horse that pulls the wagon of service. To approach service without having achieved a sense of togetherness only leads to unclear goals, politicized agendas, competitive strategies, wasted efforts, and disenchanted followers.

The condition of the wood determines its kindling potential. If that is so, this community in Acts 2 was indeed ready for the fire of God's presence to fall upon her. And it did!

Let us examine the impact of this anointing upon (1) the gathered community of faith, (2) the scattered community of Israel, (3) the preaching of Peter, and (4) the newly constitued church.

The Gathered Community

It goes without saying that Pentecost was an empowering experience. Under the power of the Spirit, God utilized a great moment in Israel's national life as the setting for unveiling his climactic promise—to tabernacle with and within his people.

Israel did not take the presence of God lightly. It represented the ultimate in human experience of which so few had been privileged to know intimately. To experience God's presence was to enjoy a privileged status, a communal conferral of respect. Moses was such a person. The glory of God's presence had overshadowed him. Its effects were substantive and contagious.

In his descent from Mount Sinai, he bore in his hands the fruit of God's visitation—two tablets of stone. They would contain God's mandates for his people. Israel was to be a nation characterized by obedience to God's revealed will. Even though Israel's prophets would constantly remind her of the peril of neglecting God's unconditional will, it would fall their lot to be casted often as a "troubler of Israel."

Their voice, however, while consistently ignored, was not lifted up in vain. There were those who heard and believed. There were those who accepted and acknowledged in their social behavior the precepts contained in God's Word. They would become a remnant in time. They would survive many fires of violence heaped upon them. (See Hebrews 11:33ff.) Their faith was in God's Word, the essential nature of which was obligatory, a command with promise.

No revival is possible without such persons of steel minds and velvet hearts. They were persuaded by God. He was their "light and salvation." He was their strength to oppose evil and advance good. They believed; therefore they were prepared to withstand any evil for what they knew to be God's will.

Every age needs such persons. Every age is beset by a cacaphony of sounds as confusing as the event surrounding the tower of Babel: deism with its alienation of God from the historical order and its idyllic optimism of human perfectionism; relativism with its denial of moral absolutes as having their genesis in God rather than human expedience or social mores; socialism with its false assumptions regarding human nature—its tendency to absolve persons of responsibilities for their behavior; religious eclecticism that seeks to structure a vibrant religious experience out of an integration of nonbiblical premises. These and other idioms have long been at war with God's decla-

21

ration of good and evil, truth and error. Every age is pushed by error to the brink of social anarchy and spiritual degeneracy by the forces of evil.

God has a stake in this world. It is his! He is prepared to equip his people to "occupy," or take control over, the kingdom of truth. For the Church is God's repository of truth.

An openness to truth, a hunger for truth, a commitment to disseminate and proclaim truth has always paved the way for great awakenings in the world. This hunger was deep. It is not surprising, then, that the manifestation of the presence of God was so profound. What happened to the disciples by the divine agents of wind and fire, the Holy Spirit and truth, attested to the continuity between Sinai and Jerusalem.

The latter was the fulfillment of the former. The written law had completed its intention—to prepare a people for service. True vines. True children of Abraham. True Israel. These descriptors are reminders that what Israel had failed to accomplished under the Law, God was indeed bringing to pass under Jesus. The emphasis in Acts 2 is upon following through on one's commitment to God—service.

These believers in Acts 2 were like bushes aflame. The Word of the Lord was indeed consuming. They could not contain it because it was a word for others. It belonged not to its possessors. It rightfully belonged to those who had not accepted its invitation of forgiveness and summons to service.

When viewed from this perspective, the phenomenon of Pentecost was and is the seed of revival. For it issues (1) a divine call to consider the "wonderful works of God" as manifested in Jesus as foundational for fellowship with him and service in the world, and (2) it provides a historical benchmark for the fulfillment of God's promise to establish for his use a people whose hearts serve as the habitation of his Spirit. This is the genius of Pentecost.

It is not the birthday of the Church, but rather a climactic moment in God's work of expanding and empowering his chosen people! Pentecost changes the way the people of God look upon their mission. The Church is a community of servants. All are enabled to share fully in the realization of God's mission. Mission belongs not to a certain segment of the Church. The Church is mission. And, missions is why the Church exists!

The Scattered Community

There was a notable impact of Pentecost upon those who shared the religious heritage of the disciples. What gives this event significance was the loyalty in which so many outside Jerusalem and Israel held it.

Like most celebrations, Pentecost served as a time of ingathering. Old acquaintances were renewed. A sense of nationhood was rekindled. The future was impregnated with a hope borrowed from the chapters of their glorious past. What quality was most in evidence in this crowd of pilgrim people? It was primarily masculine in gender, international in dialect, and devoted in their practice of reverence for God. This last characteristic explains why they were so quick to respond to Peter's preaching. Sincerity provides truth with an immediate access to the center of the self.

Here was an audience whose field was well prepared for the seed of truth.

Pentecost reveals the concern of God. The wonder of this event is that it demonstrates not only the desire of people to know God, but God's great passion for including in his kingdom all who are strangers to his covenant of love. God is surely the "hound of heaven." He is seeking those who are searching for him. They do not find him as much as he finds them.

There is a sense in which those "devout men" gathered in Jerusalem were found—apprehended. For the word of the Lord, spoken in the language of their comprehension, was attended with power. It was as though a fellow countryman had suddenly surfaced in that crowd. Each could hear the story of God's wonderful works. How amazing. They spoke without the aid of interpreters.

How could such a group of persons, with an obvious touch of commonality upon them, achieve such remarkable linguistic clarity? How? That was their question. They sought an explanation for the phenomenon itself. There could be no doubt what they were hearing was (1) miraculously conveyed and (2) wholly consistent with the story of God's mighty acts in history.

No fault was found with the content of what they heard. They were obviously familiar with the message. It in itself did not set forth any new claims. Whatever they heard was not new or controversial. They stood on familiar ground. A sense of kinship became evident by the telling of something they could hold in common.

How is that possible? What does this activity mean? Peter will address these concerns. Suffice it for now to observe that Pentecost constituted the community of faith around the habitation of Spirit whose function it is to minister the word of Jesus to others, and to gather into one fold all the redeemed of the Lord. This objective was achieved on Pentecost. The family of God is indeed one family.

The Preaching of Peter

Pentecost had a profound affect upon Peter. He, too, had occupied the same experience of those who were amazed and yet confused as to the meaning of a divine phenomenon. He, too, had stood on the edge of uncertainty. He knew from experience the immobilizing effects created by doubt. He was no stranger to ambivalence—wanting to believe, but uneasy about embracing that which the mind is not fully persuaded. Peter accepts the challenge to provide an explanation for this divine-initiated happening.

Pentecost provided the historical framework for understanding God's pursuit of salvation. Before Pentecost, the story of Israel's election and responsibility always stopped with a certain looking forward to the coming of the Messiah. Pentecost opened the window of awareness, thus enabling the "pure in heart to see God." The great anticipation was over. The great Emancipator had come. The Comforter had arrived to increase the Emancipator's reign by expanding the realms in which the emancipated honor God through Spirit and truth!

Far from adding to the religious confusion of contradicting theologies, Pentecost was a summons to hear and understand God the living Word—Jesus.

He gives the highest meaning to the acts of God in history.

Meaning is the undercurrent that drives the Church. God is not the author of confusion. He gives order. He creates light. His mission is to overcome darkness.

There are always skeptics in every crowd. They were there on Pentecost. While it is clear that some doubted the religious authenticity of what was taking place on Pentecost, there were honest, sincere seekers of truth. Peter led the way in responding to both groups.

First, Peter believed in the authority of Scripture. Pentecost revealed the trustworthiness of the word of God as normative and foundational for the people of God. In this he was confident: (1) Christian experience was to be judged or tested by Scripture, and (2) the ministry of the Church was empowered by the presence of Jesus in the person of the Spirit.

Peter, who spoke with the consent of the Eleven, invited the total gathering to consider what transpired in light of scripture. Two important considerations provide tremendous light for ascertaining the "meaning" of what happened on Pentecost.

Peter immediately linked what was then happening with what was promised to happen in the days of Joel. Truth, you see, is the foundation for experience. Joel had spoken of the "last days," an obvious reference to the days of the Messiah, which would culminate in an outpouring of the Spirit upon the people of God (Acts 2:16, also compare, Joel 2:28ff.).

For Peter, this act of corporate prophesying had its origin in God's intention, not in some phenomenon of nature. Scripture foretold it. Therefore, nothing could prevent it. Not linguistic barriers. Not lack of involvement by established religious leaders. God would keep his promise. At Pentecost, God had kept his promise. Of this Peter was convinced. "This is that," says Peter (2:16). Peter spoke as one who was wholly persuaded by the truth he proclaimed. Conviction begets confidence. Conviction has always led and preceded spiritual reforms. The reform under Ezra was largely successful because of its insistence upon faithfulness to the Law.

Ezra has been credited with reviving the study and public reading of the Law. His efforts were so effective that the returning exiles became known as a "people of the book." God's people are not bookish. They do not worship Scripture.

Their worship and conduct are evaluated in light of scripture. This is what Peter is stressing. Scripture, not wine—nor may we say tradition, or human experiences, or philosophical discourse, or sociological pattern—is a Christian's basis of authority. Conviction focuses attention not on the person but on the credibility of what is said. In an age where style is more important than substance, every Christian needs to exercise confidence in God's Word to confirm the ministry of the Spirit.

Prophecy, as it happened on Pentecost, was indicative of the ministry of the Spirit. Peter quotes from that passage in Joel 2 which spans the time between the two comings of Jesus: His first coming as Messiah and His second coming in Judgment. The one has been fulfilled: "This *is* that (italics mine). In other words, what was promised ("that") is! A new age has begun.

Yet, it prefigures an age that is yet to be. Thus, the outpouring of the Spirit represents an inauguration, a commencement of an inner reign for which past ceremonial rituals were but a sign. Thus, Pentecost was not interpreted as something denouncing the past, but the movement of God in bringing forth the reality for which the past looked with longing.

Next, Peter summoned to the witness stand none other than David, who is described as both "patriarch" and "prophet" (2:29, 30). These twin roles were stressed to demonstrate the completeness of the historical witness to the life and ministry of Jesus. Pentecost was the launching of God's call to salvation through faith in Jesus. This is the main point in Peter's response to the question, "What meaneth this?" (2:12). Pentecost is a call to faith in Jesus as both the Son of man and Son of God.

As the Son of God, his approval was given by God, not bestowed by humans. In fact, human assessments of Jesus only revealed the pitiful spiritual state of the nation and world. Contemporaries of Jesus suffered from a spiritual blindness. The obvious was seen by those whose religious backgrounds were most uninformed (Roman Centurion, Samaritan woman, publican, two blind men, children, a thief). This in itself was a sad commentary on the spiritual maturity of the religious life of his day. The power that manifested itself through Jesus left no area of human existence untouched. All realms of existence were subject to his power. Yet, this array of divine enactments was greeted with cynicism and hostility. Who can forget those chilling words of John: "His own people received him not" (John 1:11)?

Nevertheless, Peter argued that God's plans are not dictated by human acceptance or societal receptivity. The plan of God unfolds according to his exacting

Word, that which has the capacity for self-determination and flawless perception of what is needed to accomplish what God wills. Human opposition was foreseen. Human rebellion was known in advance. God need not dishonor human freedom to accomplish his will. He need not turn persons into objects in order to manipulate their actions.

God has demonstrated love for the world by setting aside his divine prerogatives and becoming sin for us. That was the purpose of his divine deliverance over into the hands of the wicked. God gave the ultimate gift, himself, as the atonement for sin. Jesus was not forced to go to Calvary. He chose to accept and fulfill God's plan of redemption.

We must never think of Jesus as a misguided enthusiast or befuddled moralist or a weak sentimentalist. Jesus died not because of weakness, but because of strength. He possessed the strength to love God with all that he had.

What happened to Jesus must be laid at the feet of those who crucified him. Human actions are never forced. They are products of human decisions. Perhaps the greatest decision any person will make concerns how he or she will relate to who Jesus is.

One thing is unmistakably clear: Jesus' death clearly confirms his humanity. He died. All acknowledge that. Spirits do not die; people do. His death was indeed a perfect sacrifice for sin. For he was tempted, but he sinned not.

The empty tomb stands as a sign of God's vindication of his suffering servant: a vindication that David had foretold with much anticipatory joy.

For the resurrection of Jesus was seen as the fulfillment of David's hope of life after death (Acts 2:26,

27). The conquest of death was a Davidic hope. The vanquishing of this mortal enemy of death, long feared and believed invincible, was seen by David as an accomplished fact centuries before it happened. Not only would death be unable to hold the body of the Messiah, but death was powerless to produce any natural consequences of decay on the body of Jesus. As the Son of God, Jesus would prevail over sin and death.

This is what qualified Peter to call David a "prophet." What he declared under the inspiration of God came to pass. God had given David an "oath" (verse 30). Thus, David took God at his word. He believed that not even death could overcome a divine promise. Through hope, David became an heir of the new age.

Next, there is the witness of the disciples. Verse 32 reveals more than a confession of faith. What began as a small consideration first posed by a group of women was soon affirmed by direct experience. Jesus was seen and heard by them. That fact they could declare on the authority of experience. What they believed was formulated out of a lived moment. Any denial of their claim must in some way first prove that these disciples were deluded or demonic. Neither claim is very tenable.

Experience has provided a context in which the meanings of Scripture give clarity to faith. The resurrection and ascension of Jesus were sensory experiences. The pouring out of the Holy Spirit was an enabling experience. He who was "by the right hand of God" (verse 33) was functioning in his office as Savior, distributing to His followers the key to his life and ministry—the presence of the Spirit. Peter quotes from Psalm 110:1 to confirm the fact that Pentecost is not the result of something a revered person such as David had done. David's tomb is yet closed. He could not, as some doubtless thought, be responsible for sending the Spirit upon the followers of Jesus.

Pentecost is clearly a result of a victory that was planned by God and consummated by Jesus. David's role is limited to that of an ancient witness. If David's faith experience was considered authoritative, how much more the experience of those who physically saw Jesus alive and ascending back to glory?

Last, there is the witness of changed lives. Make no mistake about it, Peter was preaching for a decision. He was no entertainer. The main business of the gospel is to reconcile people to God. Having stated the case for Jesus' resurrection and ascension, Peter presses home the bottom-line concern of the gospel: that is, that Jesus is what Scripture and the disciples said He is. Jesus is both God and Savior.

Salt has a purpose. It is not to be decorative or kept in a salt container. Its purpose is to enrich and enable the lives of others. As Christians across the centuries have dedicated themselves to the telling and retelling of this historically conditioned truth, persons have experienced a genuine conviction of heart.

A changed life is still a powerful testimony of the gospel's efficacy. As Peter simply set forth what happened to Jesus, he engaged in the prophetic ministry of truth-telling. Like every anointed preacher, he did not seek to punish his audience by stirring up guilt feelings. He shared with them the truth about their corporate response, as members of a historic community, to Jesus. The work of the Crucifixion was

31

not simply the deed of a few, but a decision that had a corporate consensus. That is what Peter wanted the diaspora to realize. All—no exclusions—were guilty of His death. For he was crucified by sin.

Sincere people do not fight the truth. They bow to its sovereignty. They submit to its lead and summons. They acknowledge a willingness to change directions.

"What shall we do?" was the cry that rang out from these humble quarters (verse 37). That cry has sounded in underdeveloped villages and overcrowded cities. From prison cells to public halls, penitent worshipers have cried out to God for the remission of sin. Such a cry has legitmacy. The only remedy for sin is reconciliation with God. That is possible through faith in Jesus Christ.

The Father of our Lord Jesus Christ has taken the initiative to save all who call upon the name of the Lord" (Acts 2:39). Compare this with Joel 2:32. All means all. This extravagant love is based on an ancient promise God made to all through the patriarchs and prophets. From the beginning, God has pursued the creation of a family characterized by faith. From the beginning of Israel's existence, God has sustained this creative enterprise with unmerited kindness. His mercies were seen as confirmation of his commitment to what he had promised. Israel was a beloved nation. We are all a beloved people. What should constitute a proper response to God's love?

Peter states a two-fold response: repentance and baptism. Repentance is a condition of the heart. It involves contrition, which is a genuine regret for pursuing a path known to be wrong. A sign of that contrition becomes a willingness to abandon that which dishonors God's will. A changed life becomes directly attributed to a change in direction. Repentance is not just the substitution of new rule for old one. It speaks to a deeper restructuring of the self around a new Master—Jesus Christ. Baptism is a form of a death-life proposition.

It signifies a life-style of self-denial. By this is not meant the deprivation of the self, but a purging process whereby the self is renewed, strengthened, and cleansed through the daily exercise of the denial of evil.

Baptism was the outward witness of one's inner commitment to be governed by teachings and Spirit of Jesus. It must be kept in mind that, while baptism is not set forth in verse 38 as a condition for salvation, baptism is a vital witness as to who functions as Lord of one's life.

Peter would have nothing to do with an incognito witness. In spite of the high price of going public with one's faith, Jesus was far from being a cause of shame. To own him as Lord and Savior was seen as a privilege, not a liability. This was the logical end of faith, not a contradiction of faith. The body of Christ is committed to sharing its story of redemption with the world regardless of consequences.

God's witness is singular: the outpouring of the Spirit (verse 38). The coming of the Spirit is the result of accepting the Lordship of Jesus Christ. His coming is described as more than an inducement. It is more like an endowment or covering—something that is not treated as a removable garment to be put on and taken off at will. His coming is perhaps best described as an indwelling. The two are inseparably bound up with each other; not as equals, but as unequal partners in which the greater enables the lesser to become Christlike in nature and ministry.

The New Church

Nothing must deter the church from her commitment to confronting persons with God's call to repentance and to a life-style that is founded on the values and ethical considerations of the kingdom of God (Matthew 5-7). It is upon these tracks that human destiny moves toward community instead of chaos. There is a hunger for God. There is a universal thirst for the eternal. The field is ripe for evangelism.

The gods of this world have fallen. Their false claims have only increased a desire for truth and righteousness. As the Church issues a call to repentance, it is not striking a discordant note. That message touches a sensitive and responsive cord in the depths of the self.

People want to be delivered from a life of bondage to sin. They do not wish to be abandoned in their struggle to overcome inner resistance to God's invitation to forgiveness and empowerment. Unresponsiveness is not necessarily a sign of incorrigibility. It is often a sign of entrapment. "Save yourselves," exhorts Peter (Acts 2:40). Peter is urging persons to respond in faith to the message that Jesus is both Lord and Christ. He is not suggesting that salvation is the result of human activity alone. This declaration sets forth two unmistakable convictions: (1) The first is that human nature is powerless to effect its own deliverance from spiritual bondage. Apart from Jesus' victory over sin and death, there is nothing capable of reconciling persons to God. Jesus saves! That is the bedrock of the gospel.

(2) The second conviction is that there can be no societal utopia. Human nature can be domesticated by education, that is, by acquiring socially refined skills. But human nature can neither be reconciled to God nor transformed apart from grace. Salvation is the work of grace made operative in the life of a person through an act of faith. In this light, Peter's exhortation in verse 40 becomes a plea for sanity in a world that is increasingly adopting relativistic values that undermine those eternal values proclaimed and manifested in the life of Jesus.

There is a sense in which Peter's words become a call to a life-style of non-conformity. Some will not be saved! They choose to reject God's invitation to salvation through the person and work of Jesus. They prefer to conform to the teachings of human authorities or to the social mores of the culture in which they live. They, consciously or unconsciously, create gods for their existence. They "hold" or "suppress" the truth in unrighteousness (Rom. 1:18 ff.) Salvation involves separation. This decision is never easy. There is pain in obedience. Turning from old ways is never negotiated successfully without struggle. But turn we must!

Salvation is a divine call to submit to the lordship of Jesus Christ. That is the conviction driving Peter's concern for his contempories. The lordship of Jesus was the critical issued contested on Calvary and retested by the tomb. That was one of the convictions the disciples were prepared to affirm at the expense of their lives. The lordship of Jesus Christ necessitates a singular commitment in which preeminence is given to the sovereignty of God.

This means that for the believer, all other considerations, political or religious, come under the judgment of God's Word as revealed in the life and teachings of Jesus Christ. He is the locus of God's self-disclosure. He is the Church's authority for deciding on what is God's truth. He is the Church's example of God's character.

The crucifixion of Jesus makes it clear as to the world's basic valuation of Jesus. But they were wrong about Jesus! They were wrong about "the way" to salvation. Their ethical commitments reflected the weakness of their theological understanding of God and his mission in the world. Never forget that the kingdoms of this world are domains that function primarily on the rule of self-centeredness. While self-interest is the basis of all human interaction, self-centeredness is an idolatrous ritual, a deification of some self-serving pleasure, in which the self supplants God's purposes and principles of God.

The kingdom of God lies in the opposite direction from selfishness. It dwells in the lofty realm of self-submission to the will of God. A clashing of these realms is inevitable in the courtyard of human existence. For self-centeredness and self-submission cannot coexist as equals. Salvation lies in the direction of self-submission. That is the direction in which believers are called to journey. That is the direction in which persons find God, who is the source of all goodness, truth, and redemption.

With this call to salvation, Peter underscores the fact that salvation must become personal before it can have a lasting social impact upon our institu-

36

tional life. As long as evil remains undisturbed in structures that serve the basic needs of persons, history can only repeat its tragedies and deprive itself of the experience of God's breaking into its common life with an uncommon joy.

Many of the historic revivalists knew of no personal salvation that did not involve a transformation of spiritual principles into social components of justice, freedom, and compassion. Spiritual awakenings have led to a heightening of the moral conscience with an attending commitment to alleviate conditions that degrade human dignity.

As surely as form follows function, so works follow faith. The history of revivals is replete with examples of how personal faith became the incentive for social betterment. The Church need not be ashamed of her history as an advocate for social change. She has led the way while insisting on the necessity of repentance as a precondition for true happiness.

Wherever the gospel has gone, the quality of life has risen! There is hardly an institution in the modern world that has escaped the imprint of Christian ideals. Peter understood, as every generation must, that salvation is a call that results in two-fold change: changed life and changed society. The first-century church did not accept any bifurcation of these concommitant realities. That becomes a challenge for each generation.

Through salvation, those who were perishing become God's preservers of order in a world that naturally is inclined toward disorder. The Church has been commissioned to bring each believer to maturity. Continuation is as important to God as the act of coming to him in faith. Faithfulness is the goal of Christian living. This goal cannot be reached apart from structures of ministry.

Wesley owed his success largely to the organization of fellowship cells where believers were discipled and accountability could be practiced. This is the purpose for organization: to assist believers in the execution of God's will. All are to be trained in knowing the faith and caring for one another. All are to become participants in ministry, not spectators in an entertainment show. Ministry structures that enable persons to gain a depth of commitment are insuring the continuation of its witness within its environment.

Anything lacking depth does not survive. A cut flower, as Trueblood once said, is very beautiful, but its life's expectancy is very short. Usefulness is in proportion to depth of understanding and the appropriation of faith. Here is where the Church gains her strength for ministry and mission. She is called to the ministry of preparing persons for their life-long journey in personal growth and service to others. Organization is central to this task, and every organizing effort should assess ministry structures in the light of their contribution to assisting persons and assemblies in the fulfillment of God's mission in the world.

There are those who fear organization. It is often looked upon as a human enterprise void of any spiritual sensitivities or divine principles. Organization of any task should be approached with great caution. The natural man loves power. And absolute power does corrupt.

Nevertheless, life cannot be lived apart from organization. Seasons do not just randomly come and go at will, but according to a pattern. The universe is not capricious, but predictable. There is a difference between a forest fire and a log fire in a fireplace. The one has structure to guide its operations. The former has nothing to channel its energies in constructive pursuits. Wesley was an organizer. He understood that the secret to spiritual growth lies in the continuance of those who embrace it.

Coming to faith is one thing; coming to maturity is its goal (Matthew 5:48). Translating enthusiasm into maturity and service requires a discipling process to which the entire Church is committed. So often awakenings are associated with a kind of emotional conflagration lacking light and depth. The body of Christ must never retreat from respecting emotional freedom as legitimate and essential to the worship of God. But emotions are to be grounded in awareness of truth that cannot go unanswered at the felt level.

The response of those who accepted Jesus as Lord and Christ was joyful. Truth had indeed gladdened their hearts. They were excited, and rightly so. But the apostles immediately, upon public confirmation of faith by baptism, guided them into a process in which five important needs could be addressed:

First, the need to know truth: "They continued steadfastly in the apostles' doctrine" (Acts 2:42). Loving God involves the mind. Replacing old tendencies and assumptions is the first order of business. Maturity is founded on truth, not error. For ultimately, we are what we think. Our thoughts are like hidden motivators controlling our decisions and determining our pursuits.

What should a new believer know? Much will depend on age and awareness. But this much seem clear: the church that neglects doctrinal teachings denies and deprives young believers of an opportunity to develop wholistically. Without doctrinal preaching and teaching, persons are without a defense mechanism for combating subjectivism on the one hand and bad theology on the other. Only an informed believer can withstand the onslaught of erroneous teachings and misleading charisma.

Second, we see the need to belong. Luke writes, "They continued steadfastly in . . . fellowship" (verse 42). Disconnected logs have a very short incendiary life.

Interdependency allows for the combining of potentialities—hence, the strengthening of all who share a common life. Wesley recognized this principle. His followers were required to participate in local cells for mutual edification and accountability. Independence strikes at the core of what it means to be a body. Believers need one another. Their growth comes not from what they do independently of one another, but from what they become by sharing their mutual joys and burdens. Sharing allows persons opportunities for growth in intimacy and self esteem. It gives a positive thrust to our quest for wholeness. For sharing aspects of one's pilgrimage allows others to assist in the process of authenticating perceptions. At various stages and times, every believer needs such assistance.

The secret to vibrant churches is vitalized fellowships.

Third, we note the need to remember. Acts says, "They continued steadfastly . . . in breaking of bread" (verse 42). Sacrifice is the heartbeat of the Church. The self-indulgent life has always self-destructed. Jesus modeled the life-style of servanthood—ministering to the needs of others. Self-promotion, self-aggrandizement, and self-service are all antithetical to the teachings of Jesus.

The way of the cross is purposeful suffering, which constitutes the conquest of pain by something of great value. What is of great value? Those who are wounded and need healing. Those who are oppressed and need justice. Those who spiritually crippled and need deliverance. Those who are lonely and need friendship. It is in these arenas of human need that the greatest potential exists for spiritual renewal. The Christian lives by dying to self-centeredness.

This is what recalling Jesus helps us to remember. He gave us an example of what it means to love God. He gave himself to others. The real question is not how much we do for people, but how much of ourselves we share with them. The gift without the giver is vain. Jesus gave Himself to a loving God by loving others. All believers are called on to do likewise. For life is not without its end.

Through communion we remember that we are held accountable for our response to those needs that confront us. Apathy is deadly. God's people exist to function in the world as instruments of his kingdom. Each person becomes in a very special way another's keeper.

Fourth, we have the need to be whole. Our text notes "They continued steadfastly . . . in prayers" (verse 42). Anxiety is constant menace. Life in the world is under a steady barrage of destabilizing influences. Believers live in a real world. They are not afforded special environments void of any trouble. Pain is an equal-opportunity employer!

Where do believers turn for solace and wisdom?

Where do God's people go "when the storms of life are raging?"

When trouble knocks at your door through sickness, adversity, discouragement, persecution, domestic crisis in the family, or financial setbacks—what are your instincts? Do you turn toward "home?" Do you look to God in faith? Jesus did! The upward journey requires trust which is always a pull toward the center of our certitude. Anything less only deepens our anxiety and prolongs our instability. An attitude of prayer leads to a greater consciousness of God's power and presence.

Finally, we note the need for self-discipline. In the final analysis, spiritual growth is an individual matter. Obedience cannot be imposed. The God-directed life can only emerge through the practice of submission to the will of God. People become what they practice. The best discipling program will come to naught unless there is the desire to grow, linked with a commitment to practice basic disciplines of the Spirit.

The Anointed Community

Note the marks of this anointed community.

1. Fear (verse 43). Reverence for God is a sign of spiritual maturity. This young congregation does not fear the world. They have found their peace. They know who is in control. Their life is governed by the awareness that all are accountable to God, and that God is responsive to the whole of their needs.

Such fear gets translated into respect for authority—human and divine. They understand well the lesson of history. Righteousness exalts a nation. God will not work through channels that disrespect what he has authorized for the common good. Yet, it remains to be seen what God will do when his people humble themselves and acknowledge him as Lord.

2. Unity (verse 44). Much has already been said about this. Suffice it to say that unity of heart is a gift from the Spirit. The followers of Christ would not buy into that value system which measured human worth by such criteria as wealth, position, race, party or religious affiliations. The true measure of what it means to be human is to care without impartiality. This gift runs counter to natural tendencies. But then, an anointed community is not bound by the world's values.

3. Loyalty to the local church (verse 46). Nothing grows into its potential that is not planned. However beautiful an indoor plant may be, it is less than what it could be if it is not planted in a conductive environment. So it is with believers.

Even though these early Christians have not yet been forced to worship in separate facilities, they are committed to supporting that community of faith to which they belong. In time, the differences between the Hebrews and Christians would necessitate a break in their relationship, but the principle of supporting the local church will remain. This is God's strategy for evangelism: planting and supporting local fellowships for the edification of each other.

4. Praise (verse 47). Why does the Church come together? To exalt the Lord. Exaltation takes many forms. But form is not stressed in this verse. We do not know whether they were sitting, standing, kneel-

ing, prostrated, or whatever. That is not what is really important. The critical element that motivates these human geysers of joy is their common life together in Christ. They are thanking God for the privilege of being in the family of God. And why not? It represents the miracle of divine love. What else could transform a people with so many differences into a dynamic fellowship without walls; a place where all are free to recover from their past and rediscover their neglected potentials for good? They found what they were looking for. And so can you!

Luke cannot end chapter two of Acts without reminding Theophilus that this church enjoyed two great blessings: (1) they enjoyed broad respect through the community, and (2) they enjoyed a daily in-gathering of new believers. Does the anointing of the Spirit make a difference in the life and ministry of the Church? Luke thinks so. The inhabitants of Jerusalem thought so. What do you think?

Acts
Chapter 3:
The Power of a Praying Community

"We must distinguish between abiding
experiences and changing categories."
—Harry Emerson Fosdick

If the experiences of Calvary caused a menacing
dark mood to settle over Peter's spirit, the Resurrection and Ascension restored a basic confidence that
soared to new heights on Pentecost. Peter was revitalized by the experience of the Spirit's descent upon all
the followers of Jesus. Jesus was with them in the
person of the Spirit. Of this, they were confident. As
the Master had ascended as Conqueror, now they
could live in victory through faith in his Word and
Spirit.

Peter had advanced far beyond where he was. He
had learned difficult and painful lessons under the
tutor of experience. One of those lessons had to
relate to understanding. The issue may be stated as
follows: What is God's process for developing the
"eye of faith," which involves apprehending the
things of the God? Acts 3 gives us an answer to that
question.

Prayer is God's process whereby he discloses himself and his will to those who make room for him in their heart and mind. Prayer is not a human invention. It is not a mechanism whereby a person creates out of some inner needs an object of veneration and then proceeds to embue it with certain powers. It is not a technique for human manipulation of God through acts of appeasement (1 Kings 18:26, 28). It is not a mental gymnastic exercise whereby insincerity is clothed in pious words for the sake of gaining public esteem (Matthew 6:5; compare Luke 18:11). It is not a bargaining device whereby faithfulness to lesser things somehow gets compensated for unfaithfulness to greater things (Amos 5:21-24; compare Matthew 23:14). Prayer is not an extortion game.

Prayer is an open exchange between the heart of God and the soul of persons. Perhaps more than any other discipline, prayer was the one most associated with Jesus. Peter learned from the Lord's teachings on and practice of prayer that the universe was essentially personal. God, according to Jesus, is one with whom persons can relate at the core and circumference of their being. He is to be addressed as "Father." He is the architect of human existence.

People are the bearers of God's image and the object of his love. God speaks spoke to them. He calls them by name. He care for their existence. He provides for their defense. He supplies their needs. He is acquainted with all their ways. He knows their "paths." Their journeys are marked by his awareness before the moment of their conception. Their destinies are prescribed, even though their freedom is never proscribed. Contemplations like these led the psalmist to exclaim: "Such knowledge is too wonderful for me; it is high, I cannot attain unto it!" (139:6).

That is precisely what Peter learned about prayer. It is the means by which the unattainable become attainable. Nothing is more unattainable than to scale the heights of divinity by the scaffolding of human effort. Nothing is more futile than to confront the realities of life without the guiding hand of God. Nothing more consistently links the contemporary with the ancient heroes of faith than their collective yet individual decisions to place, through prayer, their minds and heart before God as an open book. Their prayer life was motivated by two great convictions:

The first conviction is that God makes his presence available to those who approach him in sincerity and truth. Prayer expands one's consciousness of God's presence. We can only affirm or depend upon what we know is available to us. Any shifting of our awareness from a consciousness of God is accompanied by a downward spiral akin to that which befell Peter on the Sea of Galilee. Was this Peter's motive for maintaining an allegience to the discipline of corporate prayer?

Must we not affirm God everywhere we intend to honor him? Affirming God's presence is the gateway to peace and victory. That is what the Hebrews did by calling upon God for deliverance from political oppression in Egypt. That is what Moses did as he presented the unmet needs of the Hebrews in the wilderness. That is what Hannah did as she confronted her barrenness with optimism. That is what the sick and unenlightened are exhorted to do. Affirming God's presence gives one a basis for courage and a rationale for hope.

The second conviction is that God supplies the

deeper needs of those who call upon him in faith. Prayer not only expands one's consciousness, but it also enlightens the eyes of the mind. Unanswered prayers are mainly misguided prayers. Through prayer, God is given access to the inner chambers of the self. We see through his eyes.

Prayer is not predominantly a "talking" experience. It is a "telling" experience—one in which the self knows itself as being addressed by one who knows all. From this perspective, prayer becomes a listening event in which those essential categories are raised to new prominence on the scale of our awareness. The inner chambers of self are unlit. No one can be sure what inappropriate desires hide within its domain. But God knows! God as David said, is acquainted with all [our] ways" (Ps. 139:3).

Peter discovered that there is joy in being known. Had not Jesus informed him of his denial before it happened (Luke 22:31)? Does this not suggest that divine love, not divine wrath, is the dominant theme in God's dealings with his people? Is it not logical, therefore, that one should expect that the more a person participates in sincere prayer the more likely compassion for others will take precedence over their own immediate needs.

In prayer each person decides what is most important. The less one prays the more likely it is that the self will occupy center stage. Prayer will then create an imbalance in our confirmational, affirmational polarities. "I want" will eclipse "I will."

The one whose list of concerns surfaces first is the one who is likely to control the air waves. How the Church needs persons at all levels who are prepared to "wait on the Lord." When God finishes with His list, what more is there to say but, "Thanks, Lord? See you later."

A praying church is a growing church. Growth has many indexes for measurement. None is more significant than the concern of persons for persons.

As Peter and John made their way to the Temple, they were confronted with a personal request for money. This request, like many prayers, falls short of the deeper need. A man, who is described by Luke as cripple from birth, raised this petition. The request is offered in a routine manner with no regard for the ability of those addressed to supply what is asked for. It is a weak request because it is without foundation in fact. This man really doesn't expect everyone he asks to respond. Therefore he believes, like many persons today, that if you ask something enough times of enough people, you thereby increase the likelihood of obtaining it. Such a request only increases hopelessness and lengthens the shadow of discouragement. Here was a person who had settled for the fulfillment of a lesser need.

A praying church is concerned with all needs, especially the need for the recovery of faith. Faith is the means by which persons relate life to God and ready themselves to relate God to the whole of their human situation. God was beyond this man's domain. He had drawn a curtain of isolation between his world and those truths celebrated in that world within the church. While he obviously believed in the reality of God, he was not convinced that those realities were applicable to his situation. Therefore, he and those who assisted him were content to remain near but not under the wings of God's omnipotence.

Peter, like Jonathan Edwards who allegedly said, "Give me New England or I die," saw a condition that God could correct. The need for money is periodic and limited. The need for faith is constant and boundless. Peter realized that without faith history would repeat itself in some other aspect of this man's life. Something else would cripple him. Some fear. Some hurt. Some failure. Some discouragement. Some deprivation. Some calamity.

Peter had no choice but to offer this man what he possessed, that is, faith in the life and character of Jesus. Such faith rests on solid ground. For neither sin nor death could sway Jesus to desert God's will and live a life-style of rebellion. Jesus was faithful unto the end. His reward was a vindication over evil, the grave, and the world. The name of Jesus represents divine approval and authority. That name was a lifeline for Peter. It is a lifeline for the world.

A praying church is casting out a gospel lifeline to the crippled of this world. She has confidence in her God's power to save, heal, and empower for service. Peter and John did. A faith that lay buried beneath years of disuse was suddenly resurrected and applied to what previously was considered a hopeless situation. Praying churches are not discouraged by situations. They function not on the basis of circumstances but convictions. Peter and John stood solidly on the conviction of Jesus' power to deliver.

The results were gratifying, but not surprising. Whenever God can activate the potential for faith in Jesus, as the Son of God and Son of man, a great change will occur. Peter and John had anticipated that change. Wilberforce had anticipated change in England's policy regarding slave trafficking. Wesley anticipated change in the spiritual life of England and America. Sojourner Truth anticipated change in America's engagement with morally indefensible racial practices.

Change has guided God's people into the primitive regions of the world as beacons of hope: change as profound as that which happened to this lame man, a change of mind and function. This is what a praying church can accomplish—bringing persons into a personal experience of deliverance from within and without. What formerly was an unattractive landmark became a contagious witness for the Lord. This is what the Church must see. This is what she must then pray will happen in all the world.

Prayer takes on greater significance when we realize that its object, God, makes available to all what Fosdick called "abiding experiences." In every age and every arena of life, God has confirmed his power to affect change in the human situation. God's "mighty acts in history" attest to his sovereignty and goodness. God is, declares the writer of Hebrews, "a rewarder of them that diligently seek him" (11:6).

The pages of the Old Testament are replete with examples of God's vindication of His word entrusted to his servant people. His is a history of promise-fulfillment. Israel's history was a sad commentary of broken promises. Failure is not associated with any inadequacy in God. He is life's center of certitude.

The wondrous changes wrought in the lives of persons are ultimately attributable to the loving-kindness of God. He is the basis of faith. He is the foundation upon which a structure of confidence can rest with assurance. The credibility of the Church is derived from the faithfulness of God in the fulfillment of his promises. God keeps his word.

The Church has leaned on this abiding experience—confidence in God to keep his word—as she has confronted human needs. Her strength lies not in the material realm, in asthetics, in social approval, or in numerical size. Her strength lies in the quality of commitment she brings to bear upon the human needs that confront her. Each human need represents a time of opportunity and judgment. For it is not what we say about Jesus that really counts. Believing without doing leads to uninspired abstractions.

Faith involves a follow-through: action. Action, or works, brings faith to completion. It lifts faith out of the speculative realm and grounds it in the reality of service to others. Jesus had said, "Not everyone that saith unto me, Lord, Lord, shall enter into the kingdom of heaven; but he that doeth the will of my Father which is in heaven" (Matthew 7:21). In 1 John, this same thought is expressed by reminding believers that words must give rise to action. Otherwise, "we lie, and do not the truth" (1:6).

The main task of the Church is to cultivate confidence in God through witnessing, through worship services, through testimonies, through learning experiences, through training opportunities, through service to others, through life's painful visitations. All of life is an opportunity to inspire others to exercise faith in God. For through faith comes change: change in one's situation, change in one's pre-occupation, change in one's attitude toward life, change in one's perceptions and capacity for handling difficulties. Change. That is the preparation confidence brings: the miracle of change.

Prayer anticipates such changes. For no petition to

52

God is adequate that does not make room for God to be God! If God is requested to act upon a prayer, is it not reasonable to assume a positive attitude of anticipation? Whatever Jesus touched, he changed! Change is inevitable. It is a consequence of God's nature to affect redemptively whatever comes under his control. That a lame person could go from standing, to leaping, to walking is clear evidence that something new had entered this person's life and radically affected how he functioned.

What needs to be made clear is that the results of prayer are not due to any natural powers resident in persons. Most people are easily confused by miracles of change. Peter perceived that others who heard and saw the healed man were confounded as to how to account for such a miracle. He quickly issues a disclaimer: "Why look ye so earnestly on us, as though by our own power or holiness we had made this man to walk?" (Acts 3:12).

Peter speaks to that question. He indicates that the agent of this miracle was the same Jesus who was (1) glorified by the patriarchs (verse 12) and (2) foretold by *all* the prophets (verse 18) from Moses to Samuel, and from Samuel to the Latter Prophets. In short, the entire history of the Hebrews was a recital of this ancient promise of the Messiah's coming. He came in the person of Jesus. He was not able to affect this miracle of change upon the body life of Israel because of unbelief: "Ye delivered up, and denied him in the presence of Pilate, when he was determined to let him go" (verse 13). Unknowingly, they were denying the Son of God, the Holy One and Just, the Prince of life (verse 13-14). Their blindness was indeed great. For their eyes were veiled to his office and character, and to his kingdom's presence. How great was that darkness!

But regardless of the mistakes committed, God invites people to live in the present. They cannot go backwards in time and correct their misdeeds. All of us can allow God to enter our moments, the now-time of existence, and create a new story of faith. Peter never misses an opportunity to extend such an opportunity. He does so on this occasion: "Repent ye therefore, and be converted, that your sins may be blotted out, when the times of refreshing shall come from the presence of the Lord" (verse 19). The Lord's return is held up as a time of "refreshing" for those who have "turned around," reversing their response to Jesus from one of denial to one of faith.

What lies ahead for such persons? An in-gathering. Union with God. Forfeiture of this blessing is life's greatest tragedy. A praying church produces praying leaders and people whose ministries are made more effective through a discovery of God's kindnesses and truth.

Acts
Chapter 4:
The Power of a
Faithful Community

"To everything there is a season,
and a time to every purpose under
heaven: . . . A time to keep silence,
a time to speak."
—Ecclesiastes 3:1, 7

The apostolic community reflected in the Acts possessed a strong and clear sense of their mission. They knew themselves as the newly constituted people of God. This self-identity enabled them to consider themselves as citizens of two kingdoms: the one natural and the other spiritual. Each order was distinct and interrelated.

The apostles did not seek to impose their faith perspectives upon the world. Rather, each manifestation of the divine in their midst brought about questions and concerns from those who were sympathetic and unsympathetic to their cause (Acts 4:1-2).

The Sadducees and priests were concerned about the growing impact and influence of the message regarding Jesus' resurrection upon the people's loyalty to Hebraic traditions and their economic security as civil servants of a foreign ruler. In responding to those issues, this infant church faced well-organized efforts to dismantle her influence. Wickedness has made the same historically tragic yet comic response to religious movements labeled unorthodox, unenlightened, or unacceptable to the more established religious orders.

They have devised elaborate plans to crush what they often cannot equal in intellectual clarity or personal contagion. The history of religion in the world well documents the futility of such efforts. Gamaliel, a renowned teacher of the Law, Pharisee by persuasion, would give ample illustrations to verify this fact (Acts 5:37-39). Both Theudas and Judas of Galilee attempted to promote themselves and their ideas as the locus of God's redemptive work in history. Their efforts came to naught. That is the lesson of history.

God is not a historical bystander. He is actively involved in the great advance of His Word in the world. Whatever God is doing, no religious assembly or political alliance, no high priest or powerful leader can prevail against him. That was Gamaliel's advice (5:39). That was Jesus' declaration (Matthew 16:18b). That is history's message to the ages (Psalm 110:1 compare Acts 2:34). God's word is always a final word!

Faithfulness is the measure of spiritual greatness. The apostolic community knew itself as responsible to God for the stewardship of his manifold grace and gospel. Being witness to Jesus' resurrection was not a self-conceived idea. It was the hope on which the cornerstone of salvation rested. They were not seeking political solutions to spiritual problems. If anything, they were seeking spiritual solutions to all the problems pertaining to human existence. The resurrection of Jesus from the dead was, for them, an accomplished fact. They had no choice but to proclaim what God had done and its implications for personal renewal and social policies. For in the resurrection of Jesus, God confirmed his lordship and Saviorhood. In him, God comes to persons.

And through him, persons come to God. Jesus is the world's intersection where the divine and human meet for forgiveness and empowerment for service. This, the apostolic community believed and proclaimed as the only basis by which to engage in dialogue on the great moral and spiritual issues of life.

A faithful community is commissioned to share its message with the world. These followers of Christ were not "bushel Christians" (Matthew 5:15). Their ministry beyond the walls of the Temple had given them an opportunity to interpret it for a wider audience. Any dogma that cannot withstand the critique of opposing views is not worthy of one's loyalty. These Apostles were not afraid of what others thought of their convictions.

Neither were they offensive in defending their positions. What becomes clear is that God often turns our obstacles into opportunities for engaging persons in the dialogue of truth as revealed in the life and teachings of Jesus. For it is only through such exchanges that Truth, working through sincerity and humility, can form a mutual respect and hopefully create a unity of spirit and mind.

The religious movements in Jesus' day were wholly committed to service within the confines of the Temple. This isolation encouraged the erroneous compartmentalization of life into sacred and non-sacred realms. Jesus, by action and teaching, stressed the importance of planting the seed of the word in the soil of the world. The natural order was seen as his sphere of operation. Sacred and secular were merely different approaches to life: antithetical but not adversarial in their orientations.

The concept of a "base" ministry within the Church and a "field" ministry beyond the Church is well articulated by Elton Trueblood and others. In this, the Church has no option but to carry out its ministry in this duel context. That is not easy. For opposition forces persons to deal with their feelings of being comfortable.

It was against great odds that God's people have carried out their perceived assignments. None found the climate conducive to their message or concerns. None. Each was armed with courage to withstand the temptation to remain silent in the face of mounting opposition. Each paid a heavy price for doing and saying what they considered to be divinely authorized.

Exhaustion, ridicule, stoning, excommunication, public flogging, unjust imprisonments, character misrepresentation, death—these, along with dogged doubt and deep despair, have been the price paid for daring to be true to what was committed to them. Great movements are the result of dedication to great principles. History reveals those principles for which persons were prepared to die. This is the genius of all revivals. Persons found the "pearl of great price" for which they were prepared to make any sacrifice to possess and defend.

Great opportunities await the Church as she translates her message into social realities that affect human needs. Ministry to others is the goal of the cross. The ministry of reconciliation is needed where alienation exists at its worst. A faithful community cannot merely sit back and wait for the world to come knocking at its doors. John the Baptist's success came because he made his ministry accessible to people.

Jesus, while committed to a local church, was equally committed to heralding the gospel of his kingdom wherever the door of opportunity presented itself. In fact, his one-on-one ministry proved very effective in creating a broader ministry to cities. For example, the Samaritan woman began a city crusade (John 4:29,39); also the impotent man at the pool of Bethesda, in sharing his healing with certain persons, began a death crusade among Jesus' foes (5:15-16). Here were two wholly different reactions to Jesus' ministry. Yet, this is context in which ministry evolves: acceptance and faith, rejection and death.

A faithful community responds to its challenges with prophetic courage. Peter and John were certainly undaunted in the face of adversity. As they faced a large and powerful circle of leaders within the Hebraic community, they revealed signs of renewed spiritual adequacy. Their interrogators demanded to know the basis upon which the helpless man was healed: "By what power, or by what name, have ye done this?" (Acts 4:7).

Peter speaks as one whose powers are under the control of the Spirit. His reply is pointed: "By the name of Jesus Christ of Nazareth, whom ye crucified, whom God raised from the dead, even by him doth this man stand here before you whole. This is the stone which was set at nought of you builders which is become the head of the corner. Neither is there salvation in any other: for there is none other name under heaven given among men, whereby we must be saved" (verses 10-12).

These detractors could not deny that Peter spoke

his convictions (1) regarding who Jesus was and their role in his crucifixion, (2) that they were unwise builders to reject the principal stone God sent to secure the structure of salvation, (3) that there was no salvation apart from faith in the name of Jesus, and (4) that they were compelled by the higher authority of truth and experience to "speak the things which [they] had seen and heard" (verse 20).

Faithful communities live by convictions. Nothing reveals more the quality of life in a person as does his convictions. What persons are willing to be loyal to reveals the character of those persons. The inability to be faithful to convictions is by far the greatest single index for determining how flawed a person is.

Dark times provide a background for assessing a person's character. During the height of the underground resistance movement in Germany, many pastors and religious professors were faced with a decision of loyalty to state or loyalty to God. Such a tension is always inherent where persons acknowledge a duel citizenship.

The greater conflict, however, lies within the inner realm of conscience between divinely conceived "oughts" and personal feelings of "wants." Martin Niemöller had wrestled with his conscience and came down on the side of divine imperatives. He, along with other members of the Confessing Church, had resisted political control of the church and expressed opposition to the treatment of Jews by the government. For this he would be imprisoned in the dreaded Moabit Prison.

Charles Colson relates a conversation Niemöller had with a fellow cleric who was serving as chaplain of that institution: "But brother!" he said in shock.

"What brings you here? Why are you in prison?"
"And, brother, why are you not in prison?" Niemöller replied (Colson, *Kingdom in Conflict*, p. 152).

Propositions of the faith are more than pious shib-
boleths to warm the heart. Convictions are the rud-
ders of faith. They guide a person's response to the
perplexities of life. Faithfulness is the acid test of
spirituality. For through faithfulness comes fruitful-
ness. Conviction is the anvil of character. It was
through their convictions that Peter and John recognized that nothing is stronger than truth. Not sin.
Not death. Not human defiance, however large or
well equipped to mount a negative resistance. Nothing
can corral God or crush the ministry of his spirit in
the body of his people.

A faithful community finds its strength and joy in
the vindication of God's messages and the validation
of his presence.

God has always vindicated his word. Isaiah the
prophet reminded the Judeans that a season of divine
chastening would be followed by a season of divine
blessings. He anchors this prophesy concerning a
period of refreshment in the immutability of a divine
pronouncement:

> For as the heavens are higher than the
> earth, so are my ways higher than your
> ways, and my thoughts than your thoughts.
> For as the rain cometh down, and the
> snow from heaven, and returneth not
> thither, but watereth the earth, and maketh
> it bring forth and bud, that it may give
> seed to the sower, and bread to the eater:
> So shall my word be that goeth forth out
> of my mouth: it shall not return unto me

61

void, but it shall accomplish that which I
please, and it shall prosper in the thing
whereto I sent it (55:9-11).

The spoken word had indeed accomplished its intent.
In spite of the negative reaction by members of the
Sanhedrin, the word created a positive response to its
message among the common people. So much interest was stirred up among the people that the evil
intent of the Sanhedrin was restrained. They were
forced to release Peter and John or face public con-
demnation and obvious loss of public support.

A grass-roots awakening was in motion that religious dissidence could not stop. A fire was burning.
Those at the bottom and top of the social ladder
were joined in their hunger for righteousness and
social justice. A momentum was evident to members
of the Sanhedrin, thus their frantic efforts to escalate
a frontal attack on the principal advocates of the
resurrection of Jesus. But Peter and John showed no
signs of an emotional meltdown. If anything, their
trial of faith had strengthened their confidence in
God's ability to create a way of escape.

I once had an uncle for whom I hold the fondest
memory and highest affection. He was a master
checker player. Few could outwit him. I remember
asking if I could try my hand at taking him on, only
to be greeted with a smile and disarming comment.
"Sure," he said. "You can play. But remember," he
said, "I can undo any move you make!" And he
could with ease.

Perhaps that is how Christians should view God's
superintendence over the ministry of his people.
Whatever moves or strategies the adversary of our
faith initiates, God has the capacity and desire to

undo them all.

God certainly vindicated his word by enabling Peter and John to go free. Scripture tells us that "being let go, they went to their own company, and reported all that the chief priests and elders had said unto them. And when they heard that, they lifted up their voice to God with one accord, and said, Lord, thou art God" (Acts 4:23-24).

What every church needs more of is not more facilities but more testimonies of victory in ministry. Peter and John's report galvanized the church. They could see, through the eyes of David, that no human or demonic powers have ever been able to overrule God's purpose. At best, all anti-God influences have only succeeded in volunteering for cast assignments in God's redemptive drama. History's main script was written before the world began. Auditions were conducted by two spirits.

Unfortunately, many have chosen to accept parts offered them by evil influences. This was true of Herod the mad man, spineless Pontius Pilate, and other representatives from all ranks of both the Gentiles and Jews. Jesus' crucifixion was a universal conspiracy. All were involved in his humiliation by nature and class. All had indeed sinned against God.

Yet, in this process, God was at work reconciling the world to himself. Against a background of human failure, a luminous portrait of divine love shines forth. It awakens a hymn of supplication in which this emboldened church asks God, in light of the seriousness of the threats made against them, to bestow upon them the gift of boldness, a special capacity for self-abandonment.

Here was a church unprepared to give up their

mission because of dangers. They were trusting God to make them adequate to do what they believed had to be done—to "speak [God's] word" (verse 29). The Church is edified when its representatives are able to share what God is doing in the world. Such sharings make it possible for others to have their vision of God and their victories through him expand in meaning and commitment.

The gospel was sent to spread, to become a net for bringing people to God and God to people. This is the purpose of the Word of God—to reach people with the saving message of God's redeeming love. Any sacrifice is worth this. Any life devoted to this is cause has the assurance of not being in vain.

The Church is perhaps the only "institution" that can fail in its mission and remain in business. Complacency, mediocrity, and ritualism have a way of trivializing her message and fossilizing her mission. Her energies are dissipated in maintenance concerns rather than mission concerns. This will inevitably reverse the focus of the Church from being forward to one of being backward in its gaze.

This growing Apostolic community was not in any mood to sound a retreat. The great advance has captured their hearts. Now it would produce in their midst a verification of God's presence.

While these believers join in a corporate prayer, the glory of God is spoken of as "shaking" the place where they were assembled together (verse 31). This divine attestation provoked a response from the multitude. They spoke of God's mighty acts. They were not whispering. They were unafraid of who might be listening in to report them to authorities for this act of civil disobedience (verse 31; compare verse 17).

They did precisely what Peter and John said they would do. They were all prepared to fill the jails in Jerusalem!

Luke informs us that "great grace was upon them all" (verse 33). This is what a faithful church can expect: the outpouring of God's gift of love upon the corporate body. It is through love that God verifies his presence. They not only spoke God's word with boldness, but they responded to one another with unfeigned brotherly love. Their hearts belonged to God. He intertwined their hearts with one another.

What God possesses he invests in others. So unified was this community in mutual concern that their sacrifice and trust were void of selfishness. These believers were ready to advance together or die together. Is it any wonder these ordinary people accomplished great exploits for God?

Acts
Chapter 5:
The Power of a
Practicing Community

"The point of view he [Jung] lays before us is
a challenge to the spirit, and evokes an active
response in everyone who has felt within himself
an urge to grow beyond his inheritance."
—Cary F. Baynes

God has always accomplished his saving purposes
through people. Individuals are the center piece in
God's drama of redemption. The history of God's
acts of revival demonstrate this fact. Again and again,
God raised up persons whose character evoked from
their contemporaries a response of great respect that
usually was translated into a commensurate life style.
What a person is has much to do with the quality of
influence he or she exerts within and beyond a community. This does not mean that a person's testimony or witness to the content of faith is nonessen-
tial. The point being emphasized is that the quality of
life manifested by persons committed to Christ adds
authority to what is said or taught.

Any role call of persons used mightily of God
reveals a triumph of character. Ultimately, that is the
greatest good to which history bears witness—the
power of God to produce his likeness in ordinary

people. That is what revivals declare. That is what creates hope in the face of civilization's record of spiritual decadence. For no words, however eloquently stated, can rival an authentic witness to God's redeeming love.

Character is the acid test of genuineness. Not worship mannerisms. Not personal experiences. Not claims of miraculous deeds. Not pulpit persuasiveness. Not religious works. Character is God's measure of spiritual maturity. Any revival that bypasses character formation has not only missed the gospel mark, but it has missed the main point of God's self-disclosure. The call to faith is a call to "grow beyond one's inheritance"—to become Christlike.

Admittedly, such a goal is paradoxical. Its absolute attainment is impossible. The reservoir of human frailties can never be emptied, however hard one tries. Humanness by its very definition implies a condition bounded by limitations. What the goal of Christlikeness does is provide behavioral objectives that give indication of an increasing control by the Spirit within the depths of the self. Under the Spirit's influence, persons are made aware of two selves—Christ's and their's. The obvious distance between the two would create despair if it were not for the knowledge of the grace of God. That knowledge is designed to inspire faith in God's ability to enable persons to "grow beyond" their natural endowments.

The Books of Acts reveals that very fact. Here we find persons manifesting qualities of character that are the result of the Holy Spirit's in-filling. The impact of these persons upon their times validates two important considerations: (1) the claim that character is vital to revival and (2) the claim that faith and

works, loving God and godly loving, are inextricably
bound together.

Historical Witnesses
to Great Grace

1. Empowered to Encourage:
Acts 4:36; 9:27; 15:36ff.

Barnabas, who is called "the son of encouragement," heads a royal list of persons who bore witness
to the work of grace in their lives. His decision to sell
his property and place the entire proceeds into the
common treasury was an act of love and faith. Barnabas was convinced that the apostles' message concerning the resurrection of Jesus was true. But equally
convincing was the genuine concern each believer
had for the other. They did indeed love one another.
This translation of their spiritual values into social
realities removed all doubts relative to the authenticity of their experience. God was alive in them. Of
this, Barnabas was confident.

In Barnabas a corporate witness had been awak-
ened and focused in him a desire to be a servant,
much as the Levites were. Their duties related to the
up-keep of the Temple, assistant to the priests, and
distributor of funds designated for benevolence. Levites were workers. They obviously were given to the
ministry of helps.

This ministry addresses one of the primary needs
of persons—recovery from discouragement. Everyone
falls victim to attitudinal melt-downs. All experience
emotional inertia. Under the impact of discourage-

ment, illuminous flames of intentionality are reduced to intermittent signs of a diminishing presence. Yet, it was that faith in the presence of God that would cause Barnabas to extend himself as a source of caring to those in need of love and hope. Barnabas would not find a crowded field seeking to minister to the poor in spirit.

The rainbow of success does not appear immediately in the valley of the wounded. This is faith work. One must be convinced of the presence of something of an enduring nature within the wounded. Some spark. Some desire to rise from the ashes of failure. Some genuine urge to conquer a besetting tendency. Some commitment to accept and integrate a command or divine principle into the structure of one's behavior. These qualities, if present, can be revived by the touch of love, the wind of encouragement. Barnabas revealed how essential this ministry is in awakening a desire to grow beyond one's inheritance.

This ministry of encouragement also addresses one of the central needs of congregations—conservation of the saints. Discouragement is an equal-opportunity employer. Its presence can be found at all levels of spiritual maturity. The Church is often guilty of focusing upon preserving new members while older members and key leaders are inadvertently neglected. The assumption seems to be that leaders especially do not need encouragement. So often the Church assumes that her leaders are immune against depression, feelings of low self esteem, self doubt, and nonappreciation.

No institution can afford to neglect its important human resources, especially the Church. The mission of the Church requires the brightest minds as well as the deepest devotion. She must contend against a wealth of "isms" that, if embraced, would lead to a watered-down version of the faith that is neither convincing nor convicting. Revival cannot be sustained with enthusiasm. Lamp lighters are essential in the battle against darkness.

Barnabas had an eye for detecting this ability in others. He understood that a leader is the Church's primary investment. A Christian leader is the principal embodiment and developer of the key values of the community of faith. Barnabas revealed great wisdom in accepting the challenge of being an encourager of others. His labor resulted in conserving significant leaders, Paul and John Mark, for the work of ministry. Any group is impoverished if it lacks the presence and voice of a Barnabas. Such a group is likely to bemoan what is not present rather than rejoice over what is emerging within her ranks. Barnabas saw what was emerging and, like a skilled obstetrician, guided it into being. An encourager is one "who stands before," to borrow the root meaning of obstetrician, another who is impregnated with life. The Church needs the harvesters and obstetricians.

2. Empowered to Obey:
Acts 5:1-11; 9:10-22

The name *Ananias* was common in its day. Like the name *Saul*, Ananias of Damascus (Acts 9:10) was oceans apart in character from Ananias of Jerusalem (5:1). Both faced tough decisions. Both embarked upon a common destiny of faith, but they traveled by wholly different roads.

Ananias of Jerusalem resisted the leadership of the Spirit. His sin lay in the refusal to actualize what he obviously had previously agreed to do. Peter's remarks in verse 3 imply that Ananias had promised to do something—presumably, to do what other property and land-holding members of the fellowship had done: "For as many as were possessors of lands or houses sold them, and brought the prices of the things that were sold, and laid them down at the apostles' feet: and distribution was made unto every man according as he had need" (4:34-35). But later, after assessing the amount of what his property brought, he and his wife, Sapphira, finally decided not to do what they had promised. Obedience always looks easier from the side of barrenness than it does from the side of bountifulness.

Their decision, while regrettable, revealed a cancerous attitude of arrogance. They had witnessed the effects of the Spirit upon their corporate life. Yet, in spite of these miraculous manifestations of the Divine in their midst, they concocted a lie that, if successful in going undetected, would wholly undermine the very foundation of this assembly of the Spirit. That lie is that a commitment to truth is not an absolute in the fellowship of believers. God's judgment affirms the centrality of a commitment to truth among the followers of Jesus.

The results of this tragic event were amazing. First, a climate of reverence emerged from this experience (5:11). Irreverence is a form of denial. It is an attitudinal process whereby God is reduced to human proportions. He becomes a God without glory and authority: one whose will can be ignored with impunity. This lie, if institutionalized, would create a com-

72

munity of parasites rather than a community of servants. The truth is that none is exempt from honesty. Reverence toward God and respect toward all are the hallmarks of responsible membership in the body of Christ.

Next, there is an unusual manifestation of the Divine in their midst. Such manifestation takes many forms: preaching, singing, testifying, exhortations, prayer, to name a few. What Luke took pain to note is that the apostles, who were considered "unlearned and ignorant" (4:13), were greatly empowered by the Spirit for the good of the social and spiritual communities of which they were a part. As the quality of life in the community of faith rises, there is a noticeable change in the quality of its ministry.

The opposite must also be true: quality of ministry affects the quality of life in the congregation. These are coordinates. Each empowers the other. Neither is sufficient unto itself. As people and leaders work interdependently, they are able to maximize their impact upon their social environment.

Last, a climate of seriousness and praise emerges. This painful event forced everyone to assess seriously the nature of the Church. It heightened the necessity of genuineness. It compelled many to assess their motives for identifying with this assembly of the Spirit. It caused believers to affirm their faith in God as one who is sovereign in history. It led believers to dismantle the structure of fear, a crucial step in the formation of faithfulness.

This small band of believers was then ready for the great trial of faith soon to come their way. They had settled the great question of their mission (5:29). Their greatest satisfaction lay in their privilege "to suffer shame for his name" (verse 41). It is little wonder that the number of disciples multiplied.

Ananias of Damascus faced a situation similar to his name sake. He, too, was confronted with the necessity of making a choice between what was revealed by the Spirit and what his instincts were inclined to do. There ends the similarity. This latter Ananias is presented as a person of prayer. His decision making process involved the search for divine wisdom. He was acquainted with God. He immediately recognized the voice of the Lord (9:10) and gave evidence of being ready to act upon whatever the Lord said. These are the qualities of a sincere disciple of Jesus Christ: attention to prayer, discernment, responsiveness, hunger for wisdom and righteousness. One can readily see why God would entrust the disciplining of Saul into the hands of Ananias. Obedience was his trademark.

Obedience does not negate fear. It confronts fear's uncertainty with honesty and faith. Ananias did not hide his apprehension. Great men and women of God were not greatly used by the Lord because they were undaunted. Strong self-confidence was not a natural virtue. Moses was shaken by his assignment. Elijah was dismayed by the seeming insignificance of his victory on Mount Carmel. His main foe was unmoved by the carnage of her prophets.

In the face of popular support for Jesus' crucifixion, the disciples retreated behind closed doors for fear of the Jews. Jeremiah was not eager to embark upon his calling. What each shared in common was a healthy realization of his own limitations. Only as a person is willing to acknowledge a dependency upon the Lord is true success likely to occur.

74

God lighted the way for Ananias. He pierced the darkness of his mind with rays of understanding. The miracle of a vision is more than matched by the vision of a miracle—a changed person. This is what Ananias needed to appreciate. However deep rebellion may be in the life of a person, God's power to affect a change in the core of the self and then use that person mightily in the world must never be doubted! That is the essence of the Good News!

Ananias's acceptance of God's command demonstrates how faith allays fear. By acting upon what he knew, his faith increased. He accepted Saul as a Brother, or one who is beloved. He states his assignment: to be a servant through whom Saul would be blessed with sight and the indwelling of the Spirit. Obedience led Ananias to Saul. Obedience created in Saul a receptivity towards Ananias.

When the circle of obedience was complete, God's promised blessing came. Saul's sight was returned. One must be careful in drawing conclusions from this episode. This miracle of healing was a unique event in that the "scales," whatever they were, were imposed by God for a special purpose—to drive home God's sovereignty. Saul had equated God's will with the voice of human agents. The danger of this position is inevitable. It usually leads to human arrogance. This presumptuousness claims for itself what it does not in fact enjoy—divine approval. Human authority is to be tested by God's revelation through Christ Jesus. Jesus is the basis for discerning the will of God. For Saul this was an important adjustment in his theology. His eye condition became a way of illustrating what his mind needed to accept—light comes through faith in Jesus Christ.

Now, healing is God's delight. The joy of faith lies in knowing that with God all things are possible. Healings such as found in 9:18 are possible. God's power has not changed and neither has God's desire to restore human capabilities. What this incidence reveals, however, is the necessity for obedience as the means by which people participate with God in his ministry of reconciliation. Ananias's obedience to God resulted in the salvaging of a person chosen by God for a unique and pivotal role in the extension and upbuilding of the kingdom of God. The Church must always celebrate those servants who through obedience prepared others for the significant service they would render in the world. Ananias was such a person.

3. Empowered to Forgive: Acts 6—7:60

Growth always gives rise to new circumstances. Progress involves problem-solving. With the mounting of tensions between followers of Jesus and the High Priests of the Temple in Jerusalem, it was only a matter of time before the apostles and disciples of Jesus would be forced to organize separate meetings for worship and instructions. As believers converted their houses and land to cash and placed this revenue in the hands of the apostles, you have for all practical purposes the formulation of a separate community designed to further a common purpose under the aegis of Divine love (4:35).

The gospel would be tested by cultural pluralism, which is a strong antagonist to Christian unity. Diversity breeds strangeness, which in turn creates feelings of distance, a sense of uneasiness. Such feelings are natural. But then, this community was not natural. What brought these persons together across cultural and racial lines was a common response to the gospel of Jesus Christ. They were a community of the Spirit and Word. Notwithstanding, they were humans subject to all the foibles of humanity. Favoritism is a natural temptation especially in the face of great need and minimum resources.

Hellenists and Hebrews were linked by a common faith. Each group had worshiped according to the Law. They were Jews. Scholars are not agreed whether the Hellenists were Jews by birth or conversion. What is agreed upon is that there arose a problem related to the distribution food. Hellenists were not likely to have as strong a natural support base as the Hebrews in Jerusalem. Their native home would have been outside of Jerusalem. Therefore, as time progressed, they would have more of their widows in need than the Hebrews. The crisis of neglect was brought to the apostles' attention.

What followed could well serve as a procedural guideline for resolving intra-congregational conflicts: (1) A problem, which cannot be resolved by persons involved, is placed before the leadership of the church for a solution; (2) that leadership studies the nature of the problem and determines the best way to resolve the issue in question; (3) a meeting of the whole is called to present the problem and proposed solution; (4) the group is allowed to accept or reject the strategy for resolving the crisis; (5) and upon its acceptance, the leadership invokes God's blessings and confers, with group approval, authority upon

77

those chosen to ameliorate the situation.

This procedure allowed the apostles to (1) take seriously the material needs of the people, (2) concentrate their energies upon what was vital to the life of the community—ministry of prayer and the ministry of the Word, (3) avoid treating a serious issue for some in a patronizing way, and (4) keep the focus of the congregation upon its mission. The wisdom of the above is self-evident. There was no loss of momentum in mission: "And the word of God increased; and the number of disciples multiplied in Jerusalem greatly; and a great company of the priests were obedient to the faith" (6:7).

Stephen was among the other six Hellenists chosen for this assignment. Stephen's respect among Hellenists and Hebrews alike was enormous. His life was devoted to serving others. This he did with amazing results (6:8). His spiritual credentials were impeccable. Maturity highlighted his character (6:8). His stability was put to the severest test by compatriots who were eager to proved their orthodoxy to suspecting Hebraic Jews. The basic teachings of Stephen were challenged. Stephen was presented by Luke as superior to his antagonist in two crucial areas: wisdom and spirit (verse 10). He not only knew what to say, but he knew how to say it!

What could not be achieved on intellectual and personal grounds is recast and presented on religious grounds. People were bribed to say that Stephen was guilty of blasphemy against Moses and God, the Law and the Temple. Others were solicited under false pretenses to join a crusade against Stephen. As charges mounted, Stephen was brought before the Sanhedrin. As he stood before this council of elders

78

and priests, Stephen's face took on the regal appearance of angel. His soul was at peace. His inner self was unshattered by these false testimonies. Stephen was yet full of the Spirit.

This remarkable man was inwardly persuaded by the gospel that Jesus was the fulfillment of God's promise to Abraham, that Jesus was in fact the very one to whom Moses foretold and yet Jesus was God, the lawgiver. He was convinced that the Temple was made for God, not the opposite, and that their fathers' response to God under Moses and the prophets was indicative of their present response to the ministry of the Spirit. These positions caused Stephen's accusers to seek to silence him once and for all. They proceeded to attack him in mass. First, they became a raging mob. They struck out at Stephen, who shifted his focus from them to God.

Stephen saw Jesus standing in heaven at the right hand of God. He beaconed others to consider what he saw, but they had heard enough. The crowd seized Stephen and carried him out of the city in order to stone him to death. They could stop him from speaking to God. As long as he had breath, Stephen would acknowledge his dependency on God. He sensed that death was imminent. Thus, Stephen assumed a kneeling posture and cried out from the depths of his being: "Lord, lay not this sin to their charge" (7:60). With those words, "he fell asleep" (verse 60b).

Stephen's spirit of forgiveness would prove unforgettable for one person among the crowd of witnesses: Saul. Stephen had planted a powerful seed of truth in the mind of this young man, a living memory of forgiveness. Their misdeed was not glossed over. Stephen had rightly called it "sin." What was done was in violation of God's Word and Spirit. A blatant transgression had taken place. How does one find strength to forgive such atrocities? Where does the power come from to think so creatively under the burden of such pain? It comes from God. It is a work of the Spirit upon the heart of the wounded.

There is only one person who has established an account for handling sin. That person is Jesus Christ, the Son of man (verse 56). Forgiveness is the result of God's redemptive work in Christ. It represents a breakthrough in the realm of the mind and heart of a believer. Any refusal to forgive places a person in conflict with God's work and God's judgment upon failures in his or her own life. Forgiveness rests on the appropriation of grace. God does not expect his point people not to feel intense anger in the face of unmitigated and unprovoked evil.

Stephen's pain was less than the pain he knew would await the unrepentant. Thus, he was prepared to die in faith believing that sooner or later those who sinned against him would in fact seek God's forgiveness. So that their peace would not be disturbed by some nagging doubt of his feelings toward them, Stephen pronounced loud and clear what his attitude was toward them. He was freeing them of any abiding guilt for their actions. Oh, if only some parents understood the wisdom of this action.

As the Church learns this virtue, it too can help disentangle many persons caught in the web of yesterday's guilt. Forgiveness is a powerful key. How it is handled will determine the quality of ministry resident in congregational life. Forgiveness is not an option. It is an essential aspect of Christian living. To forgive is divine! Jesus took this initiative on Calvary.

80

He forgave the world its sin against him. Being God, he could forgive sin. In doing this, Jesus made forgiveness an act of unconditional love expressed toward the undeserving. It became a gift only needing to be received by faith, not a reward to be earned.

As far as Stephen was concerned, he, the offended, had every right to bequeath to the offenders the gift of his intercessory prayer for divine clemency. This attitude reflects Stephen's dying motivation—to see persons saved, not lost. He understood the awfulness of being lost. He was willing to pay the ultimate sacrifice of death in order to fulfill his ministry. But he was unwilling to remain silent in the face of lost persons. Stephen's prayer served notice that the ministry of forgiveness was no longer a special ritual presided over by the priesthood. Rather, forgiveness is inseparable from the message of Jesus. With the telling or proclamation of the story of God's mighty acts in history comes its a call to accept God's forgiveness for sins.

Naturally, many in the audience addressed by Stephen would not consider themselves lost. They were the children of Abraham and Moses by racial identity and/or religious affinity. Stephen pointed these religious persons to a higher basis for a relationship with God, namely, forgiveness. There can be no revival that does not emphasize the need and gift of forgiveness of sins.

4. Empowered to Witness:
Acts 8:5-40

Philip, like Stephen, was used mightily by God.

His knowledge of Scripture, his love of persons, his desire to see people enter into a faith relationship with God, his willingness to be spent in the service of the Lord—these and other qualities explain why Philip was instrumental in the extension of the kingdom of God.

Philip went from the ministry of distribution to the ministry of preaching the Word. Due to the persecution triggered by Saul's zeal, many disciples fled Jerusalem for safety. Philip went to Samaria where he shared the gospel with its citizens. As was characteristic of the ministry of Jesus, Philip addressed those needs presented to him. His was a wholistic ministry. No realm was left untouched.

Philip was used to bring wholeness to those suffering from demonic possession and physical infirmities. The results of this ministry were heartwarming. Many were saved, healed, and emotionally uplifted in spirit. Their seriousness of faith was confirmed by submitting to baptism. Even the city's leading sorcerer, a man believed to possess "great power of God," accepted as truth Philip's preaching concerning the kingdom of God and Jesus as the Christ (8:10, 12). His conversion and baptism emphasize the fact that what happened in Samaria affected the entire city. Here was a classic case of mass evangelism.

The apostles, upon hearing what had happened in Samaria, sent two of their leading representatives, Peter and John, to confirm the report. Most scholars believed that the Holy Spirit was not poured out upon the Samaritans in order to assure unity between the church in Jerusalem and the church in Samaria. Peter and John proceeded to lay hands on the Samaritans. As they prayed, the Holy Spirit was given and received. A long-standing division between Jews and Samaritans was healed. Strongholds of hostility were destroyed as a new, unbounded fellowship sprung into existence.

What centuries of theological scrimmages could not accomplish, a mass revival did. Philip's labor in Samaria paved the way for subsequent outreach efforts in Samaritan cities. This gift of witnessing to large numbers of people is special. Philip was an evangelist. His ministry and gifts lay in presenting the claims of the gospel to unreached audiences. The Church has not suffered an extinction of evangelists, but she has suffered from not emphasizing the importance of this ministry to the work of the local church.

Philip returned to Jerusalem and was soon directed to travel south toward Gaza. What he discovered upon reaching Gaza was an Ethiopian charge d'affaires who was a convert to Judaism. Having led a city to Christ, Philip was then used of God to lead a single person to Christ. From mass evangelism to personal evangelism, from large crowds to no crowds, the transition was no problem for Philip. He was not concerned with numbers. He was equally at home with one as with many. What mattered most was his commitment to sharing the gospel wherever the Spirit led.

Both settings require a knowledge of Scripture. Both settings demand a love for persons, skill in communication, spiritual discernment, and boldness. In addition to these, personal witnessing requires skill in interpersonal relationships, which includes a sensitivity for timing and patience. The Spirit led Philip to a person who was seeking to know God's will. This miracle was not greatly appreciated. Jesus had told the disciple, "Lift up your eyes, and look on the fields; for they are white already to harvest" (John 4:35). Philip was instructed by the Spirit to "Go near, and join thyself to this chariot" (Acts 8:29).

Is this God's way of reaching persons? Is he actively involved in placing us in situations where we can assist others in knowing him better? Absolutely! Personal witnessing need not be feared. God directs us to persons who are most susceptible to our witness. His task is to guide us. Our task is to seize such opportunities in faith. That is what Philip did. He did not rely on clever phrases or detailed explanations. He simply preached Jesus. Christ is the cornerstone of faith. He is the subject foretold by patriarchs and prophets. Without faith in him, there can be no salvation (John 14:6). Philip, having fulfilled his assignment, was directed elsewhere. But he had set in motion a spark that would eventually begin incendiary fellowships throughout Africa.

5. Empowered to Grow: Acts 9:32—11:18

Growth is a sign of life. With the persecution of Stephen, believers were scattered abroad. Everywhere they went they faithfully witnessed to the lordship of Jesus (8:4, 12, 25, 35; 9:20; 10:36; 11:20). Consequently, many persons, primarily Jews, turned to the Lord. It had happened in Judea, Galilee, Samaria, Lydda, and Saron. No one could doubt the seriousness of these followers of Christ. Their mission was clear. Their strategy was sound. Their message was

84

simply stated, and its truth was convincing and compelling. The Spirit of the Lord was gathering in one fold a new people.

This growth resulted in a multiplication of churches. Indigenous fellowships emerged as people turned to God. This local unit enabled the harvest of the Spirit to implement the Lord's command to "teach all nations . . . to observe all things whatsoever I have commanded you" (Matt. 28:19-20). Not only is the local fellowship a center of worship, but it is a center of education. Both are important: a place of meeting for renewal and healing and a place of equipping for ministry and mission.

These fellowships did not define their mission narrowly. Their mission, to proclaim the gospel of Jesus Christ, necessitated that they embrace the whole person and not just isolated dimensions of the self. For a person's deliverance extends to the whole of that life. This explains in part why the growth of the early church was so enduring and decisive. Persons were not merely introduced to Christ and abandoned. Rather, they were introduced to the applications of Christ to the whole of their lives. This integration of the gospel into the broad network of human needs revealed its relevancy and distinctiveness.

Not all growth is healthy. This reality is undeniable. In an age given to appearance, image, and cultic hero worship, the church's need for self monitoring is crucial. The temptation to function by lesser values is great. In a climate where being number one has reached demonic proportions, the ability to resist dishonesty will depend on the willingness of leaders to engage in a moral audit of their own values and personal stability.

The concern for growth, reaching the world for Christ, must always be balanced by a concern for quality of life. Since corporate life is reflective of the life of its key leaders, the imprint of a leader will have lasting consequences for good or evil. Peter's pilgrimage in honesty is therefore a refreshing example of what gives a movement its greatest impetus—a heritage of dedicated and devoted Christian lives.

For all of his considerable weaknesses, Peter was committed to growing spiritually. When confronted with an option of walking or not walking in fellowship with Christ on the night of Christ's betrayal, Peter was quick to accept whatever was required of him by Jesus (John 13:9-10). Fellowship with Christ was Peter's highest desire. He would prove this during his encounter with the risen Christ after his humiliating defection from the faith (John 21:15ff.) He would now be tested again in Caesarea.

The gospel of grace is a commanding gospel. It demands allegiance to the teachings and spirit of Jesus. In a world characterized by racial hostilities, the gospel of the Kingdom calls persons to a new ethic: the ethic of unconditional love. Scripture makes it clear that this ethic cannot be actualized apart from the experience of grace. Peter knew this experience. He was a living witness to the graciousness of Christ. He had spurned the divine warning of his impending crisis of faith. He abrogated to himself arrogance. He reaped a shattered self whose confidence was shaken. He deserved rejection. He received mercy and confidence. With time, this experience of grace would stimulate the ascendancy of honesty as a driving force in his life.

Someone has rightly said that "people must be

judged not by the heights to which they attain, but the depths from which they have come." Peter came from great depths of ignorance concerning himself. He is not alone in this. How many great ministries have become shipwrecked because their principal leaders failed to manage their wayward temptations? How many congregations have perished in a wilderness of disenchantment due to immaturity on the part of their leaders? Many leaders would be wise to consider Fosdick's charge to his congregation:

> I adjure you, do not be easy on me as your minister. *Hold me up to high standards.* Here in America, so prosperous and self-complacent, it is going to be easy in this generation to preach respectability, but to preach real Christianity, that searches personal life and social relationships, will be hard. *Hold me to it. And as I ask you not to be easy on me, I ask you also not to expect me to be easy on you"* (Robert M. Miller, *Harry Emerson Fosdick: Preacher, Pastor, Prophet* [New York: Oxford University Press, 1985], pp. 200-201. Italics mine).

That is what great servants have in common. They aspire to be held to high standards.

For Peter, this meant coming to grips with his feelings of racial exclusiveness. Peter's Jewishness was never more apparent than on the occasion of his visit to Cornelius' house. As was stated previously, God prepares his people for their journeys of faith. He spoke to Cornelius and then to Peter. Each was given instructions. Each obeyed. In their coming together, Peter suddenly discovered the meaning of his vision received at Simon the tanner's home in Joppa. It all

made sense now. The sheet of unclean animals represented the Gentiles. Jewish tradition forbade the
association of Jews with Gentiles. The reason was
more religious than racial, but with time, racial feelings replace religious motives. But from the beginning of the Hebrew nation, this was not so.

Abraham was called to become the father of many
nations (Genesis 12:1ff.) Until Jesus, most Jewish
persons thought that this Fatherhood would be realized by all Gentiles' becoming Jewish converts. Jesus
changed all of that. Jesus found more faith outside of
his beloved Palestine than within (Matthew 8:10). He
said the same was true of Elijah and Elisha (Luke
4:25-27). Peter comes to this same understanding.
God's family is indeed universal. Jesus died for all.
He opened a new way for all to be reconciled to God.
Peter declared in the presence of Gentiles and Jews,
"God is no respecter of persons: but in every nation
he that feareth him, and worketh righteousness, is
accepted with him" (Acts 10:34-35).

This represented a giant step for Peter. He had
confronted his convictions and found them wanting.
He had acknowledged his feelings and found them
wrong. He bowed to divine revelation. His willingness to grow is attested to by his readiness to move
beyond previous boundaries of understanding, thus
dismantling the structure of wrong assumptions and
misguided traditions. This advance into Caesarea
marks another epoch in the history of the Christian
church. This advance did not come without conflict.
Traditions die hard. But Peter's personal testimony
of his own inner struggle and the miracle of the coming of the Spirit upon these Gentiles convinced others that this was indeed a genuine act of God in

accordance with his historic mission (11:8, 15-18).

The gospel belongs to the world. Jesus came not merely to be the Savior of the few, but the Lord of all. This is the purpose God is committed to fulfilling in history. Who, says Peter, is prepared to "withstand God" (verse 7b)? None but the foolish and misguided. God has only one fold! The work of revival is a testimony to God's ability to bring together under Christ all who "believe on the name of the Lord Jesus Christ" (verse 17). Thank God for servants who by their testimony and example were committed to a life-style of continued growth in knowledge and being.

6. Empowered to Establish: Acts 9:1-31; 13:1ff.

The Book of Acts has been referred to as the Acts of Peter and Paul. These stellar servants did more to shape the character of the early church than any since their time. The imprint of their labor and lives has left an indelible impact upon the world's understanding of the Christian faith.

Paul's religious heritage as a Pharisee, intellectual abilities, command of languages, and record of selfless service gave the early church a dynamic leverage for interpreting the life and teachings of Jesus. Paul lived in both worlds: under Moses and under Jesus. News of his conversion seemed an idle tale. His persecution of the Church had been fueled with a seemingly total disregard for any persons who embraced the teachings of Jesus. All were treated alike—none received compassion (Acts 9:2).

His experience of Jesus as risen Lord marked the turning point in his life. It was as though he had stepped out of a great darkness into a marvelous light. Everything took on a new perspective. His accountability to Jesus was clarified. His mission in life became clear: to bear the name of Jesus to the Gentiles (9:15). His authority was grounded in the reality of his experience and the removing of his "scales" of ignorance so that the truth of Scripture might be fully understood. A new world had dawned in the eyes and heart of Saul. Instead of being prepared for a search-and-destroy mission, Saul was recommissioned, this time by God and not persons to announce the good news concerning Jesus Christ to Gentiles. He was given no promise of a smooth sailing. In fact, the opposite was stated. Saul could expect great opposition. And it was not long after his conversion that his life was targeted for destruction (9:23). Death would be a constant shadow. Nevertheless, Saul would never swerve from the path designated by God.

What can Paul teach us about revival?

First, Paul (the Greek translation of the Hebrew *Saul*) would never lose sight of his appointment. Time and again, his credentials as an apostle and his sanity would be challenged (Acts 26:24; 2 Corinthians 13:3). His record of hardships place him in the forefront of those who were "persecuted for righteousness' sake" (Matthew 5:10; compare 2 Corinthians 11:23-27). Paul considered the "care of the churches" to be a greater concern to him than his physical welfare (2 Corinthians 11:28). What enabled him to weather the stormy seasons of his ministry? Undoubtedly, the answer is to be found in his assurance of a divine appointment. In spite of what happened to him, Paul would never lose sight of his chosenness. That is the same spirit whereby all the reformers and revivalists have approached their respective assignments. Each felt the call of God on them. They took comfort in the knowledge that their lives belonged to God. As Paul Harvey would say, "And now you know the rest of the story."

Next, Paul had a good grasp of the Lord's mission in the world (Acts 26:17-18). The central problem with humankind lies not in rule and tradition-keeping, but in blindness: ignorance of God's intent and true identity. Paul came to appreciate the fact that blindness was a spiritual problem. God's mission was essentially a saving mission. The work that God had chosen Paul to do lay in truth-telling. Jesus was the truth. His experience had confirmed what his eyes were blinded from seeing in Scripture.

The truth about Jesus was indeed dynamite. Its power opened the eyes of those who in faith welcomed Jesus as Lord in their hearts. It also affected a radical change in values and virtues, in the depth of the self. Here was God's way of bringing in his kingdom. The sword of truth was God's weapon. Love was God ethic. Humility, not the power of coercion, was God's method of operation. Paul embraced this mission with enthusiasm. For him, the redemption of humanity was the only viable alternative to social chaos and human lostness.

Also, Paul valued God's strategy of extending his

mission through the local church. Paul did more than raise up churches. He established leaders for the work of ministry (Acts 15:36). The importance of the local assembly in the economy of God is central to all God's transactions.

The effectiveness of this fellowship depends (1) on her interdependent relationship with ministries in touch with the needs beyond her border and (2) her accountability for the stewardship of her resources and the faithfulness of her teaching. Sound leaders produce sound communities of faith. Paul made himself available to church leaders. His teaching and encouragement did much to settle disputes and clarify the faith. The authority of his influence ought not to be ignored. The ministry of tested and wise servants is sorely needed as support for young leaders and troubled congregations. National bodies must continually ask not what the local congregation can do for them, but what both can do together to strengthen the local church and minister to the world.

Last, Paul believed it was possible to win the world for Christ. There is an optimism that radiates from the life of the Apostle Paul. He approached each opportunity with a sense of expectancy. He understood the Master's ambitious plans of going "into all the world." He could not be stopped by persecution or rejection. Paul's life is a fitting testimony of what a person can do if he or she first believes it is possible. Paul actualized what he declared to the Philippians: "I can do all things through Christ which strengtheneth me" (4:13). What he did through the grace of God is amazing.

Each missionary journey resulted in incendiary fellowships adorning the landscape of history. Pockets

92

of darkness were a cause for lighting the candle of hope. The Savior had come. Of this, he was a witness. Only God knows the extent of the fruit of his labor. This much is known: Paul was committed to going as far as he could with the message concerning Jesus Christ. Each port would become a springboard to another (Romans 15:24). As was said of another, Paul was "willing to go any where as long as it was forward." His lasts days would be spent in house arrest in Rome. His luminous life created lasting memories in the minds of those who felt the fervor of his heart. Up to the end, Paul was seeking to win one more for Christ (Acts 28:23, 30-31).

His confidence was never stronger. For his faith was joyfully rooted in the eternal and unfailing word of the Lord. His prayer was: "For to me to live is Christ, and to die is gain" (Philippians 1:21). Herein lies the gateway to revival for our day—the fellowship of fire. May each reader experience a call to that fellowship anew.

> May thy rich grace impart
> strength to my fainting heart,
> my zeal inspire;
> As thou has died for me,
> O, may my love to Thee
> pure, warm, and changeless be,
> a living fire."

> —Ray Palmer

Epilogue

As you have discovered, this book is an attempt to look at the subject of revival through the eyes of Acts of the Apostles. Principles embedded in Scriptures provide a significant place of beginning for those who desire to see the wind of the Spirit awakening persons to faith and ministry. It has happened often in history. It will continue to happen wherever persons are willing

- to recapture a vision of God's greatness.
- to rededicate themselves to the faithful witnessing to God's redemption in Christ Jesus the Lord.
- to reaffirm the message and values of the kingdom of God.
- to make the salvation of persons their ultimate concern.
- to practice a life-style of humility and compassion.
- to prepare a people for the celebration of God's victories in history and the consummation of God's fellowship beyond history.
- to pray for the Spirit's anointing. Having done all, pray for revival to begin in you! And when it does, the awakening has indeed begun. Who knows how far it can reach and how long it will last?

A Study of Revival in the Book of Acts

I. The Power of a Caring Community (Chapter 1)
  A. The Gospels: God's acts of compassion

  B. The Book of Acts: Luke's continued review of caring people
    1. What was God's genuine concern?
    2. God raised up spokepersons.
    3. Spreading the gospel—revival—was a response to the Holy Spirit's presence.
  C. Revival and Christian faith. Faith rests on the belief that:
    1. Christ is the Messiah.
    2. the living Christ is Lord.
    3. the Kingdom has come.
      (a) Obedience and anticipation are its principles.
      (b) The promise of the Kingdom is the baptism of the Holy Spirit.
      (c) The Kingdom's preoccupation is doing the will of God.

(d) The purpose of the Kingdom is to restore our power.

(e) The priority of the Kingdom is prayer.

D. Evil will not prevail—Christ is Conqueror.

E. God's community has a great "bullpen."

II. The Power of the Anointed Community (Chapter 2)

A. The importance of Pentecost

B. The impact of the Holy Spirit's anointing at Pentecost

1. The impact on the gathered community
   —Persons were empowered and prepared for their part in revival.

2. The impact on the scattered community of Israel
   —The Pentecost ingathering provided a new outlook on how to respond when they returned to their homes.

3. The impact upon Peter's preaching
   —He interpreted Pentecost and the task facing the church.

4. The impact on the newly constituted church; Pentecost launched a response to the need:
   (a) to know truth
   (b) to belong
   (c) to remember: Christ, his life, his message, and his commands
   (d) to be whole, unified
   (e) for self-discipline

C. The marks of the annointed community

1. A reverent fear of God

2. Unity

5. Empowered to Grow
6. Empowered to Establish
C. Paul Teaches Us About Revival

Notes

KEEPER'S GOLD

Recent Titles by Judith Cook

BLOOD ON THE BORDERS
DEATH OF A LADY'S MAID
KILL THE WITCH
MURDER AT THE ROSE
SCHOOL OF THE NIGHT

DEAD RINGER *
WORM IN THE BUD *

* *available from Severn House*

KEEPER'S GOLD

Judith Cook

This first world edition published in Great Britain 2004 by
SEVERN HOUSE PUBLISHERS LTD of
9–15 High Street, Sutton, Surrey SM1 1DF.
This first world edition published in the USA 2004 by
SEVERN HOUSE PUBLISHERS INC of
595 Madison Avenue, New York, N.Y. 10022.

British Library Cataloguing in Publication Data

Cook,   Judith,   1933
    Keeper's gold. - (John Latymer mystery series ; 3)
    1.   Latymer, John (Fictitious character) - Fiction
    2.   Ex-police officers - England - Fiction
    3.   Murder - Investigation - England - Cornwall - Fiction
    4.   Detective and mystery stories
    I.   Title
    823.9'14 [F]

    ISBN 0-7278-6130-1

Typeset by Palimpsest Book Production Ltd.,
Polmont, Stirlingshire, Scotland.
Printed and bound in Great Britain by
MPG Books Ltd., Bodmin, Cornwall.

Acknowledgements

My thanks to Ken Ainge for his usual invaluable help. Also to Anna Tyack, Finds Officer at Truro Museum, for her assistance on the workings of the new Treasure Act and the protocols for those who discover buried treasure. Also the staff of the Morrab Library in Penzance for the use of their reference books on the bronze-age archaeology of the area. The Department of Culture and Sport's *Treasure Annual Report for 2001* and *Information for Finders of Treasure* proved very useful too.

Author's note: St Mellick is a composite of several 'saint' villages on Bodmin Moor, and neither Lanwithen and its museum, nor indeed Keeper's Tump, exist, although all other places mentioned do. Keeper's Tump is based on the bronze-age barrow where the Rillaton Cup was found in the nineteenth century.

Judith Cook, Newlyn, Cornwall, 2004.

Prologue

A dank, unpleasant mist had come down quite suddenly during the last few minutes and he was beginning to shiver. He looked at his watch. It was now nearly half past twelve and the meeting had been arranged for midnight. The instructions he'd been given had been explicit, which, in the circumstances, had caused him some amusement. He was to drive down into Cornwall, take the main road across Bodmin Moor until he saw the sign pointing to St Mellick, then turn off. After reaching the village, he should drive straight through until, about half a mile out the other side, he'd see a small cottage on his left and a footpath sign. He must then follow the path on foot for about 300 yards or so until he came to a hillock on his left and two standing stones on his right. Then wait.

An eerie howling from one direction was answered by another from the other side of the moor. Common sense told him it was foxes, not the pack of the Wild Hunt, the Barguest down on holiday from the north country, or the Hound of the Baskervilles; and anyway, the Baskerville Hound had supposedly operated on Dartmoor. He was not an imaginative man but if he had to stay here much longer he'd begin to believe anything. He looked at his watch again. Twenty to one. Should he go or should he stay? It had taken him hours of driving to get here and all he wanted now was to go to bed. He unzipped the small, soft-topped case he had brought with him and peered inside to comfort himself that its contents, the reason for his being in this godforsaken place, were still safe.

He began to walk up and down, trying to keep warm. The hillock on his left was in fact a bronze-age barrow. It was clearly marked on the ordnance map and he'd discovered that,

1

like many ancient sites, it had attracted its own myths and legends over the centuries. It was said that it hid a secret of some kind, a secret which was protected by 'The Keeper', a being in a golden mask, and that dire misfortune befell anyone who disturbed him. Added to that, the standing stones on the other side of the path were known locally as the Guardians. According to the intermediary whom he'd met in London, the place had been chosen to make use of the legend, but he'd not seen the point, nor why the transfer couldn't have taken place there and then without his having to slog down to St Mellick. Presumably there was some thinking behind it, other than simply making him sweat for his money, but for the life of him he couldn't imagine what it was.

He peered again down the path to the main road. Still no sign of life. He'd had enough. He'd go back to his car and drive off. He'd given them their chance and they'd blown it. He wasn't all that bothered, there was always Plan B. He'd put that in hand first thing in the morning. Deep in thought, he didn't hear a sound until he was suddenly grabbed by the shoulder from behind. The unexpectedness made him jump, then he realized his long wait was finally at an end. 'And about bloody time too!' he protested as he turned round, then stood transfixed as he looked into the blank golden mask facing him. It was the last thing he was ever to see.

One

Tourists did not beat a path to the door of the Lanwithen Museum, not even those energetic souls striding out on walking holidays on Bodmin Moor, let alone the coach parties which regularly stopped off at Jamaica Inn as part of a tour of 'du Maurier country'. As was the case with many small provincial museums, it had been founded towards the end of the nineteenth century by a local benefactor, one who, this being Cornwall, had made his fortune on the backs of the tin and copper miners who now lay two-deep in the graveyards along the north coast, most of them dead by the time they were forty. While some of the smaller museums had come under the umbrella of the county authority, modernizing them-selves in the process, Lanwithen Museum had moved little with the times and remained in private hands, run by a trust. Something to do with the original terms of the bequest, curator Matthew Turner was told by the trustees when he'd applied for the post.

On the other hand, Lanwithen town itself had seen some-thing of a change in its fortunes over recent years, due in part to the famous chef with the fish restaurant a few miles away on the coast, close to which was a village which had suddenly become trendy, where most of the cottages were now owned by the wealthy as second homes. So, Lanwithen, once little more than a single dreary high street, now boasted antique emporia, boutiques and shops with tasteful fascias selling expensive luxury goods. But the new wealth had not trickled out as far as the museum, a bleak, double-fronted granite building with the words 'Lanwithen Museum' and the name of its founder, 'Elijah Tregorren', carved over the door in large lettering.

3

To go inside was to walk into a past age. No effort had been made to update its contents or make it more attractive to visitors. Rooms, smelling of damp and lit by what appeared to be a couple of sixty-watt bulbs, were full of old-fashioned exhibition cases made of dark wood and dusty glass, containing such objects as a handful of bronze-age and iron-age relics from the moor, pieces of Samian ware (unlikely to have been found locally), a few pieces of mediaeval pottery, and a great many lumps of tin and copper ore and other minerals found in the mines. A large room at the back was full from floor to ceiling with old farm implements, and one end was devoted, according to a faded card, to the 'History of Lanwithen', a history which appeared to have stopped around 1908.

At first Matthew Turner, who had barely scraped a lower second degree in history and archaeology, could hardly believe his luck when he was informed that he'd been shortlisted for the post of curator, since his only experience up until then had been working in the storage department of a city museum in the north. He'd travelled down to Cornwall for his interview feeling on top of the world and full of enthusiasm, some of which lasted even after he had been shown the museum and its contents. Should he be lucky enough to get the post, he told himself, he'd soon alter all that. To his amazement he was offered the job, and eagerly accepted. He never did discover how many other contenders there'd been, nor indeed if there'd actually been any, but as month followed month he soon realized that there was so little money available that nothing was likely to change in the foreseeable future, another detail which had been rapidly skated over when he was interviewed. There was a small income from the original bequest, an even smaller grant from the local authority, which could be cut off at any time, and the money taken on the door. That was about it. Other than a part-time secretary who came in three mornings a week, his was the only full-time paid post; everyone else worked on a voluntary basis, which meant they had to be treated with kid gloves and a great deal of tact. Heaven forbid any one of them didn't think she was sufficiently valued.

With great difficulty he'd persuaded the trustees to go for a lottery grant, but after several months of waiting their proposal had been turned down. Time passed. He began scanning the situations-vacant columns in the relevant periodicals, appling for several, but he was not even shortlisted for any of them. He began to think of Lanwithen Museum as some kind of waiting room for hell in which he would be stuck for life, gradually growing as grey and dusty as the exhibits around him. Then, after an evening slumped in front of the television, he'd had an idea. While watching one of the many popular archaeology programmes, he saw in a flash that what was needed to put the museum, and himself with it, on the map was a well-publicized television dig somewhere local, which would attract the punters, possibly make the papers, and actually bring in some money. It should be easy: Bodmin Moor was littered with archaeological remains of all kinds.

He ransacked the shelves of mouldering papers and maps in what passed at the museum for its library, to see what sites were known to have been excavated by enthusiastic amateurs in the nineteenth century, or properly qualified professionals in the twentieth. He was looking for those which appeared to be still untouched, and discovered, to his relief, that there were dozens of them. Fired with enthusiasm, he wrote off at once to the companies responsible for *Time Team* and *Buried Treasure*, suggesting they look at one or other of the barrows on Bodmin Moor. The responses had been lukewarm: *Time Team* were fully committed for the next two seasons but would bear his request in mind; *Buried Treasure*, as its name implied, needed to be absolutely sure beforehand that they would find just that, or that it had actually already been found, before they'd even consider such a project. Could he guarantee a hoard of some kind?

It's no good, he thought, I can't stand much more of this. He decided he'd give in his notice at the end of the month then go back up north. It wouldn't be the end of the world if he couldn't find another museum job; after all, he had no wife or family to support. He'd take an IT course or something. He went back into his tiny office and began composing his resignation letter in his head.

One of the volunteers, a Mrs Pengelly, was on the admission desk when a man, carrying a brightly coloured zip bag over his shoulder, strode in through the door, leaving it swinging behind him. He looked around, then stomped over to her.

'Where's the fellow in charge?'

'Mr Turner, the curator, is in his office,' she replied, reluctantly putting down her knitting. She put his age somewhere in the mid-fifties. He was overweight, with a heavy-featured red face. She thought vaguely that he might be a farmer.

'Tell him I want to see him. Look sharp!'

She stood up. 'I'll *see* if it's convenient. He's a very busy man.'

The man guffawed loudly and looked around again. 'In this dump? I doubt it.'

'You don't have to wait if you don't want to,' she replied, needled.

'No, I don't. But I reckon your "curator", or whatever you call him, must have some kind of qualifications for the job.'

She marched into Turner's office and told him about the visitor. 'Such a *rude* man. If I were you I'd get rid of him right away.'

'Is he local?'

She thought for a moment. 'Not right local here in Lanwithen or I'd have known him.' Mrs Pengelly's family had lived in Lanwithen for generations. 'But from the way he talks he is Cornish, I'm certain of that. I thought straight off he might be a farmer but I'm not sure now. He looks a bit like those folk who used to go overseas from here years back, make a bit of money, then come home to settle down. They used to call they Cousin Jacks.'

Turner stood up. 'OK, I'll come out and see what he wants.' But before he could do so the door burst open and their visitor erupted in. He glared at Mrs Pengelly. 'How long does it take you to tell him there –' he nodded toward Turner – 'that someone wants to see him urgent?'

'There's no need to speak to my staff like that,' snapped Turner. 'Right, you can go, Mrs Pengelly. Thank you.' As she left the room he turned to his unwanted guest. He retreated

6

back behind his desk. 'Very well then. I'm afraid all I can offer you to sit on is that stool in the corner if you'd like to pull it over here.' The man did so. 'And now perhaps you'll tell me who you are and what this is all about.'

'The name's Smith,' replied the man. 'Brian Smith. And I want to know what you make of these.' He unzipped the bag and took out two objects, both wrapped in newspaper. He carefully unwrapped the first one and set it down on Turner's desk a tiny, exquisite, gold cup or beaker, about four or five inches high. He then unwrapped the second and laid beside it a magnificent torque, a necklace made of very fine plaited gold wire, its ends decorated with enamelwork. Turner thought he was going to faint. For a few minutes there was complete silence.

'How on earth did you get hold of these?' he managed, finally.

'Metal detecting,' responded Smith, with a self-satisfied smile. 'It's become my hobby since I took early retirement and come back down to Cornwall.'

'Good God!' Turner picked up the little cup and turned it round. Even on a dull day it positively glowed. 'It's even finer than the Rillaton Cup.'

'What's that?'

'A handleless cup or beaker like this, found by a farm labourer in a barrow in Linkinhorne parish in 1837.' He ran a finger gently up and down it. 'That too had corrugated sides like this. Apparently there were other things there as well but they vanished shortly afterwards.' He put it back on the table and picked up the torque. 'As for this . . .' He shook his head. 'You say you found both of them while metal detecting? Where?'

'Don't know as I can tell you that.'

'If you can't, then you'll have to go somewhere else.'

Smith paused. 'Very well. They're from Keeper's Tump, over to St Mellick.'

Turner thought for a moment. 'Keeper's Tump? That's a bronze-age barrow, isn't it? Did you actually get inside somehow?'

Smith looked genuinely blank. 'How come I could've done that?'

'The mound is hollow inside, if the earth hasn't all fallen

in. It covers a burial, a grave.'

Smith shook his head. 'Thought it was solid myself. Climbed up on to it with the detector and it suddenly started pinging away. Dug down a bit and there they were.'

'Together?'

'That's right. First I found the cup, then the necklace thing.'

'I find that hard to believe.'

'You saying I stole them? So, it's a grave. Don't they find such things in these old graves?'

'They do, but not, so far as I'm aware, in the earth on the top, though funny things do happen and it could be that the grave was robbed in the past, the robber panicked and then hid the treasure . . . except for one thing . . .'

'What's that?'

'I'll need to look it up and check it out, as it isn't my period, but even if they'd been found inside the grave they couldn't both have been put there originally. You see, one is at least five hundred years older than the other. Quite possibly even older than that!'

Two

'Goodness, I didn't realize you'd *all* been in the police force,' observed Jack Maynard in some surprise. A recently acquired and now regular customer of the Taste for Murder bookshop in Bristol, the partners had felt it might be a good idea to take him out to lunch to keep it that way. They'd chatted mainly about books and the book business throughout the meal and had now reached the coffee stage.

'*I* wasn't,' Kate Berry informed him. 'It's John and Keith who were with West Midlands Police. Keith was a detective sergeant and John—'

'Reached the dizzy heights of chief inspector,' added Keith Berry. 'For different reasons we both took early retirement. Kate and I started the bookshop when I left the force and John joined us about six months ago.'

Maynard turned to John Latymer. 'Found life too dreadfully dull, did you, with nothing much to do?'

'Actually I had a job. I was a tour manager for Becketts Literary Tours, but after a couple of years of trailing round the country, I felt I'd had enough of it.'

He hoped he wasn't sounding too churlish. He was fully aware that Maynard really was an excellent customer and definitely one to be encouraged, but, as he'd told Berry after meeting him for the first time, he found him somewhat precious. He couldn't decide whether the camp manner was assumed or whether Maynard really was gay. He held some kind of consultancy post in London which obviously paid well, since it enabled him to live in Holland Park and buy lots of expensive books, but he was also heavily into Feng Shui, meditation and crystals, while his taste was for gothic novels, a genre the shop was adding to its specialities.

Latymer was enjoying being part of A Taste for Murder and during the last six months he'd learned a great deal more about book dealing and selling. The shop had a section for new books, looked after by Kate, but it was primarily devoted to second-hand and rare stock, along with book searches. However, outside the world of the bookshop, things were not so good. The break-up of his marriage back in the spring meant that he was now living alone in a flat once again. Admittedly it was a nice flat in a pleasant place but he was finding it a solitary existence, a condition exacerbated by the fact that he'd recently had a really bad cold that had left him feeling overtired, depressed and prone to the nightmares from which he suffered from time to time.

As to the reason for the break-up, his wife, Tess, had been the prime mover, in one respect literally, since she'd insisted they sell their house in a pleasant Gloucestershire village and move nearer to Taunton so that she could be close to her daughter Diana, who was expecting her first child. But what had really driven them apart was his becoming involved in an attempt to discover the real identity of a dead man, a quest which had led Berry and himself to the Solway coast and the discovery of a drugs racket and two murders, not to mention a political cover-up. Tess had been devastated. It was a second marriage for both of them and, as she told him, she'd never have gone through with it if she'd thought for one moment that, now he'd left the police force, he'd become mixed up in crime again. After all, it was his police work that had broken up his first marriage. If they were to stay together, then it was on the understanding that his essay at detection was a one-off, and when he'd assured her that was indeed the case, he'd really meant it. But within a relatively short time he and Berry had become involved in yet another mystery, following which he'd resigned from his job to join Keith and Kate in their business and Tess had promptly moved to Taunton. The divorce had gone through shortly afterwards.

Funnily enough, to his surprise, she'd rung him the previous week. He wasn't sure why. Everything was fine, she told him, in answer to his enquiry. Diana was now back at work and likely to be promoted, as was Peter, and she was looking after the baby for her in the daytime until they found a really suitable person to look after him; something which was, apparently, proving difficult. But, in spite of her past enthusiasm for living near Diana so she could help out, she didn't actually sound all that happy with the situation she now found herself in. He'd managed to restrain himself from saying *I told you so*, and vaguely agreed that they should meet up again some time.

Another nail in the coffin of his marriage had been his tentative relationship, if such it could be called, with Fiona Garleston, to whom he'd felt drawn during his foray into private detection in Scotland. He'd seen her several times during the last six months, both at her home on the Solway coast and in Bristol, but, even though he was now free, the situation didn't seem to be getting anywhere, partly because he couldn't bring himself to ask her if she would ever be prepared to leave Scotland to live with him.

'You're very quiet, John.' Maynard was looking archly at him across the table. 'Got the blues?'

Latymer suddenly became aware that conversation had been washing around him for some time without his taking any part in it.'

'I'm sorry,' he apologized. 'I admit to being miles away. I've had a bad cold and it's really laid me out.'

'I told him he should take a couple of weeks off and have a holiday,' declared Kate. 'He's had quite a hard few months, not least learning the business. It's nearly the end of September and things will quieten down now a little until the run-up to Christmas. It would be a good time to go, John, and there are some real bargains going in the way of holidays in the Canaries, Greece and so on. You'd still get some sun.' Latymer mumbled a suitable response. It sounded all right in principle, but the last thing he felt he wanted was a solitary vacation on one of the Costas or the Greek islands. Unless he could persuade Fiona along . . .

'Wait a minute, I've got an idea,' broke in Maynard. 'Do you know Cornwall at all, John?'

Latymer replied that he did, a little. 'Some of the literary

11

tours used to take in what they call "du Maurier country", mostly around Fowey, because of its connection with the novels. I've also been down to Penzance a couple of times.' He didn't add that the second occasion had involved a corpse.

'Ah,' declared Maynard, knowingly, 'but "du Maurier country" isn't the proper Cornwall, the real Cornwall, nor is Penzance.'

'Are you Cornish, then?' asked Latymer in some surprise.

'Not exactly. Well, no, as a matter of fact, I'm not. But I feel *drawn* to Cornwall and the Cornish. What I meant was, do you know the *real* Cornwall, not the fiction of Manderley or the tourist traps along Mount's Bay.'

'And what is the real Cornwall?' enquired Berry.

A misty look crossed Maynard's face. He seemed to be staring into the distance at some unseen prospect. 'The real Cornwall,' he responded, dreamily, 'is the savage north coast, the grandeur of Bodmin Moor.'

'All I saw of Bodmin Moor was from the coach when we crossed part of it to get to Jamaica Inn for lunch, and that's on little more than a glorified traffic island nowadays. From what I did see, it looked pretty bleak to me,' Latymer told him.

'That's where you're wrong, you see. Once you know it, you realize it's far from bleak. I bought a cottage there last year at St Mellick. A delightful village and the people are *so* friendly. Make you really feel one of them. What I was going to suggest was, why don't you borrow it for a couple of weeks? From what I'm told, early October's usually good for weather in Cornwall. It's very peaceful but there's a pub and a post office and a shop in the village.'

'And the cottage?' persisted Berry, ever practical.

'Basically a two-up two-down, but the last owner built a charming little conservatory on the back, which catches a lot of sun.' He gave a reminiscent smile. 'There are mod cons, of course, electricity, hot water and so on, and you'll find most of the things you need.' He paused. 'But perhaps you'd better take bedding and towels, as what's there in the way of linen might have got rather damp. I've simply been too busy to get down there for a little while . . . Oh,' he added, 'and there's no phone. I've not bothered having a line put in, since most people have mobiles these days.'

'Are you sure you'd be happy for me to use it?' Latymer found himself asking, although he was already having doubts.

'Of *course*! I hope I'm not selfish. I assumed when I bought it that I'd offer it to friends when I wasn't there myself.' He looked at his watch. 'Goodness, I must love you and leave you. I promised to call in on someone the other side of Bristol before I drove home.'

Berry looked across at Latymer and winked. 'Do you want us to suggest a route?'

Maynard laughed. 'I hardly think so. I'm quite capable of reading a road map. It's quite simple, I go straight through the city centre.'

'Well, it's up to you,' said Berry, 'but to get through Bristol city centre and come out in the right place, most visitors need a native guide!'

Berry paid the bill and they made their way out of the restaurant. Maynard shook hands with Berry and Latymer and kissed Kate on both cheeks. 'Well, see you soon, and look out for that first edition of *The Monk* for me, Keith. And John, the cottage is yours if you want it.'

Latymer tried to appear enthusiastic. 'I'll give your kind offer some thought if I may, Jack, and give you a call before the end of the week.'

'Fine,' responded Maynard. 'If you do decide to go, you won't regret it.'

'The *real* Cornwall,' snorted Berry, after they'd returned to the shop. 'You're dead right, he really is precious. If you do go down there you'll probably find the place draped in velvet curtains strung with crystal beads and all the furniture arranged in odd ways. You never know, he might have a mirror over the bed! But he's a very good customer and he pays on the nail.'

'It's an idea though,' said Latymer.

Keith nodded. 'Look, I've a big old road atlas here some-

13

where, let's see where St Mellick is before you finally make your mind up.' He rooted about on a shelf. 'Yes, here we are. It's a few years old but I don't suppose much has changed.' There was no one in the shop so he spread it out on the counter and turned to the back. 'It'll be with the rest of the saints . . . good grief, there's dozens of them just in Cornwall . . . Austell, Blazey, Buryan, Breward . . . Clether . . . Enoder, Endellion, Mellion . . . Veep! I must have missed it . . . here we are, St Mellick, page three.'

Latymer shook his head. 'Who on earth were St Breward, St Clether and St Veep? I've never heard of any of them.'

'I suppose they must be part of what they call the standing army of Celtic saints. I read about them somewhere. Some are supposed to have crossed over from Ireland floating on leaves, and I think one came in a sieve . . . it's Christianity all mixed up with Celtic folklore. Anyway, here's St Mellick.' They both peered at the map. 'See, it's north of the main A30. It looks as if the most straightforward way is to turn off at that B road there –' he pointed to a junction – 'and it should eventually take you to St Mellick. It's not all that far from Lanwithen, which is supposed to be quite smart nowadays, and it's within shouting distance of Padstow and the famous fish restaurant. You know, it could be just what you need.'

Latymer returned to his flat that night and immediately rang Fiona. He thought it unlikely that she'd be prepared to drop everything and take off for the wilds of Cornwall with him, since she lived in a pretty isolated spot herself all year round, however, he lived in hope. But there was no reply and, from the number of clicks on the answerphone, she must have been out for some time, so he emailed her, since she was usually a good correspondent. However, there was still no reply the next morning or the following evening. She must be away. He felt unaccountably hurt even though she had every right to go where she chose when she chose. Finally he made up his mind, rang Jack Maynard and arranged to take him up on his offer. He'd go down to St Mellick at the end of the following week.

Maynard giggled. 'Mind you don't come across any

bodies, John. Keith's told me how you're always falling over them.'

'I wouldn't put it quite like that,' Latymer assured him. 'Not only is it highly unlikely but it's the last thing I need.'

Three

It was clear that Matthew Turner's statement had come as something of a shock to Smith. 'What are you getting at?' he demanded.

'I'm not "getting" at anything. What I'm telling you is that these two objects are from different eras. They're as far apart from each other in time as something made the year Columbus discovered America would be from something made now, possibly even further. Say 1066 and now. There's no way they could have been buried in the same grave, not to mention the fact that grave goods are found inside graves and barrows, not on top. They must have been deliberately buried there much more recently. Did the earth look disturbed, was that why you used your metal detector there?' Smith shook his head. 'Well, perhaps they were found back in the nineteenth century, like the Rillaton Cup, and someone hid them there but never came back for them. But that still wouldn't explain away two such different objects.' He looked across at Smith. 'Have you informed the coroner?'

'Why would I do that? I've found gold not a sodding body.'

'Because that's legally what you have to do if you make a substantial archaeological find, which this most definitely is.'

'Then what?'

'Well, up until recently the finds would've come under treasure trove, but now there's a new law in operation . . . I've a leaflet about it here somewhere . . . Yes, it's here. It's called the Treasure Act. There's a whole list of things to which it applies, but the only one that really concerns you is the section on objects more than three hundred years old and made of gold or silver. I can't date these exactly but I'll certainly confirm that they're well over three hundred years old, in fact

16

the cup must be nearer three thousand. And there's no doubt they're made of gold. So, you register the find with the coroner and then you'll be directed to the finds liaison officer . . .'

Smith stood up. 'Do I have to listen to all this garbage? All this red tape? I came in here to see if you could tell me what they were and how much they were likely to fetch, I can see for myself they're some valuable. I don't want a load of tripe about coroners, liaison officers and acts of Parliament.'

Turner tried to hold on to his temper. 'Suit yourself. But if you don't inform the coroner, under the new act you could find yourself liable for a five-thousand-pound fine, three months in gaol, or both.'

Smith slumped down again on the stool. 'All right, get on with it.'

'I think the nearest finds liaison officer is in Truro, based in the county museum. If the items had been found on private land and you'd had the owner's permission to metal detect, then he'd have to be involved as well, for he'd be due a percentage of the profits if and when the goods are sold.' He paused. 'In fact, you might still get into some trouble. I don't suppose you bothered to find out the status of Keeper's Tump, whether it's on common land or land that's privately owned?' It was clear from Smith's face that the thought had never crossed his mind. 'Even putting aside the question of who might own the land, Keeper's Tump must be a scheduled site and you should have asked permission from the relevant authorities before going metal detecting on it, then—'

But Smith wasn't listening. 'How much do you reckon they're worth?' he broke in, stemming the flow.

'I haven't a clue. The liaison officer might be able to give you a very rough idea. The officer will then send them to the British Museum for safe keeping, their advice and, if everything's above board, to see if they want to make an offer for them. There'll also have to be an inquest to confirm the find is treasure, which you can attend to explain how you found the stuff. That's up to you. Don't worry, it's not like a murder case or a sudden death, there's no jury or anything. Then it'll be valued by the official Treasure Valuation Committee, but you can also have it valued independently yourself if you want.

When it's all been satisfactorily agreed, the BM, or any other interested museums, are given a set time to come back with an offer and, if you accept, you'll then get an ex gratia payment or reward.'

'But this lot could take years!'

'It says here it usually takes about twelve months.'

'Twelve months! I wish I'd never come here. I suppose, now I've shown them to you, you'll go shooting your mouth off all over the place. I'm sure I could have sold them myself without all this rigmarole. Who'd know so long as I was careful? Then I'd have got all the money.'

Turner shook his head. 'You'd never get away with it. Word would get round in no time among those who know about these things, and the penalty you'd face then would be far more severe.' But even as he was speaking, a plan was beginning to form in his mind as he realized that out of the blue had come an opportunity which must be grasped at all costs. He did his best to look more sympathetic. 'I can see how frustrating it must be for you.' He paused. 'Look, I've just had an idea, though it will depend on both you and I keeping quiet about this for a little while. And, in spite of what I've just told you, it will mean not telling the coroner, at least not straight away.'

'And what's that?'

Turner explained that he'd been trying for some time to interest one of the television archaeology programme makers to do a dig based somewhere in the area, but hadn't been able to come up with anything sufficiently enticing. Smith was unimpressed. 'I can't see the point of it. Anyway, what's in it for you?'

'A great deal,' Turner told him. 'I'm desperate to get out of Lanwithen and into a better job. Something like this would publicize the museum, get people in, bring some money into the place at last. Not that we could make an offer for the cup and the torque, we'd need to actually *win* the lottery for that, not just get a grant from its proceeds, but more to the point, it would give me a decent profile, look good on my CV, allow me to aim for a post in one of the major museums. I know this goes against everything I've been saying, but what I'm suggesting is this: you hang on to the stuff, making absolutely sure it's safe and that nobody knows about it. Nobody. Got that? Or we'll both be in trouble. Then I try again to get the telly people interested. This time I'll be specific and suggest they excavate Keeper's Tump, telling them all about the buried treasure legend.' He warmed to his theme. 'If all goes well and we get a unit down here, then they'll find you waiting for them. You tell them that when you heard they were coming to make a programme about Keeper's Tump, you couldn't resist trying out your metal detector and, lo and behold, look at what you've just found.'

'Suppose they don't believe me?'

'They might well not, but they're unlikely to turn down the chance of making a programme about such a spectacular find. I suppose you could say we're all conning each other in this game. It won't matter after that if they don't find anything else when they actually do the dig, not when it can be made to look such a success. You also tell them that you brought the objects to me straight away to find out what they were, and that I told you that you'd have to inform the coroner, which you now propose to do. Then the whole process will start rolling. There'll be masses of publicity and you'll do well out of it. If the BM don't want it, which I'm sure they will, other museums here and abroad will be competing with each other for the stuff.' A thought struck him. 'I'll just take a couple of photographs. It's as well I left my camera here the other day.'

'I don't want no photos taken,' said Smith in alarm.

'It's only so that I can look up similar objects, where they were found, their provenance – and perhaps get an idea of their value. It'll help us both in the long run.'

Smith still looked far from happy. 'What if someone sees the photographs? What about when you get the film developed?'

'I doubt it would mean much to the average bored operative working a developing and printing machine. And if someone did say anything I could easily pass it off as pictures I'd taken of finds in another museum.' He looked at his watch. 'I'll tell Mrs Pengelly she can go for lunch early, then I'll

19

lock up and we'll put the things in behind the glass in one of the old showcases. That'll make it look as if I'm telling the truth.' He was surprised to find how easily lies now tripped off his tongue.

He came back from seeing Mrs Pengelly out of the front door, to find Smith fidgeting in his chair. 'You got a toilet here?'

Turner pointed towards the back of the building. 'There's one out there for the staff. Go past all that old farm stuff and it's the door on the left.'

As soon as Smith was safely inside, he whipped out his camera and took several detailed shots of both objects, ensuring that by the time Smith returned he was standing outside the office door, camera in hand. They walked through into the museum proper. 'That case over there will do. It's not locked, there's nothing in it anyone would want.' He rubbed his pullover sleeve against the glass. 'That'll do. If it looks a bit grubby it'll help make it look as if they've been there for ages.' He took half a dozen shots then handed the artefacts back to Smith. 'If we'd proper security here I'd suggest you left them with me, but the fact is that we haven't.'

'Don't make no difference if you had, I wouldn't leave them with you, not even if it were like Fort Knox here. I'm not letting them out of my sight until I have to.' He put the cup and the torque back in the bag in which he'd brought them, then grabbed hold of Turner. 'What if you don't get no telly people down here? How long am I expected to hang about?'

'I'll . . . I'll tell you if that's likely to happen,' spluttered Turner, trying unsuccessfully to break loose. 'Then you can go to the coroner and tell him you've just found the stuff. I won't say anything.'

Smith released his grip. 'All right,' he said, grudgingly, 'but don't you leave it go. If you do, then it's all off.' At which he walked out of the museum without another word. Turner watched him go down the road to his car with mixed feelings. He couldn't decide whether Smith was just an unpleasant individual with a bullying nature or something more sinister. He was already beginning to have doubts about his bright idea;

20

the whole plan hinged on his having to trust someone he didn't know and didn't much like the look of.

He'd begun trying to contact the archaeology programme makers that same afternoon, ringing up first Channel Four's *Time Team* then the BBC, who'd run the series on buried treasure. In each case he was asked to submit a formal proposal. When he demurred over the time this would take, pointing out that it was nearly August and by mid-October the weather on Bodmin Moor was unlikely to be suitable, *Time Team* repeated what they had said in their original letter to him: that they were committed months in advance and that this kind of project took a considerable time to set up. Nor were the BBC any more encouraging, but eventually the umpteenth researcher or producer to whom he spoke suggested he try a new production company who, she understood, were about to embark on a series of archaeology programmes for Channel 5.

'They're called Crayford Productions, the guy who started it is Peter Crayford. I can give you their phone number if you like. Mind you, I've no idea where they're at or even if they're in the market for ideas.'

In fact Crayford Productions had no guarantee they were going to be given the green light to go ahead at all. Pete and his partner Dave, who was also the cameraman, hadn't found the commissioning editors at Channel 5 particularly enthusiastic. Yes, they agreed, popular archaeology programmes did seem to do well, yes, archaeology was now pretty sexy, but was there room for another? *Time Team* had an actor/presenter already well known to television audiences long before the series was dreamed up, as well as experts who over the years had become familiar faces. While the BBC, presumably with the youth market in mind, offered a pretty, young, excitable presenter whizzing about all over the place enthusing over everything. What could Crayford Productions offer that was different?

Pete did his best. He was sure, he told them, that there was room for one more. After all, the other shows didn't run for fifty-two weeks of the year and anyway he felt they could offer a new angle. 'We thought we'd take a look at places with legends surrounding them; no one's done that so far as I know and there must be some unexcavated sites with myths attached. You'd attract both those who like popular archaeology and people who like creepy stories, ghosts and the supernatural.' Eventually, after more meetings and constant telephone calls, he'd managed to extract a small amount of development money to make a pilot programme. No promises, though, that it would lead to anything more definite.

Pete, Dave and Duncan, their one researcher, had spent the next couple of weeks going over every site they'd previously considered, trying to decide which one it should be for the crucial pilot. A number were ruled out straight away, since they'd require more in the way of workers and machinery than they could afford. Time was now rapidly running out if they intended getting something in the can before the winter. It was then that Duncan took the call from Matthew Turner, curator of Lanwithen Museum in Cornwall.

'The guy seems really excited,' he told Pete. 'It could be just what we're looking for. He says there's this barrow on Bodmin Moor called Keeper's Tump. Apparently legend has it that there's gold in there guarded by someone or something called the Keeper, and that you venture into it at your peril. So far as he's aware it's never been excavated. Then he more or less hinted that if we did go down there we wouldn't be wasting our time. I thought we might see what Adrian thinks. Shall I see if he can come in now?'

Adrian was the archaeologist who'd agreed, somewhat grudgingly, to become their expert if and when they finally filmed a dig. He heard Pete out in silence then commented, 'Bodmin Moor's pockmarked with barrows and stone circles and God knows what, but most of the good finds have actually been made further west, towards Land's End. Also, it sounds as if this Keeper's Tump dates from the early bronze age, and if that's so, it's bound to have been robbed in antiquity, whatever your source tells you.'

'But Duncan was certainly under the impression that the museum curator knew more than he was saying,' Pete insisted.

22

Adrian snorted.

Appalled at the prospect of his precious pilot programme slipping away, Pete came to a decision. 'Well, I'm going to go for it. Or we'll still be sitting here this time next year.'

Adrian sighed. 'OK, if that's what you want. Find out all you can from the curator and I'll make sure we have permission from the relevant authority to mess around with what must be a scheduled site, even if it's more or less unknown. When are you planning to film there?'

Pete picked up a clipboard containing a rough schedule. 'It's going to be really tight now. Let's see, we're already into August. I thought the first week in October. The weather's still supposed to be quite good down there then. I'll send Duncan off straight away to do the initial research, see exactly what it is and where, find out what we're going to need in the way of equipment and help, accommodation and so on. Then Dave and I will go down and have another look before the end of September.' He frowned. 'And we'll need a presenter, but it can't be anyone well known. The whole project's on a shoestring. Right, so that's settled. I'll do as you say, call the curator and see what else I can find out. You never know, this might be the making of all of us.'

Adrian looked at him and slowly shook his head. 'Dream on!'

But somehow, in the end, Pete achieved his aim. Duncan had returned impressed with the site itself as a location, not to mention the legend of the Keeper – and the curator of the Lanwithen Museum had been extremely helpful and keen. In fact he'd even pointed to a spot amid the furze on top of the mound, where he would suggest digging. Thus reassured, Dave and Pete also drove down to Cornwall to see Keeper's Tump for themselves and meet Turner, who was indeed, as Duncan had told them, most enthusiastic. A date was fixed for the beginning of October, at which time Crayford Productions, plus their archaeological expert, hired-in geophysics man, a handful of students prepared to work for nothing and a presenter still to be decided on, would move in on St Mellick.

Four

By the time Latymer finally set off for Cornwall, he was wishing he'd never agreed to take up Maynard's offer. At the time, he'd agreed with the Berrys that it might be a good idea to have a short break and get away from it all after a year during which he had changed jobs, become involved in a particularly gruesome murder, and his marriage had ended in divorce. It would give him time to think. But now it had come to it, time to think was the last thing he wanted, he did too much of it anyway, especially in the small hours when all too often he'd find himself awake with the same thoughts going round and round like a carousel in his head until finally he fell into an unpleasant, dream-haunted sleep about an hour before he ought to get up.

Hindsight is a wonderful thing but at least he'd never regretted making a career in the police force, even if he'd chosen to leave it well before he needed to. A few weeks earlier he'd run into an old colleague who was still in the force and wanted to know what he was doing. Latymer told him.

'So, you've gone in with Keith? I'd heard he was running a crime bookshop somewhere, but I'd no idea you were involved as well, though you two always did work well together. But I must admit I'm surprised.'

Latymer enquired why.

'Well, it's the kind of thing I could imagine old Keith doing. Do you remember how he used to chase up Victorian copies of the *Police Gazette*? But it seems a sort of, well, a sort of *sedentary* life for you. Presumably once you'd left us you found yourself with too much time on your hands.'

Latymer explained that for two years he'd been a tour

manager for Becketts Literary Tours but had become bored with it. He considered saying something about his and Berry's ventures into private investigation, then decided against it, knowing only too well what the professional policeman thought of the private investigator.

'Well, must get on,' declared his ex-colleague, after they'd made a vague agreement to meet up one day for a drink together. 'I'm on the way to collect my wife, she's been visiting her mother.' He stopped short. 'Good heavens! Of course, you remarried! How is the wife . . . Tessa, isn't it?'

'Fine,' responded Latymer, and left it at that. The last thing he wanted was to discuss his dismal personal life, another subject which regularly came to haunt him during the night watches; no woman contemplating a relationship with him was likely to be encouraged on learning that he'd two broken marriages behind him. Looking back on it, he realized that the seeds of failure had been there from the start. After his last few years of pressure and overwork as a detective chief inspector based in Birmingham, a cosy life in the country with Tess, able to please himself at last, had seemed an enticing prospect. Until, that was, his unintended first brush with murder had led to his waking up one day feeling guilty that the prospect stretching before him seemed to offer little other than stifling middle-age: a straightjacket rather than comfortable domesticity.

No, he told himself sternly as he drove out of Bristol and on to the M5, this wouldn't do. He needed a short holiday. If the weather was as good as he'd been led to believe, he'd be able to go for long walks, put the gloomy thoughts out of his head and, hopefully, tire himself out sufficiently to sleep well. Unfortunately, however, the weather wasn't looking at all promising and, as he approached the notorious motorway interchange – known to West Country drivers as the 'car park' – he wished he'd taken Keith's advice: that, as it was Friday, he should take the whole day off and avoid the lemming-like weekend westward rush of the second-home owners. He crawled slowly through the maze of the interchange only to discover, once on the other side, that there'd been an accident on the motorway a few miles further towards Exeter which held him up even longer. He spent the next hour fuming in several miles of standing traffic, debating whether or not to come off at the next turn-off and go straight back home.

When things did finally start moving again, he decided to press on. Dusk was falling as he reached Exeter and by the time he was crossing Bodmin Moor it was dark, misty, and raining solidly, with visibility so poor that he almost missed his turning off to St Mellick. Nor was finding the village as easy as it had looked on the map. Finally he hit the right road and, following Maynard's instructions, drove through the village and out the other side, having noted thankfully that there was indeed a pub, that its lights were on and that it offered meals and bed and breakfast. There was nothing else on the road as he peered through the windscreen searching for the public footpath where he'd been told to turn off. He nearly missed the signpost, since it was leaning over at an angle. The writing on it was almost indecipherable, appearing to say the footpath led to 'Ke—r's ump'. Maynard had told him that he would be able to park outside the cottage, which he would then see on his left.

He pulled up outside it, leaving the headlights on to show him the way to the door, and squelched over to it. In view of what Maynard had said, he was disappointed to discover that it was anything but picturesque. He turned the key in the lock, opened the door and felt for a light switch. Lit by what appeared to be only a 60-watt light bulb, the interior looked unbelievably bleak and there was an overpowering smell of damp. He'd decided to bring a duvet with him as well as the bedlinen and towels suggested by Maynard. It had obviously been a good idea, since even if the cottage boasted such a luxury, it was probably damp enough to give him pneumonia, which led him to ponder dismally what state the bed or beds would be in. Maynard had said that he hadn't been down to the cottage himself for a few weeks, but it didn't look as if anyone had been near the place for far longer than that. Keith had described Maynard's London flat, on the one occasion he had seen it, as extremely grand, full of beautiful antique furniture with the fingerprints of an expensive interior designer all over it. That being so, they'd both assumed that his second home would be similar, expensively converted and tastefully decorated and furnished. Instead of which, the paint was flaking off the walls and the furniture looked as if it had been acquired from downmarket second-hand shops.

There was, he saw with some relief, a wood-burning stove, which was something, but there didn't seem to be any logs for it. Well, he was here now and would have to make the best of it. He went out and unpacked the car. He'd brought the necessities – tea, coffee, milk, bread and so forth – but decided to leave them in their box after taking a look at the kitchen, which could only be described as squalid. Either Maynard or whoever he'd lent the place to previously hadn't even bothered to clean up after themselves. He gingerly lifted the lid off the pan which was standing on the Calor-gas stove, then replaced it quickly. It would take a forensic pathologist to decide what was under the thick grey-green mould. Thoroughly disheartened, he went upstairs, dreading what the bedrooms would be like, but at least the larger of the two was reasonably clean and tidy, although the bed did feel damp. He came back downstairs and looked around. The prospect of spending the evening, let alone the night, in the place was appalling. If this was 'the real Cornwall', the Cornish could keep it. He switched off the lights, locked the door, got into the car and drove to the pub.

There were only a couple of other cars in the car park. He open the door marked 'Public Bar' and went in, blinking in the light. A log fire was burning in the grate and the landlord was standing behind the bar chatting with a handful of drinkers who looked like locals. 'Can I help you, sir?' he enquired as Latymer made his way towards him.

'I hope so,' declared Latymer. 'I sincerely hope so. Have you got a room for the night?'

An hour or so later, after a substantial meal of steak-and-kidney pie, he was feeling more himself. He was still amazed that Maynard's cottage was in the state it was, but possibly things would look better in the light of day. If the weather improved he'd open the windows. Whether it did or not, he'd buy some logs and light the stove – then he could bring the mattress downstairs to dry it off. By the time he'd finished his meal, there were hardly any more drinkers in the pub, no doubt the weather was putting people off. He went to the bar to get another pint.

'You down on holiday?' enquired one of the locals who'd been sitting on a bar stool ever since he'd arrived.

'That's the general idea,' Latymer told him.

'Touring round?'

'Don't mind Harry,' broke in the man standing next to him. 'He always wants to know everything about anyone coming into the village, before anyone else does. Then he can tell the rest of us. We call him the St Mellick bugle!'

Latymer laughed. 'Actually I'll be staying in a cottage I've been lent. But it was so dark and dismal when I got to it that I thought I'd try for a bed here tonight.' He turned to the land-lord. 'And tomorrow night too if that's all right. After which I should have made it more habitable. It looks as if no one's been there for ages.'

'Which one's that then?' asked Harry.

'It's out on the Lanwithen road. You turn off to it where it says Public Footpath.'

The men at the bar exchanged glances with the landlord. 'That place!' exclaimed Harry's companion. 'We haven't seen no sign of life there for months. I bet it's running with water; you can't leave houses empty around here long without they get full of damp. Funny fellow, him what owns it.' He turned to the landlord. 'Keeps himself to himself when he is here, doesn't he, Jim.'

'Hardly ever comes in the pub,' the landlord agreed. 'Got a big, expensive car though.'

'You looking for peace and quiet, then, coming out here, Mr . . .?'

'Latymer. John Latymer.'

'Mr Latymer. I'd have thought you'd have done better over to Fowey or down St Ives this time of year.'

The landlord leant across the bar. 'If you are looking for peace and quiet, you're going to be in for a surprise. I can put you up tomorrow night but not after, because I've got people from the television booked in from Sunday for at least a week, and it's likely to be anything but quiet and peaceful here. Especially for you.'

28

Latymer stared at him. 'Why me? It won't affect me if some drama's being filmed down here.'

Before the landlord could answer, Harry did it for him. 'But it's not a *drama*,' he informed Latymer triumphantly. 'It's one of they archaeology programmes and they'm doing one of they three-day excavations at Keeper's Tump.'

Latymer was even more bewildered. 'What on earth is Keeper's Tump?'

The landlord smiled. 'One of the old prehistoric barrows. It's about a quarter of a mile further on from where you're staying. You'll have a seat in the front row.'

Why on earth hadn't Maynard mentioned it, wondered Latymer; but then, if he'd not been down to St Mellick for ages, he probably didn't know. Well, all he could do was see how it went and, if staying in the cottage made life impossible, he'd do what Harry suggested and find somewhere in Fowey or St Ives. He was just about to leave the group and take his beer back to his seat when Harry addressed him again. 'You'll not have heard the stories then?' he persisted.

Escape was beginning to look impossible. 'What stories?'

'Why, about Keeper's Tump. And the Keeper. They do say that it's guarded by the Keeper, an ancient warrior in a gold mask, and that you mess with what's inside at your peril. It'll be interesting to see what happens to they telly people when they disturb him.'

'It's only an old tale,' said his companion. 'There's lots of them all over Cornwall. They do say a stone circle near Penzance is called the Merry Maidens because a group of girls danced on Sunday and were turned to stone. Then we've the Hurlers and the Cheesewring on the moor here. I shouldn't let it worry you.'

In spite of everything, Latymer did actually sleep well that night and woke in the morning determined to make the best of it. As for the film people, well, he was planning to be out a good deal and it wasn't as if they'd be filming right on his doorstep. The weather had improved, the skies had cleared and the sun was shining. After breakfast he drove to the small supermarket outside Lanwithen for further supplies, picked up

29

two bags of logs from a nearby garage and returned to the cottage. He opened the windows, lit the stove, brought the mattress down to put in front of it and set about tackling the kitchen. He scraped out the gruesome substance in the saucepan and washed it thoroughly; at least the water heater worked as, happily, did the television set, and he'd brought a small radio with him.

The conservatory, about which Maynard had spoken so lovingly, turned out to be little more than a lean-to attached to the back of the house. Another sign of lack of occupancy was the row of uncared-for dead plants along the window ledge. Rain had come in between the roof and the house, leaving patches of mould everywhere. An ugly set of plastic chairs and a table were pushed against one end of the building, again not the kind of thing he would have expected to find. There was a door opening out to what might have been intended as a sitting area but which was completely over-grown. He was contemplating this when he heard his mobile ring in the kitchen. It was Keith.

'Just thought I'd make sure everything's OK and you got there all right. Nice cottage and everything?' Latymer gave him a graphic description of what he'd found on arrival and how he'd had to take refuge in the local pub. Berry sounded puzzled. 'I'm amazed. You can't believe how posh his London place is and I thought the cottage was bound to be the same. It sounds like a complete dump. Are you going to stay there or find somewhere else?'

'I'm not sure. Oh, and there's another thing. Apparently there's a film unit arriving on Sunday to make an archaeology programme about a prehistoric monument a few hundred yards from here. There's some legend attached to it about a superman in a gold mask who sees off intruders.'

He could hear Berry laughing. 'Well, don't try and find out if it's true. I suppose you haven't come across any bodies yet? Nothing in the woodshed – if there is a woodshed?'

'There's a stone building used for storage out the back and I've just put a couple of bags of logs in it, but the only bodies there were those of a few spiders. And there's nowhere to hide one in the house.'

'Well, let me know if you decide to move out,' said Berry, 'and do try and have a proper holiday. The bookshop's ticking over perfectly well without you.'

Getting everything clean and decent took him most of the morning, after which he made himself a scratch lunch then went outside to explore. The obvious place to go was Keeper's Tump and he set off towards it. The footpath now narrowed, with the remains of a dry stone wall on one side and rough moorland covered with large stones on the other. He wondered how the television crew were going to get their equipment to where they were going to film. As is the way in Cornwall, the mist and low cloud had suddenly vanished, leaving a watery sun shining in a clear pale-blue sky. The moors rolled away on each side of him now as far as he could see, still with patches of colour from late heather and pockets of gorse. There must be farms or cottages further out for in one place he could see poles carrying electricity and phone lines across apparently empty countryside. Above him larks rose in the sky and he heard the calls of lapwings, something he couldn't remember hearing for a long time. There were also a surprising number of crows, as well as wheeling seagulls.

Keeper's Tump itself, when he reached it, was not all that impressive. He left the path and walked round it. A group of crows were perched on the top of the mound, taking off, as he disturbed them, cawing loudly. He reckoned the mound itself was about twenty feet across and around fifteen feet high at its highest point, possibly even a little higher. Presumably a good bit of it must have been built of stone but now it was entirely covered in bracken and gorse. It was slightly flatter on one side, which he assumed must be the entrance, and he went over to investigate. It looked as if the vegetation there had been pulled away at some time, then put carefully back, for the gorse was withered and brown. No doubt the television people must have been down to investigate the site thoroughly before embarking on the actual filming, and would need some idea of how easy it was likely to be to get into the burial chamber inside.

He shivered suddenly. The place had a definite atmosphere, and not a pleasant one. He didn't think it was because he'd been told the story about the Keeper. He didn't consider himself to be a particularly fanciful person and while investigating his last case he and Fiona Garleston had walked to the top of Meon Hill, near Stratford-on-Avon, where, in the 1940s, a man had been the victim of a bizarre murder with overtones of witchcraft and the supernatural, yet neither of them had felt anything strange or unpleasant there.

He made his way back to the path and after walking a little way turned and looked again at Keeper's Tump. From where he was standing, at a sharp bend in the path, it looked almost as if the power line to the farms also led to the barrow. Some of the crows had returned to the mound, dozens of others were now strung out on the line like spectators along a processional route. What was that saying he'd come across when he'd been up in Scotland? The crow road! That was it, the crow road. It meant the road to death. He shook himself. This was getting ridiculous, what he needed was to go somewhere loud and brash. He got in the car and drove to Newquay.

Five

Matthew Turner was becoming increasingly alarmed. Throughout the weeks of negotiations with Crayford Productions, he'd remained in touch with Smith, keeping him informed whenever there was anything concrete to tell him. Smith had been his usual surly self throughout, but hadn't given him any hint that he wasn't still going along with their plan; at least, he'd never said anything to the contrary. But then, when Turner started trying to contact him to tell him the date the film unit was to arrive, and discuss how the two of them should play it to ensure the maximum effect, there was no reply, not even a message service. It would seem Smith had switched off his mobile phone and Turner had never given him his landline number, always supposing he had one.

When Duncan had arrived to do the initial research, Turner had gone out to Keeper's Tump with him and given him all the information he'd managed to assemble on the archaeology of Bodmin Moor in general and the barrow in particular. It was as well he did, as it was obvious that when he finally saw Keeper's Tump Duncan had found it disappointing, and it was with some difficulty that he was finally persuaded that the excavation really would be worthwhile. 'Look, I think I can safely promise that,' Turner had told him. 'I've been through everything and there are no records anywhere that it's been investigated before.' But in spite of these reassurances, the researcher had seemed so doubtful that at one stage Turner had almost decided to show him the photographs then swear him to secrecy; almost, but not quite.

When it came to the practicalities, he'd had to agree that there would be a real problem getting people and equipment to the site. 'Though you'll be able to drive your vehicles off the road, Duncan, and park them just outside that old cottage we passed on our way here.'

'What if they object?' he'd queried.

'According to the locals it's semi-derelict, no one's been near it for months. But other than that, as you've seen for yourself, there's only the path.'

'I suppose it might just be possible to get a four-by-four up here.' He'd stepped back and looked at the mound again. 'So, what about the spot you keep on about? Have you seen it yourself?'

Turner had had to admit that he hadn't, but that he knew someone who had.

When he returned to London Duncan was questioned closely on what the difficulties regarding the site were likely to be, and the chances of success in turning up something really interesting. He had to report that Matthew Turner had seemed somewhat vague now it had come to the actual event, particularly with regard to the area where he'd originally implied there might be finds. 'I simply couldn't make out why he was so sure, but I do feel in my bones that he knows a good deal more than he's saying. I wondered if he or his nameless friend had already found something, which is why he's seemed so certain. But he assured me umpteen times that he'll have the man himself there ready and waiting for us before we start.'

It was taking Pete Crayford all his time to get the enterprise together at such relatively short notice, and on a shoestring, and now something close to panic was setting in. He'd originally assumed that there'd be time for himself and Dave to go down to Cornwall before filming started, but it was now looking increasingly unlikely. He was having difficulty with Adrian, who thought they should have waited until a better subject turned up, and he still hadn't contracted a presenter. Also, he was still working out how many volunteer students they were going to need and if it would be possible to have some local assistance as well. All in all, he felt the only solution was for Duncan to return to the site, take lots of photographs and sort out all he could. 'We're going to have to trust you on this one,' he concluded.

Duncan was far from happy but could see his point. 'There's no doubt it would've been much better if you could have gone down and seen the site for yourselves, but I'll do my best. I can send pics back to you and you can tell me straight away if you need any more, or want something different. However, I also need some idea of how you plan to set up and do the shoot. I'll check if it's possible to get a four-by-four to the site, and confirm the local accommodation I booked provisionally. Before I go back, I'd better show Adrian all the gen I got on the archaeology and see what he says. There must be things he also needs to know well in advance.

Pete agreed. 'And find out who this curator's friend is and talk to him. It's not good enough to have him turn up when we get there. It seems a bit dodgy to me.'

But Duncan had been unable to do so. Turner had lied, claiming that his informant was away at present and he didn't have his mobile-phone number. Duncan didn't believe him, but given the time pressure, was forced to leave it at that. Now filming was only days away and Crayford Productions were due to arrive at the weekend. Pressed yet again by Duncan, this time over the phone, for information on the 'hot spot', Turner again reassured him everything was going to be all right, that his man would be there and there was nothing to worry about.

Staring bleakly out of the window of his office on the Friday before Crayford Productions arrived, Turner was finally having to face up to the fact that there was every chance it wasn't going to be all right, and that he was now in the nightmare position of being unable to contact the person whose cooperation was crucial to the success of the enterprise; and this after he'd done everything possible to make it all happen. What on earth was he going to say? Would he be able to get away with showing them the photographs? But even if he did, would they believe such valuable items had actually been found at Keeper's Tump? He still had doubts himself. It was as well he'd managed to take pictures of them separately as well as the shots Smith had agreed to, which made it look as if the pictures had been taken in a museum somewhere else. But if the deception eventually came out, where would it leave him? Almost certainly without a job and pretty well unemployable anywhere else.

After making the cottage as habitable as possible, Latymer decided that he might as well stay on for a few more days at least, as it might even be quite interesting to see how a televised three-day dig was put together. Then he planned to spend the rest of the time touring around, possibly taking a detour home through Dorset to look up some old friends. He realized the film people must have arrived when he passed the pub towards the end of Sunday afternoon and saw a white minibus bearing the legend 'Crayford Productions' parked in the pub car park alongside a battered-looking four-by-four.

The bar was somewhat busier when he went in for a drink that evening, presumably because the locals were curious to see the strangers from London. He assumed that the film people must be the small group sitting round a table at the end of the bar, but surely there must be more of them somewhere? He'd envisaged dozens of people and far more vehicles.

Harry was in his usual place on a bar stool. 'Here's Mr Latymer now,' he announced loudly as Latymer made his way to the bar. There was an immediate silence as both film unit and locals stopped talking and looked at him. He stopped short, embarrassed to be the centre of attention. A tall man in a reversed baseball cap detached himself from the group at the table and came over to him holding out his hand. 'Mr Latymer? Pete Crayford of Crayford Productions. I believe you already know we're down here to film a three-day dig at Keeper's Tump, though in actual fact it'll take at least a week. We need tomorrow to set up, after which we do the dig, then we have to tie up the loose ends, possibly extra shots and so on.' He paused. 'I hope I'm not disturbing your quiet evening drink, but the landlord said you might be able to help us.'

'I knew there was to be a programme about Keeper's Tump,' Latymer agreed, 'but I can't quite see how I can help you.'

Pete gave a reassuring smile. 'Look, do you mind joining us for a little while? If you'd like to go over to our table, I'll get you a drink.' Since it seemed churlish to refuse, Latymer made his way across the bar as the film unit made room for him. The crew was indeed a small one for such an ambitious enterprise. In quick succession he was introduced to Dave, the cameraman, Jim who 'did sound', Duncan, the unit's researcher, and Adrian, the team's tame archaeological expert. The only woman involved was the presenter, Rosie Hartnell, a bored, sulky-looking young blonde woman with a childish voice. Rosie had not been Pete's first choice, nor even his second or tenth, as her experience had been limited to standing in for other people on breakfast shows and some children's television, but his choice was severely limited by time and money. Once contracted, it soon became apparent that she not only knew little or nothing about archaeology, she didn't even want to know.

A few minutes later Pete returned with a pint, set it down, then explained the problem. 'I understand you're staying in the cottage by the path to the site. Our researcher, Duncan here, was told that it would be empty, that no one had been near it for ages, and we assumed therefore that it'd be OK to park the crew van, the four-by-four and any other vehicles we might need outside your place, rather than leave them on the road for hours at a time. We're hoping to get the four-by-four up to the site. Duncan thinks it's just about possible.'

'It won't be easy,' Latymer said. 'I expect he's told you that the path's quite narrow in places, with the remains of a broken-down wall on one side and rough ground with quite large stones or boulders on the other. I can see it would be useful to be able to do so, otherwise you're going to be carting all your equipment up there on foot. Well, I don't see any reason to object to you parking outside the cottage, so long as you make sure I'm not boxed in. I'm supposed to be here on holiday.'

Pete smiled. 'Thanks very much. Rather than leave the van with all kinds of stuff in it out on the road for hours, I'd visions of having to keep it here. We'll do our best not to get in your way and you'll be very welcome to come along and see what's going on.' He then explained to Latymer how they'd been contacted by the curator of a local museum and decided to make Keeper's Tump the subject of their pilot programme for Channel 5. 'I'm afraid we've not been absolutely frank with him,' he admitted. 'We've rather led him to believe that this is the first of a series but we're by no means certain if it will even be shown at all!'

'But then he's not been entirely upfront with us either,' broke in Duncan. 'He looks mysterious and suggests there will almost certainly be something to find at the site and says he'll be bringing some detecting nut with him on Monday to tell us more. But Adrian isn't at all convinced.'

'I'm not,' confirmed the archaeologist. 'I'm convinced all they'll turn up is a couple of old tins or a bit of broken farm machinery.'

Latymer finished his drink, thanked them, then made his way home. He felt torn. There was no doubt that he'd now lose any peace and quiet he might have had, but on the other hand the excavation was bound to be interesting and the film crew seemed a lively bunch. He made himself some supper, watched television, then went to bed, only to wake sweating in the middle of the night from a nightmare in which he was led stumbling between rows of raucous crows towards Keeper's Tump by some being he couldn't distinguish.

The unit arrived bright and early the next day and Latymer went out to greet them. The weather was fine and mild, quite different from that on the day he'd arrived. Pete looked at the cottage. 'I take it this place isn't actually yours?'

'No, it's not. I've been lent it by an acquaintance, one of our bookshop customers. He described it in glowing terms, raved on about how this is "the real Cornwall" and the cottage some kind of luxury retreat. In actual fact it's pretty much of a dump, and if this is the real Cornwall, I think I'll settle for the holiday one in future.'

'A bookshop? Whereabouts?'

'In Bristol. I've recently gone in with a couple of friends.'

'That's pretty courageous. I understand the big chains have the market more or less sewn up.'

'There's still room for the specialist outlet.' He was about to elaborate when a small coach pulled up at the side of the road and a number of young people in anoraks and woolly hats began getting out. 'Sorry, I'll have to leave you,' said Pete. 'These are the students who are here to help with the actual heavy work. What we're intending to do today is make a thorough exploration of the site, ensure we know exactly where the entrance is and loosen everything up so that we can get in there quickly tomorrow. We're also expecting a local chap from English Heritage to turn up sometime just to check us over, and Matthew Turner, the curator of the Lanwithen Museum, with his mysterious chum. If you're still here when they arrive, would you mind directing them to the site? OK,' he called out to the assembled company, 'let's get going.'

He climbed into the four-by-four, Dave, Jim and Rosie squashed in the back, everyone else following behind on foot as it bumped cautiously off down the path. By the time the next two visitors arrived, almost simultaneously, there was nowhere to park except on the road, which annoyed the expert from English Heritage, who gave the impression that he considered the enterprise a waste of his time anyway, while Matthew Turner looked like a man who wished he could be anywhere but where he was. Of his informant there was no sign. Now admittedly intrigued, as much by the cross-currents he could feel as the event itself, Latymer explained who he was and offered to take them up to the site.

The expert thanked him. 'You've had a look then? It's all quite pointless, you know. They're not going to find anything, whatever you might have told them, Turner. The grave's bound to have been robbed in antiquity, not to mention the fact that the whole thing is only supposed to take three days. I'll be amazed if they even find any bones. It could take them that long just to get inside without bringing the whole lot down on their heads.'

'Actually I think they must already have employed someone to do some advance work,' Latymer told him. 'I meant to ask the director about it when he said something about loosening up the entrance ready for filming, but then he was called away. I don't know much about these things but it looked to me as if the area around what could be the entrance had already been disturbed, which would make sense given their timescale. I know they had someone down here earlier, so presumably it was done then.'

'Do you know if that's so, Turner?' enquired the expert.

Turner shook his head. 'They've not said anything to me.'

'If they've already done some work on the site, then we should have been fully informed. Their resident academic must have been told that when he sorted permission out with the authorities. What exactly did you find there, Mr Latymer?'

'As you'll see in a minute, the mound is thickly covered in coarse grass, bracken and gorse. It looked to me as if some of the vegetation had been removed a little while ago then carefully replaced over what I assume is the entrance, though I could be wrong about that. But it certainly looked as if some of the gorse had actually been uprooted. It was going brown and came away in my hand when I touched it.'

'You're very observant,' commented the expert. 'Unusually so.'

'Possibly it's because I used to be a detective,' commented Latymer, feeling patronized.

By this time they'd reached the mound. It looked strange to see so many people in such a lonely spot, but at least the invasion had done something to dissipate the atmosphere Latymer had previously found so chilling. For a couple of hours he watched the activity, the careful outside shots, the decisions being made about what should be done when. Soon even he could see that, far from being a positive asset to the show, Rosie was turning out to be a disaster. Her trendy outdoor clothing looked inappropriate, she was constantly tossing her hair out of her eyes in an irritating way and seemed incapable of keeping in her head even a loose idea of what she was supposed to say, despite a script having been provided for her the previous evening once it was recognized that improvised commentary was completely beyond her, however good the subsequent editing might be. Thankfully it wasn't his problem, thought Latymer, as he made his way back to the cottage. He decided to make the best of the weather and drive over to the south coast. If he took the ferry from Fowey to Bodinnick he could take the coastal path around a creek to Polruan, pick up another ferry from there back to Fowey and have a pleasant lunch. He'd pay another visit to the excavation the next day.

Fowey was as pleasant as he remembered it from his literary-tour days and in the end he'd stayed on into the evening, had a good dinner, then driven home, gone to bed late and slept heavily. So, he was only just getting up when he heard the vehicles arriving outside the following day. He watched as Pete Crayford addressed everyone, obviously reminding them what they were to do, after which the foot soldiers moved off down the path. While Latymer got himself some breakfast, he heard raised voices and couldn't resist going over to the window. Pete, quite clearly annoyed, was arguing with the museum curator. 'So, where in God's name is this bloody man you promised?'

Turner looked wretched. 'I don't know. I just don't know. I'd been in touch with him ever since you said you were definitely coming and he was supposed to have been here yesterday.'

'Can't you get hold of him? Surely you must know where he is?'

'That's the trouble. I don't. And he isn't answering his phone.'

'But at least you must have his address. Can't you go and see if you can find him?'

Turner shook his head. 'He never gave it to me.'

Pete shook his head in exasperation. 'He was having you on, wasn't he? Making out there's something there when there isn't. That is, if he ever existed.'

Turner frantically assured him that he did, but Pete refused to be pacified.

'There'll only be a few sardine tins, left after someone's picnic. It looks to me as if we'll be lucky even to find that. Well, I can't stand here all day. I've got a job to do if I'm to save the whole thing from becoming a complete shambles.'

'What shall I do, then?' ventured Turner.

'Don't tempt me. It's up to you. Go or stay, I don't bloody care unless you can find mystery man and get him here this morning.'

*   *   *

41

Some time later Latymer himself went along to the site. It was a really beautiful day, the landscape bathed in the wonderful translucent light that floods Cornwall in the autumn. Every gorse bush and rocky outfall was etched against the rolling landscape under the clear blue sky. It was the nearest to Maynard's 'real Cornwall' that Latymer had seen it. By the time he reached the mound, the vegetation had been completely cleared from the entrance, revealing several large stones, and Rosie was standing outside. It took her half a dozen attempts to put across the simple fact that this was the entrance and they were about to remove the stones and investigate the mound's interior. Pete came over to Latymer, shaking his head. 'She's going to have to go, she's absolutely hopeless.'

'What'll you do?' enquired Latymer.

'Get Adrian to do it. He may not be pretty but he's both knowledgeable and capable of putting stuff across. I should have employed him to do that from the start. For one thing it would have saved us money, but the received wisdom is that viewers want good-looking female presenters.'

Latymer looked across at the mound. 'I see you've loosened all the stones. I suppose you won't know exactly what you'll find until you go in.'

Pete grimaced. 'That's my real nightmare: that we go in and find most of the original roof has fallen in and that, even if there is any space, there's nothing in it. But neither Adrian, nor the grumpy expert from English Heritage who was here yesterday, thinks it has. They both climbed up on the mound and walked over as much of it as they could. As to the stones, they'd already been loosened. I understand you told the English Heritage man that you thought we might already have made a start.'

'I'm sorry if I was wrong. It just looked to me as if someone had already been there and I assumed it was you.'

'That's OK. I told the expert that all Duncan had done was make sure we'd know where the entrance was and I think he believed me. Now for the big moment. Right, get the rest of those stones out, and be careful, we don't want everything above crashing down. Adrian . . .?'

Adrian went over to the entrance. 'If they're careful, it should be OK. It looks as if there's stone here at both sides, with a capstone across, and the stones already loosened were merely blocking up the entrance to keep intruders out. See? There's the bottom of the capstone, then loose earth, then the smaller stones. Start by taking a few of the top ones out.' There was silence as the first few stones were removed by two students, who were filmed doing so, and then passed the stones on to others behind them to be carefully stacked and recorded by a postgraduate who was making careful drawings. The stones came out with extraordinary ease, given the age of the site. Above them the crows, disturbed from their usual resting place, wheeled and cawed in the air above.

As the final stone on the top row was removed, the two students stopped suddenly. 'Go on, go on!' bawled Pete. 'Don't stop. We're still filming.'

'But there's a nasty smell coming from the hole,' one of them called out.

'The air in there's probably stale after all these years. Do get on, it's going so well, we're soon going to be able to look inside.'

The work continued until the entrance was clear. By now everyone had become aware of the smell.

Pete wrinkled his nose in disgust. 'Well, smell or not, we'll see if it's possible to get inside. Bring the lights over, will you?'

The lights were set up facing into the entrance. Pete and Adrian bent down and slowly disappeared into the dark opening. Everyone else, including Latymer, clustered around to see what was going on. The smell was now becoming positively nauseating, a smell unpleasantly familiar to Latymer. The chill feeling he'd experienced before returned in force.

'Well, the roof's not fallen in,' called out Pete from inside. 'There's some kind of a chamber in here. But the smell is appalling. Some animal must have got in somehow and died. As to finds, can't see anything obvious, can you, Adrian? No pottery or bones. Oh, there's possibly something over there. Adrian's going to take a look.' There was a silence, followed

43

by a stifled shout, then a white-faced Pete emerged from the entrance, followed by an equally shaken Adrian, who was promptly sick.

'What is it?' demanded Dave. 'What's the matter?'

'There's a body in there,' managed Pete.

Dave laughed. 'I thought that's what you wanted to find. Any gold with it?'

Peter, grey-faced, could only shake his head. The thought struck Latymer that Mr Smith, having taken the crow road, would appear to have kept his appointment after all.

Six

There was a moment's stunned silence, followed by a babble of noise. Then Adrian moved forward. 'Are you sure?'

Pete shuddered. 'Quite. Do you want to go in and see for yourself?'

Latymer reacted automatically and without a moment's thought. 'No, you mustn't. No one else should go in there.'

'Why not?' demanded Dave. 'Who are you to take it on yourself to tell us what to do? The star of a TV crime series?'

'Because, if what you say is true, this is now a crime *scene* and the fewer people that trample in there the better. And no, I'm certainly not a TV crime addict, but I did use to be a police officer.'

Dave shrugged. 'You're the expert then, I suppose. So, what do you suggest we do now?'

'Ring the police immediately and tell them what you've found.'

Dave produced his mobile phone and did so while Pete looked on, aghast. 'But what about the filming? What on earth is going to happen to my schedule once the police get involved?'

'You could hardly go on filming with a rotting corpse inside the barrow,' commented Latymer. 'It obviously never occurred to whoever put it there that within no time there'd be hordes of people down here, and a film crew.'

'OK, we'll do as you say,' said Dave, finishing his phone conversation. 'They're sending someone along. I think they thought it was some kind of joke at first.' He looked across at Latymer. 'The officer I spoke to said the same as you, that nobody must go back in there until the police arrive, and that

45

no one must leave here either, as they'll need to take details and statements from everyone.'

'Where are they coming from?' enquired Latymer.

'Bodmin. It shouldn't take very long.'

The next twenty minutes seemed interminable. The students, now very subdued, clustered together in a group, the male members of Crayford Productions deep in discussion as to the future, if any, of their project, while Rosie, ignored, sat by herself on a rock. Also on his own, standing staring out across the moor, was the museum curator, Matthew Turner, looking thoroughly shaken. Latymer, as onlooker, was aware of the incongruity of the scene, the glorious autumn weather, the disparate group with its high-tech electronic equipment, the ancient barrow with its legend, and over all, the stench of a very modern corpse. The crows, disturbed by the film unit when it had first arrived, had settled back on top of the barrow as if waiting for something. He didn't like to dwell on what that might be.

Pete looked impatiently up the path then shouted, 'They're here!' Two policemen, a sergeant and a constable, were walking rapidly towards them. 'Got here as soon as we could,' the sergeant called out breathlessly as they arrived, 'but there's no way we can get a squad car up that path.' He introduced himself as Sergeant Johns and his colleague as Constable Pender, then added, 'Anyone know who owns the cottage back there?'

'I'm staying in it,' Latymer informed him, 'but it belongs to someone called Maynard who lives in London.'

'Well, we can take the details from you later. I take it you're involved in the filming?'

'No, I just happened to be here on holiday. I was watching out of interest. Mr Crayford is the man in charge.'

Pete explained to Johns how he and his cameraman had entered the barrow, preparatory to setting up the necessary lighting, to see if there were any obvious finds. 'Naturally we wondered about the awful smell. I thought some animal might have got in somehow or other and died in there. We'd no idea . . .' His voice trailed away.

'Very unpleasant for you, sir,' commented Johns, then

produced a powerful torch, beckoned the constable to follow him, and both men disappeared inside. Nobody spoke. A few minutes later they reappeared, the sergeant shaking his head. 'Yuk, what a stink! I reckon he must have been there well over a week, but forensics will be able to tell us more. Now, will you all stand back. It's probably too late now, but the less people trampling around the entrance, the better. Constable Pender will start taking details from you, while I report back. We need to know who he is. Whoever put him there removed much of his clothing and anything that might easily identify him, but it could be that someone here actually knew him.' After going aside to call his boss, he returned shortly afterwards to announce that the various cars and the crew van parked outside the cottage must be removed to the road to allow nearer access for police vehicles, and that he would accompany the various drivers to see that this was done.

He pointed to the four-by-four. 'And it would be useful if that vehicle could be used for bringing people up here until we get a suitable one ourselves. Detective Inspector Anderson will be here soon, along with the police surgeon and the people from SOCO – that is the scenes of crime officers. Headquarters will try to find somewhere in the village where we can set up a base, and in the meantime you must all remain here. Your time won't be wasted. Constable Pender will carry on taking your details until DI Anderson arrives.'

'But surely *I* don't have to stay in this awful place now I've told the police officer what he wanted to know,' wailed Rosie. 'I've nothing to do with any of this. I'm just the presenter on the programme.' She tossed back her hair in a familiar gesture and gave Johns a carefully crafted wavering smile.

'Sorry,' he responded, briskly, 'it doesn't matter if you're only the sweeper-up. It applies to everyone.' At which she flounced off and returned to her rock.

'I suppose I'd better move my own car as well,' said Latymer. 'Anyway, I'd like to make sure everything's OK at the cottage. I imagine Mr Crayford can give us all a lift?' Crayford, grumbling under his breath, got into the four-by-four and motioned to them to get in. 'You're welcome to use the cottage for any immediate need you might have until you

47

set up an incident room,' offered Latymer, as they rattled off down the track.

Johns looked slightly surprised at the use of the professional term, but thanked him. 'I imagine the DI will want to talk to you anyway Mr . . .' He looked across at Latymer.

'Latymer. John Latymer.'

'He'll obviously be interested in anything you might have seen or heard since you've been in the cottage, as well as any details you can give us regarding its owner. Do you know him well?'

Latymer shook his head. 'Apart from seeing him in our shop, I've only met him properly once, which was when he offered to lend me the cottage for a short holiday. Other than that, we spoke on the phone a couple of times when I was fixing up to come here.'

'What kind of shop is that then?'

'A bookshop, in Bristol. In partnership with two friends.'

They arrived outside the cottage and the drivers began moving their vehicles out on to the road. 'Sorry to have to ask you to move your car too, Mr Latymer, but it's going to be quite a squeeze to get everything in.' Crayford was standing fuming by the four-by-four. 'I've a whole load of equipment up there. I'm going to need this to collect it.'

'You'll be able to do that once we've taken DI Anderson, and anyone else who needs a lift, up to the crime scene. We should have something suitable of our own anytime. Now, if you wouldn't mind joining your colleagues . . .?' Crayford stomped off up the path, followed by the drivers, cursing heartily as he went.

'Nasty business, though,' commented Johns. 'It must have been quite a shock.'

'It certainly was. I imagine poor old Crayford must be tearing his hair out. They were down here making one of those TV programmes about a three-day dig and this was only the first real day of filming.' Latymer unlocked the cottage door. 'Come in, if you like. I take it you're waiting for your boss.'

The two men went in, to be greeted by the familiar smell of damp. 'I hope you're not being charged over the odds for

48

this,' remarked Johns, looking around. 'It's hardly what you'd call luxurious, is it?'

'You can say that again. When I got here and saw what it was like, I nearly turned round and went back home. Luckily I was able to camp out at the pub for a couple of nights until the film unit arrived. I must admit I was quite amazed at the state of the place.'

'Why was that? Mind you, it isn't what I'd choose to spend a holiday in.'

'Because Maynard had cracked on about how charming and comfortable it was, and my partner, who's seen his flat in London, says that it's the last word in luxury, full of expensive furniture and pricey antiques, so I was expecting something pretty good here too. If you think it's grotty now, you should have seen it last Friday night! Anyway, you said you'd want his address and phone number. I haven't got his address, though I can get it from my partner, but I do have his phone number here somewhere.' Latymer rooted out his filofax and gave the number to Johns. 'All I know is that he lives in Holland Park.'

'No sign of recent occupancy, I imagine?'

'Definitely not. I don't think anyone had been down here for weeks, possibly months.'

As he spoke, another squad car drove in through the gate, followed by a blue Golf – which Johns told Latymer belonged to the police surgeon – a transit van bringing in the SOCOs and, at a discreet distance behind, a plain undertaker's van for the body. 'You've been really helpful, Mr Latymer,' said Johns. 'Right on the ball. I wish we came across more people like you.'

Latymer gave a rueful smile. 'Possibly that's because I used to be with West Midlands police. I took early retirement,' he added, seeing the sergeant's expression.

'That certainly explains it. Once things settle down, I'd be interested to know why you left the force.' He looked out of the window. 'I see the DI and his driver are here.' He paused. 'Er . . . there's just one thing perhaps I'd better mention. I shouldn't really be saying this, but DI Anderson's a bit, well, abrupt. He's relatively new down here, joined us about six

49

months ago, and he's been having a bit of trouble settling in. I just thought I'd warn you.'

Latymer thanked him then followed him out to meet the DI, who greeted the sergeant with a grunt and a sour face. Having been shown Crayford's vehicle, he motioned to his driver to get behind the wheel and to Johns to climb in the back; then he noticed Latymer. 'Who are you?' he barked.

'Mr Latymer is staying in the cottage and has offered to let us make use of it if we wish,' Johns explained. 'He needs to come back with us, as he was also there when the body was found.' Anderson grunted again, then turned to the police doctor, who was taking his bag out of the boot of his car. 'You'd better come too, doctor.' Latymer and the doctor climbed in the back with Johns and they rumbled off up the path, Anderson talking over his shoulder to the sergeant as they went along.

'Bit tough on you when you're supposed to be on holiday,' commented the doctor after Latymer had explained who he was.

Latymer grimaced. 'And I was supposed to be having a stress-free break. From the smell, I imagine it's going to be pretty unpleasant in there. I haven't seen the body, of course, but I'd agree with the sergeant that it's probably been there well over a week.'

'You've some medical knowledge then?'

'A little. I used to be a police officer,' he added, quietly.

'Does DI Anderson know that?' enquired the doctor, equally softly. Latymer shook his head. 'It'll be interesting to see how he reacts to it when he does,' mouthed the doctor, as Anderson turned his head as if to demand to know what they were talking about. However, before he could say anything, his attention was distracted elsewhere, since they'd reached the site. Anderson immediately jumped out and made his way over to the now increasingly impatient group of people still standing around a short distance away from the entrance to Keeper's Tump.

'Have you all given the constable your details?' There was a murmur of assent from most of them. 'OK. Then all those who have can go for now, but I want all of you to assemble

50

outside the church in the village at five o'clock sharp, by which time we'll have sorted out an incident room where you can be questioned properly. Got that? I still need the two who found the body to remain here, along with anyone else who hasn't yet given their details to Constable Pender. Is everyone here to do with the filming, constable?'

'Almost all of them, sir,' Pender replied, 'except for Mr Turner, who's the curator of Lanwithen Museum, and Mr Latymer there, who's been staying in the cottage.'

'Very well, I'll talk to you two shortly, the rest of you can go.' He turned to Johns and the doctor. 'Right, we'd better get started. Oh, and in view of the particular circumstances, there's a forensic pathologist on his way.'

It would have been routine in his day, thought Latymer, to call in a Home Office pathologist for almost any suspicious death, but a new system had recently been brought in, which meant that police forces had to pay forensics experts themselves, rather than their being paid by the Home Office. The change had resulted in a pathologist not always being called, as cash-strapped police forces grappled with rising costs.

'I need to get back to the museum. How long do you think they'll keep us here?' asked Turner as the policemen and the doctor disappeared inside the barrow. He was obviously very much on edge. 'I can't imagine why they'd think I'd know anything about it.'

'Possibly because I told them the dig here was your suggestion,' snapped Pete Crayford. 'Perhaps that's why, and after all you did more or less promise us finds, or we wouldn't be here in the first place. You and your precious local informant! And you think you have problems? What about us? They're never going to let us film now, and what the hell am I to say to our sponsors? The whole thing's a bloody nightmare. Adrian told me we should have hung on for something better, he was dead right. Anything would be better than this.'

Turner said nothing but looked, if anything, even more fraught, and Latymer felt certain that there was more to his unease than impatience to get back to the museum, or a reaction to Crayford's anger. He wondered if it had anything to do with the missing informant who'd let Turner down so badly.

From what Crayford had implied, both on Sunday evening in the pub and just now, a great deal must have been riding on what this man might have had to tell them. All of which suggested that Crayford Productions fully expected they'd discover something remarkable. This led him back to his earlier notion, that it was the missing informant who was lying dead in the burial chamber. It made some kind of sense, but if so, why? No, he must get a grip on himself, it was too easy, too fanciful. He felt deeply frustrated that he wasn't able to see the scene of crime for himself, and was trying to think of a way of offering assistance that might enable him to do so, when a police Land Rover came slowly into view.

At the sound of the vehicle, Johns appeared from the entrance and called over to the driver to ask if he'd brought the lights he'd been asked for and, if so, if he'd bring them over to the entrance. The driver shouted his assent, opened the back door, let out the SOCOs to whom he'd given a lift, and began unloading lighting equipment. 'I'll have to go back for a couple more people and some more of their equipment. The screen's still down there.'

'OK', returned Johns, going over to the lights.

'I'll give you a hand with these, Latymer offered, and together the two men carried the equipment to the entrance. Johns went inside with the lights, Latymer, craning over his shoulder, following behind with rolls of cable.

The scene inside was luridly lit by torchlight, and Latymer was able to get a view of the blackened body, bits of which appeared to be missing. The police doctor was just finishing his examination. 'I'd say he'd been dead ten to twelve days,' he was saying. 'He seems to have had a crack on the head but it's hard to say if that's what caused his death, I think probably not, but then the body's pretty far gone. Not just the decomposition, which one would expect, but it looks as if a variety of creatures have been at it too, hardly surprising seeing where it is. As well as missing parts of the extremities, there's damage to the chest area as well. Altogether very nasty. I think you'll have to leave anything else to your forensic pathologist when he does the post-mortem. But I can certainly certify he's well and truly dead.' He stood up. 'Well, if you've no

52

more need of me, I'd like to get back. I've a surgery full of people to get through this afternoon.'

He made his way to the entrance. Anderson also stood up to see him out, then caught sight of Latymer. 'What the hell do you think you're doing in here?' he bellowed. Latymer explained that he was just helping the sergeant carry the lights. 'Well, you'd no business to do so. Get out!'

Latymer retreated swiftly to allow passage first to the doctor then to Anderson. The driver of the police Land Rover was just about to return to collect the rest of the men and their equipment as Anderson emerged and called to him to take the police doctor back to his car.

'How much longer are you going to keep us here?' demanded Pete. 'So, Dave and I found the body? That's about it. As soon as we did, we called you to tell you about it. We've both told the constable what he wanted to know, and I'd appreciate it if you'd now let us get on with our lives. I'm going to have to spend all afternoon on the phone as it is, trying to explain to the people in London that the project's buggered. If we promise to meet you outside the church with everyone else, can we go? And I'd like to take our equipment back to the pub with us, it's not going to do it much good lying around here. You've got your own transport now.'

Anderson had a word with Johns then nodded reluctantly. 'Very well. But you'd better be sure you'll be there.' Pete and Dave immediately loaded up their four-by-four and drove away as Anderson turned his attention to Turner. 'So, you're the curator of the local museum and this whole thing was your idea.'

'If you mean that it was me who suggested doing a programme about Keeper's Tump, then yes, but Crayford Productions were already looking for a suitable site when I contacted them. I'd tried to interest several programme makers in doing something down here. Archaeology programmes are very popular and I thought it would do both the museum and the tourist industry here some good.'

'Why Keeper's Tump?'

'Because, so far as we know, it's never been excavated before, and also because of the legend.' Anderson looked blank. 'It's said that it has a guardian called the Keeper, and that misfortune befalls anyone who disturbs the grave.'

'Well, misfortune certainly befell the unfortunate bastard in there,' commented Anderson. 'And what's all this about the fellow who claimed there was treasure buried hereabouts, but never turned up? Is it true?'

'What? About the treasure or the man?'

'Both.'

'He didn't actually claim he'd found treasure, only that he was sure there was some.'

'What do you know about him?'

Turner went even whiter, if that was possible. 'Very little. Except that his name's Smith.'

Anderson gave an exasperated snort.

'Plenty of people really are called Smith,' snapped Turner. 'You only have to look in the phone book. He first turned up back in the summer to ask if I knew anything about Keeper's Tump. I told him that he shouldn't mess about as it's an ancient monument and he should get permission. I said I was hoping to get a TV programme interested in doing a dig here, and that it would be sensible to leave things alone until I knew the outcome. We'd then get permission to examine the site, everything would be official, and he could come along and we could all see what there was to find.'

'And he agreed?'

'Oh, yes. No problem,' lied Turner.

'What was he like?'

'Oh, middle-aged, heavily built, nothing outstanding to look at. At first I thought he might be a farmer. One of my volunteers said he spoke like a local man who'd been away and "got on", and that figured with what he told me: that he was a retired businessman who'd recently returned home.'

'My sergeant tells me you've not been able to find him and that you don't actually know where he lives. Weren't you taking a chance on his keeping his word?'

'I didn't think so. We'd been in touch by phone right up until a couple of weeks ago. Look, please can I go now? I've no help this afternoon and, if I can't get back, the museum can't open.'

Anderson sighed heavily. 'Very well. You'd better get off then. You don't need to come back to the village tonight, but I'll need to talk to you again.'

Turner set off towards the road at a brisk trot, almost into the path of the returning Land Rover. First out was a smart-looking man carrying a bag. 'I asked your man for a lift, seeing as I couldn't get my own car up here,' he told the waiting policemen. Then he saw Latymer. 'Good God! DCI Latymer. But I thought you'd given all this up, John?'

'Dr Mike Evans,' countered Latymer. 'And I have, Mike. Sort of.'

'Can someone tell me what the bloody hell's going on?' thundered Anderson.

Seven

'It was worth it just to see Anderson's face!' Mike Evans settled back in his chair in the lounge of the Atlantic Bay Hotel in Newquay as his coffee was put in front of him. He and Latymer had arranged to meet up that evening for dinner after he'd finished his examination and seen the body removed to Truro for the post-mortem. He'd been able to reach the site so quickly, he explained to Latymer, because, when the police contacted him, he was already in the county, attending a conference in Newquay. 'I'm actually based in Exeter and, although theoretically it should only take an hour or so to get to Bodmin, it often takes a good deal longer. Anderson was lucky in that respect, but it's a bloody difficult site. I don't envy the SOCOs, either the site or the man in charge.'

Latymer grinned. 'I take it you don't care too much for Anderson.'

'No.' He smiled back. 'And I'll tell you why later. He certainly didn't take to you!'

It was true to say Anderson had not. He'd questioned Latymer closely about the cottage, who it belonged to, whether anyone had stayed there recently, even though at one stage Johns intervened to point out that they already had the information. When Latymer had proffered some information of his own, Anderson rapidly became irritable. Latymer explained how he'd noticed signs of disturbance at what he'd taken to be the entrance to the Keeper's barrow, and that he'd assumed it must have been done on behalf of the film unit to save time when they arrived. However, when he'd mentioned it to Crayford Productions, they'd assured him that they hadn't authorized anyone to touch anything until after a local expert had visited the site with them. Yet someone obviously had

56

tampered with the stones in the entrance, for, when the archaeology students had started to unblock it, they had come away far too easily. The assumption must be, therefore, that it had been done by whoever put the body in the grave. To which Anderson had responded to the effect that this was merely surmise. When Latymer went further, referring to the coincidental disappearance of the mysterious local expert, and tentatively suggested the possibility that he might be the corpse, Anderson had become increasingly cross, demanding to know if Latymer was trying to teach him his job.

Latymer had tried to be placatory, assuring him that he was only trying to help, since he'd just happened to be around at the time. 'I can do without that kind of help,' Anderson had snapped. 'What would you have said if some retired ex-copper insisted on giving you the benefit of his wisdom when you were at the start of a major investigation? One who'd presumably taken early retirement when the job got too much for him.'

'I might well have found his – or indeed *her* – advice useful.' Latymer could feel his own temper rising. 'I was only trying to be helpful. I thought you might actually like to know that an ancient site, which allegedly has not been touched for a couple of thousand years, had been broken into before the filming even started. Also, since the sergeant informed us all that there was no identification on the body, it occurred to me that it might possibly be that of the only other person we know about who had a special interest in that particular site. I apologize if you'd already come to the same conclusion.'

Anderson scowled. 'Thank you, but I think I can manage without your assistance. I suggest you go away now you've given us your personal details, and get on with enjoying your early retirement. Things have moved on since you left the force. If I need to speak to you again I know where you are.' At that he'd stalked away to greet the police photographer, who had only just arrived.

'I felt like telling him that some things might have changed in the last few years, but not the emergence of the kind of arrogant bastard the force throws up from time to time,' Latymer admitted, looking out over the Atlantic from the restaurant window, the waves caught in the lights of the town as they curled in across the wide, flat, beach. It was difficult to associate murder with so much peace.

Evans agreed, but added, 'I suppose to some extent you're bound to miss it. You really were considered one of the best, you know. And here you are now, running a bookshop with Keith Berry, but then, you two did work together a good deal, if I remember rightly. And a crime bookshop too. I don't suppose there are all that many run by two ex-policemen. Does he still feel the old itch too sometimes?'

It was then Latymer told him a little about the two unofficial cases with which they'd recently become involved. 'The last DI I came into contact with actually asked for my help officially, on a consultancy basis.' He paused and pulled a face. 'Just about the last thing Keith said before I left was not to trip over a body! The first case came about because I'd just happened to be in Cornwall with the literary tour people I was working for, shortly before a corpse was washed up just outside Newlyn harbour, bringing with it unforeseen repercussions; and the other after the terrified son of one of my then neighbours called me out in the middle of the night to say he'd found a dead man on top of a hill near Stratford-upon-Avon. I didn't go looking for either of them.'

'But you couldn't resist it.'

'Right. When it came to it, I couldn't. Now, tell me why, in particular, you don't like Anderson.'

'I've only been down here a couple of years. I'd had enough of Birmingham, it was a good time for the kids to move schools, so when this job came up based in Exeter, I took it. Compared to the midlands, Cornwall and Devon haven't a high percentage of suspicious deaths, a good many of the PMs I do are on the victims of accidents or suicides. Anyway back in April or May or thereabouts, I was called down here by Anderson, who'd literally only just joined the local force, following his promotion. The body of a man had been found on a beach near here, at the foot of a shallow cliff. From the appearance of the body and the place where it was found, he could have jumped, been pushed, or stumbled over by accident, though, if the latter, he must have been drunk, for by then it was staying light quite late and there were street lights not far away, which gave some light almost as far as the cliff path. The edge would have been impossible to miss.

'If it was murder, then whoever did it must have assumed that, if they pushed the victim over, then the sea would finish him off and sweep the body out to sea. But he must have been a stranger with little knowledge of tides, for they were at neap: that's when the sun and moon pull against each other and the difference between high and low water is at its most minimal. So, it's possible the water was only two or three feet deep, even if the victim went in at high tide, which would then drop rapidly. The same would apply if he'd tried to commit suicide there.

'Anderson was waiting on the beach when I told him this, to which he replied that he didn't know pathologists considered themselves to be tide experts and, if he wanted that kind of advice, he'd ask for it. Before I'd even had a chance to examine the body, which had been removed from its original position to avoid its being covered with water again, he assured me that it was almost certainly either accident or suicide. I pointed out that, if it was a suicide, then why on earth did he choose a low cliff above a sandy beach, when on either side there were cliffs a hundred feet or more high, towering over jagged rocks and deep water!

'At which he again reminded me that my job was confined to discovering, then confirming, the cause of death, which must almost certainly have been by drowning. The police doctor had already confirmed that superficial injuries were caused by his fall, a conclusion which appeared to me to be correct.'

'*Was* he drowned?'

'No. He wasn't.' Evans paused briefly. 'I put Anderson's attitude down to the fact that he'd only recently moved to a strange force in a strange place and might therefore be feeling somewhat insecure. I understand his last post was in Milton Keynes, which is about as different from Cornwall as you can get. As to the corpse, at that stage nobody had any idea who he was. He was wearing a black T-shirt and jeans, and there was nothing in the pockets, although a credit card with his fingerprints on it was later found in the grass at the top of the cliff. Anyway, I did the PM and discovered, as we removed the T-shirt, which had been soaked in sea water of course, that there was some blood on the front of it, and the reason why soon became apparent when the body was stripped. He'd been stabbed through the heart. The weapon used was something like a stiletto, long, thin and pointed. It had gone into the heart, leaving only a tiny hole on the surface of the skin. There would have been very little bleeding at the time.

'Anderson didn't attend the post-mortem but bustled in immediately afterwards, full of himself, booming out that he trusted I'd be able to confirm the man had drowned and that foul play wasn't suspected. I told him I couldn't do that, since it was definitely murder, as he'd be able to see for himself. Had it not been plain to all present that this was indeed the case, I think he still might have tried to argue the odds. My own feeling is that he'd wanted a nice tidy death by drowning (which could be put down to suicide or accident), with everything then tied up in double quick time. As it was, he was landed with a full-scale murder enquiry, for which he appeared to blame me. If you want to know more about the details of the case, then it was pretty well covered in the local papers at the time.

'It turned out eventually that the victim was a man called Harry Groves from Stockwell in south London, with a record of petty crime. Other than that, little was known about him. Anderson started crashing around making enquiries in the villages nearest to where the body was found and got nowhere. Even if he'd been more tactful and the victim a local man, he'd probably have found it difficult anyway, since he'd be regarded as a "foreigner", as they say down here, and, from what I gather, they're a particularly clannish lot in the moorland and north-coast villages. A local farmer was murdered near here a couple of years ago, everyone knew him, nobody liked him, there must have been some ideas as to who did it, but to this day the local police have never picked anyone up for it. Funny place, Cornwall.'

But not the only one, thought Latymer, recalling the Warwickshire murder which had featured in his last essay into private detection, a murder about which local people were still not prepared to say anything, over half a century after the event. He drove back to the cottage in a thoughtful mood. Evans, after carrying out the post-mortem in Truro, would be returning to Newquay, since he was due to deliver a lecture in the afternoon. He looked at his watch as he went into the house. Eleven thirty . . . Would Berry be up? He decided to risk it.

Berry answered the phone himself. 'I actually rang you earlier this evening to see how you were getting on. Decided to stay on, then?'

'For a day or two,' Latymer told him. 'I'm glad I haven't dragged you out of bed. Look, have you ten minutes to spare? There's something I feel you'd better know.'

He woke up the next morning determined to follow up some enquiries of his own. Berry, after finally accepting that Latymer wasn't having him on, had listened attentively to what he'd had to say. As well as giving him the basic facts, Latymer explained how it looked to him as if just about everyone involved was concealing something. He felt certain that the museum curator knew more than he was saying and that he'd concealed information from Crayford Productions, who, in turn, had deliberately led him to believe that they were fully financed and that the programme on Keeper's Tump was the first in a major series, rather than a shoestring pilot which might never be transmitted at all. Also that he felt, looking back on his first two evenings in the pub, that in reality the apparently friendly locals sitting chatting at the bar took a pretty dim view of 'they lot from up-country' coming down to their neck of the woods and messing about with one of their ancient sites. As to the investigation itself, it appeared it was in the hands of a newly appointed, bad-tempered and apparently inept DI who'd taken against him straight away. Berry asked if he wanted him to drop every-thing and come down for a couple of days, but Latymer urged caution. He wanted to look further into it first, look up the details of the first murder and also see if he could find out anything more from the museum curator. He intended to make Lanwithen Museum his first port of call in the morning.

Matthew Turner, after opening up the museum the following morning, was sitting in his office feeling tired out and physically sick, having been roused from sleep at about three o'clock that morning by the ringing of the telephone. The flat was over a shop in the town and the phone was downstairs in his hallway. He switched on the light and stumbled out of bed. The only reason he could think of for a call at such a time was that one or other of his parents was seriously ill. He made his way down to the phone as fast as he could, pulling a jersey over his head as he went, and picked up the receiver.

'Mr Turner?' enquired a voice he didn't recognize.

'Yes? Who's that?' The caller was silent. Turner raised his voice. 'Are you there? Who is it?' Still silence. 'What do you want?'

'The photographs, Mr Turner.'

As his head cleared, Turner went cold. He tried to sound offhand. 'What photographs? Is this some kind of a bad joke? What in God's name do you want to talk about photographs for in the middle of the night? I'm not a photographer and, if I was, I wouldn't appreciate being woken up at this godforsaken hour to arrange a sitting.'

'You know very well which photographs I mean, Mr Turner.' The voice was a strange one and the line not very clear; it was difficult to tell whether it belonged to a man or a woman. 'I want those photographs. I must have them. I suggest we arrange to meet tomorrow evening and that you give them to me.'

'You're crazy,' blustered Turner. 'Stark, raving mad! I'll report you to the police as a nuisance caller.'

'I shouldn't do that,' responded the voice. 'How are you going to explain to them just what's been going on? Just what you've been concealing. Think about it.' He paused. 'I'll give you until the end of tomorrow afternoon to come to a sensible decision, then I'll ring again to confirm where we should meet.'

'What if I don't agree?'

There was another pause. 'I don't imagine you'd like me to have to come and *fetch* them, would you? Oh, and I'm sure our mutual friend Smith would send you his regards . . . if he could.'

There was a click as the line went dead. Frantically, Turner dialled 1471 to learn that he was called that morning at ten past three, and that 'the caller withheld their number'. He put the phone back in its cradle and sat down on the floor. Oh God, he thought, what have I got myself into?

So it was that, when Latymer arrived at the museum that morning, the day's volunteer helper informed him that the curator was not feeling well and couldn't see anybody. 'It's hardly surprising.' Her eyes glowed. 'Did you hear Radio Cornwall this morning? About that murdered body they found at Keeper's Tump over to the moor? Poor Mr Turner was there when they found it, he'd been helping they TV people with the filming. I should come back again some time when he's feeling better.'

'Perhaps you could tell him it's John Latymer,' insisted Latymer. 'I was there yesterday as well. And I really would like to have a word with him.'

The volunteer looked doubtful. 'All right, I'll go and tell him and see what he says. But, you know, they shouldn't never have interfered up there. You've heard about the Keeper, have you? It's right what they say, you come to grief if you disturb him.' She went over to the office door, knocked, and went in, returning a couple of minutes later. 'He says to go in. I shouldn't stay too long, he's looking some bad.'

Turner was huddled up in his chair, his face grey. 'Why have you come? What do you want?'

'I wanted to talk to you.'

'Why?' Then a look of sheer terror crossed his face. 'Did *he* send you? He said he'd ring again this afternoon, but it's only half past eleven. Have you come instead of him?'

'Nobody's sent me,' declared Latymer. 'I'm here entirely of my own accord. You look terrible, what on earth's the matter?' Turner looked at him as if he were about to burst into tears. 'I really do think we should talk,' said Latymer, more gently. 'Something's obviously very wrong.' As he spoke, his mobile phone started ringing. 'Excuse me a moment, will you?'

It was Mike Evans. 'I'm probably not supposed to tell you the results of the post-mortem but, in view of who's in charge, I thought I'd like to pass the result on to someone with a bit of nous. Because something very odd seems to be going on in this neck of the woods. The victim did have a crack on the head, but the police doctor was right, it wasn't sufficient to have caused his death. The body was in far worse condition than that of the man I told you about, the dead man found on the beach, but the cause of death was exactly the same: a blow from a stiletto-type dagger right through the heart.'

'So, there must be a connection?'

'Happily, that's your business, or rather Anderson's, I suppose, not mine. But, for what it's worth, I'd say yes. You don't often come across a stiletto as a murder weapon in this day and age. Well, good luck. I must get back to Newquay. See you soon. Possibly at the inquest?'

Latymer apologized again to Turner, then tried to pick up the conversation where it had been left off. 'I was just asking you why this business has upset you so much, apart from the obvious shock of finding a body on the site. Who did you mean when you asked if "he" sent me? Who's going to ring you this afternoon?'

Turner swallowed. 'Oh, it's nothing, no one,' he said, hurriedly. 'That is, it's nothing much. Actually, it's the builder who did some work here . . . about an unpaid bill. The trustees are certain they paid it, he says they haven't. He says if it hasn't been sorted by this afternoon, either he or his mate will be round demanding it in person. I don't fancy any unpleasantness, that's all.'

He's lying through his teeth, thought Latymer. 'Well, if that is the case, I imagine it can be sorted out quite easily, so I shouldn't let it worry you. What I really wanted to ask you is if you know more about this man Smith than you're letting on.'

Turner struggled for control, then shook his head. 'As I told the police, he just walked in here one day out of the blue, claiming that he was sure there was something really good buried there.'

'Why did he want to tell you about it?'

'Because he wanted to know what kind of items might turn up in or around a bronze-age barrow. There are several on the moor and, back in the 1930s, a farm labourer did find gold at the one near Rillaton, not far from here. But most of the spectacular finds have been further west, as I told him. Also, I told him that I'm not a bronze-age expert.'

'And you believed him?'

'Why not? He seemed to know what he was talking about. As I told the chief inspector, I'd been trying to get a TV programme to do something down here for ages, and it seemed just the thing: an interesting site with a legend attached and the possibility that there might be something really interesting there. I know that, with hindsight, it sounds a bit naïve. But I did manage to persuade Smith not to do anything else until we knew whether or not we could get some TV people interested.'

'Shouldn't he have informed the authorities? I know there's a new law about this, though I'm not sure of the details.'

'He didn't have to do anything unless he'd actually made a find. Then he'd have to tell, first the coroner, then the local Finds Liaison Officer in Truro. I explained all this and also told him that he should get permission before detecting on, or immediately around, an ancient site.'

Latymer looked across at him. 'Are you sure, absolutely sure, that there's nothing else? That he didn't, perhaps, actually show you something he'd found there, just to whet your appetite?'

'No. Nothing like that.'

He's still lying, thought Latymer. He's also very scared. Turner stood up. 'Look, why the hell are you asking me all these questions? You're not in the police any more. Will you please go away? I'm not feeling at all well.'

'I know I've no right to expect answers from you,' agreed Latymer, 'but I'm becoming increasingly concerned, because I think that, even apart from the murder, which is bad enough, there's something very unpleasant going on down here, and that it involves your Mr Smith. Has it occurred to you that it just might be his body inside that bronze-age barrow? You say that for weeks he was closely involved in what was going on, but then he suddenly disappears just when it's all about to happen. But no, I'm not a policeman any more, it's up to Anderson and his team, and my advice is to be as frank as possible with them.' He also stood up, ready to go, and took his card out of his pocket. 'The phone numbers are those of the shop and my flat in Bristol, but I've written that of my mobile on it for you. If, for any reason at all, you feel the need to contact me, please do so. I'll be around for a few days yet.'

He drove away convinced that Turner was concealing possibly vital information he was too scared to divulge. He was one very frightened man. It was also clear he was under pressure. The story of the unpaid builder's bill was obviously untrue, so who was leaning on him and why? Had Smith originally offered Turner some kind of deal in return for his help, a deal that Turner had reneged on, and it was Smith he was expecting to hear from that afternoon . . . which meant he couldn't be the corpse.

Perhaps Smith had started out by offering Turner a cut if he helped him sell some stuff, but then the curator had suggested that bringing in a TV company would be a better idea. Using such a well-publicized excavation would give the supposed discovery legitimacy, which in turn would lead to a good price without any risk. Turner might well have pointed out that artefacts would be difficult to sell on the black market without the authorities getting wind of it, which was true – though, as Latymer knew from experience, some people did get away with it. There were collectors whose lust for a particular item was such that they'd do anything, pay anything, to possess it, even if it had to be kept locked away in a safe and never see the light of day again. Well, he'd gone as far down that road as possible for the time being. He decided to visit the offices of the *West Briton* in Truro and look up the details of the body on the beach. Like Evans, he felt sure the two deaths had to be connected.

Turner watched him go with mixed feelings. Perhaps, after all, Latymer really was what he said he was and his offer of help a genuine one. At least, if he'd taken it up, he'd have had some support. But what would it do for his employment chances if he'd admitted that Smith had brought in two priceless artefacts which couldn't possibly have been found together in Keeper's Tump, unless they had recently been reburied there – and that he'd persuaded him to do nothing about it until he was able to arrange maximum publicity? Then he thought again of the chilling phone call in the night and the cold voice informing him that Smith would send his regards 'if he could'. If he could? Was Latymer's surmise right, was it Smith's body in Keeper's Tump? Round and round it went in his head. The museum closed for lunch and he usually had something to eat in the pub or the one small café in the town, but he didn't feel like eating. He decided to go back to his flat. Once safely inside, he made himself a cheese sandwich then forced himself to look at the answerphone. To his relief there were no messages.

It was with extreme reluctance that he returned to the museum at two o'clock. It was Wednesday and there was no help on Wednesday afternoons, since it was early closing in the town and a quiet day. He sat at the desk by the door, jumping every time anyone came in. But the good weather of the previous two days was fast disappearing, it was starting to rain and there were few visitors. The afternoon seemed interminable. What was he going to say when his night caller rang again? And he was certain that he would. Four o'clock, half past four, nearly five and still no phone call. Perhaps, after all, it was just a sick joke.

Dead on five he checked that everything was in order, switched off all but the entry light, put his coat on and went towards the door. As he reached it the phone began to ring. He stood still, rooted to the spot. Perhaps they'd give up if there was no reply, assume he'd left the building. But suppose the caller was ringing on a mobile from just outside? After a while the ringing finally stopped. He made up his mind, put the lights back on in the library, went in and, removing some dusty volumes from the middle shelf, retrieved the envelope in which he'd put the photographs and their negatives. Then, once again, he checked the museum and turned out the lights. As he reached the door, the phone started ringing again. He almost fell out on to the step outside, locked the door behind him and looked frantically around. It was raining hard by now but, so far as he could tell, there was no one about. So far, so good. Whatever he might feel about Latymer, he was now desperately in need of help. He leapt into his car and shot off into the murk towards Latymer's cottage, praying he'd find him at home.

Eight

Turner left his car on the road and almost ran up the path to the cottage. A police car and van were parked outside, so presumably the police were still working up at Keeper's Tump, but there was no sign of life within. To make sure, he walked round to the back of the building, but there were no lights anywhere and the back door was securely locked, as was that of the conservatory. As he stood considering what to do next, he saw the lights of a vehicle coming down the path and stepped back out of sight. With the weather now closing in rapidly, the police had given up for the day. The Land Rover dropped off a couple of scenes of crime officers and the drivers of the other two vehicles, after which all three drove away, leaving him alone in the dark.

He'd found the whole area around Keeper's Tump pretty eerie when he'd visited it the first time in broad daylight, but now the uneasy feeling he'd never really shaken off returned in force. However far-fetched, the idea of a supernatural warrior in a gold mask lurking inside the mound was not a pleasant one. There was some kind of a shed behind the cottage and, as there was no lock on the door, he went inside to wait; at least he was out of the rain. But time passed and there was still no sign of Latymer. He rang his mobile number several times but without success. What should he do? Go back to his flat only to receive yet another frightening telephone call? He decided the best thing would be to spend a couple of hours in the pub, but changed his mind on seeing that the Crayford Productions vehicles were still parked in the car park. Evidently the police had required them to stay on. In desperation he drove to Bodmin and had a meal in a pub, then, seeing that it also offered bed and breakfast, booked himself in for the night. Eventually, just after eleven o'clock, he finally managed to reach Latymer, who naturally assumed that Turner was calling from Lanwithen. The young man was in such a state of panic that Latymer was quite unable to disentangle what his problem was and suggested therefore that since it was now very late, they meet up in the morning.

'Whatever it is, I'm unlikely to be able to help you with it now,' he asserted, firmly; 'I'll give you a call first thing in the morning,' and he rang off before Turner was able to explain that he wasn't in Lanwithen. Oh well, there was nothing more he could do. At least his night caller was unlikely to break into the pub looking for him

Latymer had spent some time going through the papers detailing the story of the discovery of the body on the beach the previous April. Although murders in the Devon and Cornwall police area were relatively few compared to many other places, the story hadn't even received significant local media coverage once it was confirmed that the corpse was that of a lowlife villain from London. There was a fairly wide-spread assumption that the murder was connected with drugs, attention being drawn yet again to the fact that the county had a considerable problem, as Latymer knew only too well. So, what better motive for murder? Perhaps, so it was speculated, the victim was a dealer who'd either fallen out with his counterpart in Cornwall or reneged on some deal and suffered the consequences. Either way it was good riddance to bad rubbish. Anderson was questioned on a number of occasions as to the progress (or lack of it) made on the case; finally, when coverage had dropped almost entirely away, making the senior policeman's classic statement when they see the likelihood of catching a killer disappearing into thin air: 'The net is closing in!' Latymer noted that the murder had taken place at the end of April, some three or four months before Mr Smith had paid his dramatic visit to the Lanwithen Museum.

His next port of call was Truro Museum, which had a selection of artefacts excavated locally, but nothing which might be described as priceless treasure. He enquired about this and was told by an attendant that most of the really valuable objects

70

were now in the British Museum. Among these were three gold lunulae, 'Probably ornaments for neck or breast,' he was informed, two found at Harlyn Bay and the third near Boscastle. Other valuable pieces had been found further west in the Penwith area.

'I've heard of something called the Rillaton Cup,' said Latymer. 'Can you tell me anything about that?'

The attendant reacted with enthusiasm. 'It was found by a workman in a bronze-age barrow on Bodmin Moor sometime in the 1800s. The cup was in there along with some human bones, a bronze dagger and beads. Everything else has disappeared except for the cup. I think we've a photograph of it somewhere, if you're interested. I'll just ask one of my colleagues in the office. He might like a word with you himself.'

He reappeared a few minutes later with a young man who introduced himself as the finds liaison officer. 'I understand you're interested in the Rillaton Cup? Here's a picture of it, it is rather splendid. Unusually, it wasn't actually found inside the barrow but in a cist, a small rectangular burial pit, on the edge of the mound above ground level. It's not known how the finder came across it.'

Latymer looked at the small gold object. 'It's beautiful,' he commented. 'Have many others been found?'

'No, they're extremely rare. One was discovered in Germany and another in Switzerland and that was about it until, out of the blue, in 2001, yet another turned up near Ringlemere in Kent. It was discovered by someone using a metal detector. Unfortunately it's pretty squashed and was probably run over by agricultural machinery, which is a great pity, but it's a splendid find all the same.'

'Do you think any more are likely to surface?'

He shrugged. 'Who knows? Most of the barrows and graves were robbed in antiquity, but you never know. Are you interested in metal detecting then? Belong to a club?'

'No. It's just that I'm staying in a holiday cottage close to the barrow called Keeper's Tump, which was about to be excavated by a television team until . . . possibly you know what's happened? Perhaps they were hoping to find another one there.'

71

'I heard something about a body being found inside the mound. It must be infuriating for the telly people, though I really do have serious doubts about these speed digs. But they must have been romantic optimists if they really expected to come across a gold hoard, just like that. In fact, I'm doubtful if they'd have found anything at all in Keeper's Tump. Apart from anything else, it's too easily accessible from the road.' Latymer thanked him and went back out into the street. It was raining steadily. Faced with returning to his unwelcoming base or being forced to spend the evening in the pub with Crayford Productions, he decided, in spite of the rain, to have a look around Truro, then get something to eat and visit the cinema, which he noted was showing *The Lord of the Rings – The Return of the King*. Somehow, given that the trail was leading to the appearance of mysterious gold objects, it seemed appropriate.

He returned home, drank two large malt whiskies, then slept heavily, his dreams laced with images of gigantic elephantine beasts carrying pagodas on their backs, a gold ring which somehow became the Rillaton Cup, and vast battles, accompanied by a great deal of noise, which went on and on right up to his own front door. Struggling awake in what felt like the middle of the night, he realized the noise really did come from his own front door, on which someone was frantically knocking. He picked up his watch and squinted at it. Good God, it wasn't yet seven o'clock. Sleepily he made his way downstairs, cursing as he went, and opened the door to find Turner standing shivering on the step. 'Hell's teeth, what are you doing here?' he exclaimed. 'When I said I'd ring you first thing, I meant as soon as the museum opened – and I fully intended to do that. There was no need to come over and wake me up at the crack of dawn.' He yawned, then, seeing the young man's crestfallen face, said, 'Very well, now you are here, you'd better come in. But what on earth's the matter? What could there possibly be that couldn't wait until nine o'clock?'

'I wasn't at home,' said Turner, 'and I wasn't going to go back to my flat or the museum until I'd seen you. I came over here last night and waited ages. I kept trying to ring you but there was no reply. In the end I stayed over in Bodmin for the night. I didn't dare go back.'

'Why not?'

'Because I'm frightened someone's going to kill me.'

'I see. Well, put the kettle on while I get dressed and then you'd better tell me all about it. And the truth this time.'

Half an hour later, in halting tones, Turner described how Smith had walked into the museum one day, bringing with him two artefacts he claimed to have discovered metal detecting on or around Keeper's Tump. 'I've got photographs of them here.' He drew out the envelope and removed the pictures. 'See? That one's a cup like the one found in a barrow on Bodmin Moor ages ago, and the necklace thing is called a torque.'

Latymer could hardly believe his eyes. The gold cup was almost identical to that photograph he'd been shown of the one found at Rillaton. 'Good grief! I don't know about the torque but, from what I understand, gold cups like this one are incredibly rare. Together they must be worth a fortune. Did you really believe him when he said he'd found them metal detecting?'

'Well he *could* have done, it's just about possible, but what worried me was the fact that he claimed that he'd found them buried together.'

'And that's significant?'

'Yes. You see, they date from considerably different periods, the cup is hundreds of years older than the torque, so they couldn't *originally* have been buried together. I wondered if perhaps some unofficial excavator or a farm worker had found them separately and hidden them away, reburied them even, expecting to come back for them, but never did. Which is what I told him.'

'What did he say?'

'That he'd heard this strong signal, dug down, and found them buried together. That's certainly possible.'

'You didn't suggest he alert the relevant authorities, then?'

Turner sighed heavily. 'I know that's what I should have done. All right, it was wrong of me, but I'm desperate to get a better job and get out of here and I'd been trying for ages to get a TV company to come down and do a dig and put both me and the museum on the map. I gave Smith all the right stuff about reporting it to the coroner and the finds liaison officer and so on, and then it struck me that, if he'd just hold on until I was able to set something up, we could rebury them where he said he'd found them, and the TV people's discovery would ensure a spectacular find that would do us all some good. Smith had sort of hinted that he'd try selling the stuff secretly, but I persuaded him that my way would ensure he got a substantial reward for them and everything would be legal and above board. It would be for the experts to argue over how they came to be together in the same place.'

'It didn't occur to you he might have stolen them?'

'No, it didn't. I'll admit that I thought he might not be telling me everything, but if two such valuable pieces had been stolen recently from any of our national collections, then I'd probably have known about it. I don't always read them, since we're such a minor outfit, but we regularly receive circulars about the loss of far less important items. Anyway, he finally agreed, also that I could take some photographs, although he wasn't all that keen about that.'

'Weren't you taking a risk getting the film developed?'

'Not in Newquay at the height of the season. Hundreds of films go through the processors every day. It would need something like pornographic pictures for an individual reel to be noticed.'

'So, what's all this about being murdered? Have you been directly threatened?'

Turner shivered. 'I had this phone call in the middle of the night before last, from a man (I think it was a man) with a really scary voice. Somehow he knew about the photos and told me I must hand them over to him at a time and place to be agreed. If I didn't, then he'd come and fetch them. He didn't directly say I'd be harmed if I didn't, but the inference was obvious. He said he'd ring again at the end of yesterday afternoon to fix up the meeting. Nastiest of all, he said something about how Smith would have sent his regards "if he could". By the time it got to five o'clock yesterday, I'd begun to think it might have been a sick hoax after all, but then the

74

phone began ringing. It rang and rang. So, I got in the car and drove over to you.' He looked at Latymer. 'I suppose I'd better go to the police.'

'You must. You should have told them all this as soon as the body was found at the site. I'm aware that Anderson isn't a very sympathetic character, but for your own sake you will have to be as open and frank with him as you have with me.' Latymer looked again at the photographs. 'I'm not at all sure what this is all about, but I think you've got yourself involved in something very nasty indeed.'

'What about the photographs?'

'Give them to the police, of course, though – since I see you've several – I'd like to hang on to one myself, to make some enquiries of my own. Let Anderson have the rest. I imagine he'll give you a hard time – I would have done. You might also ask him if he can put a trace on your phone in case your caller calls again. If he does contact you again, tell him you've given the photographs to the police, so there's no point in pursuing you any further. Now, we'll have another cup of coffee, then I'll come back to the museum with you. It's better if you ring the police from there rather than here, Anderson's made it quite clear he doesn't want any help from me.'

As he and Turner arrived outside the museum in their respective cars, it was immediately obvious something was amiss. A police car was parked in front of the building and a constable was standing outside the main door with a man Turner recognized to his horror as Josiah Trembath, a local solicitor and the chairman of the board of trustees. 'Oh, there you are at last, Turner,' he barked as Turner ran up the steps. 'Where the hell have you been?'

'I stayed over in Bodmin last night and – er – overslept. What's happened? What's the matter?'

'There's been a break-in,' the constable informed him.

'But I locked up properly last night,' said Turner, horrified. 'I double checked, I always do.'

'The intruder got in through one of the back windows,' explained the constable. 'It wouldn't have taken much effort to force it, the frame is quite rotten.'

75

'If that's the case, Turner, why weren't we informed about it?'

'You were. I told the trustees. In writing. I understand it was discussed twice at meetings, but no action was taken,' responded Turner, angrily.

Trembath's face reddened. 'Don't you take that tone with me! The refuse men discovered what had happened when they came round the back at half past seven this morning. And where were you? Not in your flat. Presumably you were away all night.'

'What difference does that make?' raged Turner. 'I don't sleep over the shop. There's nothing in my contract to say I can't spend a night away from home.'

The constable was growing impatient. 'You'd better come in and see the damage.' He looked enquiringly at Latymer.

'This is Mr Latymer. He's on holiday down here and . . . and I'd arranged to show him over the museum. He wanted to know more about the area. I'd like him to come in with me, if that's all right.'

They trooped in through the hallway and into the museum proper, then stopped short at the chaos in front of them. Books had been thrown off shelves, drawers pulled out and emptied, the glass fronts of some of the cases forced open and their contents strewn on the floor. Turner went through to the office and could hardly get in through the door for the files from the filing cabinet. The desk drawers had also been emptied out but Turner was relieved to see that the computer, the only one the museum possessed, was still in place.

'I imagine it'll be difficult for you to know what, if anything, has been stolen, until you've had time to go through it,' commented the constable. 'Was there anything here of special value?'

Turner shook his head. 'No. There were some artefacts from excavations in the area, odds and ends of iron-age pottery, a collection of various ores from mines, old agricultural implements and items like miners' helmets donated by various individuals, but nothing worth breaking in for.'

Trembath glared at him. 'You make it sound as if the museum has nothing of any value.'

'I'm not saying that. There's plenty of things of local interest but nothing truly valuable in financial terms, not even in the store room.' He turned to the constable. 'Do you think it could be down to local vandals breaking in for the sake of it?'

The constable shrugged. 'Could be. Look, I've been on to CID and asked them to send someone along, but it might be some time as they're a bit stretched just now. You'd better wait until someone gets over here from Bodmin before you start cleaning up, though there's nothing to stop you checking if anything has gone missing. You don't need to stay here, sir, unless you want to,' he continued, turning to Trembath.

'Well, I'd like to get back to the office,' the chairman agreed. 'Not least because I must contact the insurers. I'll try to get hold of Mrs Pengelly and see if she can organize a clean-up. I think I might be able to persuade the trustees to pay them for their time, given the circumstances,' he added, pompously. 'As for you, Turner, I'd like to see you in my office once everything is in hand.'

He and the constable left together as Turner and Latymer began threading their way through obstacles lying all over the floor. Turner shook his head. 'I don't know where to start.' He paused. 'Do you think it could have been someone looking for the photographs?'

'Well, comforting as it might be to put it down to local yobs, it has all the hallmarks of someone looking for something specific, possibly the photographs. Unless you still aren't telling me everything and you've got the cup and the torque hidden away here. If so, you'd better see if they're still there.'

'Good God, no! Smith would hardly let me touch them, even when he was present. I'd never have been able to persuade him to leave them behind. As to there being anything else to tell, there is one other thing, but I don't suppose it's important. Smith never told me where he lived but, during one of our phone conversations, he said something which made me think it was somewhere near St Day in 'a handy croft' ... I didn't take much notice at the time. Perhaps I should mention that too, in case it might help the police to trace him.'

By the time Sergeant Johns arrived an hour or so later,

Turner was almost certain nothing obvious was missing. 'CID are pretty well tied up with the Keeper's Tump business,' he explained, 'so I offered to come over and see what's happened.' He looked around. 'What a mess!' If he was surprised to see Latymer there, he didn't say so.

'Nothing seems to be missing,' Turner told him. 'Could it be kids breaking in and trashing the place? The constable thought it a possibility and I seem to remember a couple of schools near here got done over not long ago.'

'It's a possibility,' Johns agreed, 'but I'm not sure . . .' He walked round the room, carefully stepping over the contents of the cases and the heaps of paper. 'It could be they were looking for something specific. But if you say nothing appears to have been taken, then what could it be?'

Latymer and Turner exchanged looks. 'It's time you told Sergeant Johns what you've just told me,' said Latymer. 'And apologize for not admitting what you knew earlier.'

So Turner told his story yet again, produced the photos and handed them to the sergeant. Johns stared at the objects. 'Phew! These must be worth a small fortune! You're not saying this stuff was hidden away in here, are you? The DI's going to go through the roof as it is. Why the hell didn't you tell the truth straight off?'

'Because I was scared. No, of course they weren't here. Look, as I've explained to Mr Latymer, when I suggested the idea to Mr Smith, it didn't seem all that wrong. The cup and the torque would still have turned up, but they'd have done so on television and made us a lot of publicity. I never dreamt it would end up like this.'

'I don't imagine you did, but it was a bloody stupid thing to do.'

As the sergeant was speaking, Mrs Pengelly and another of the volunteers appeared, laden with brooms and cleaning materials. 'Mr Trembath's sent us in to help you clean up,' she declared. 'He says you're to be sure to make a list of anything missing or broken and to put the bits somewhere safe. Dear lord, it's some old mess you've got here! Who in the world would've done such a thing?'

'It'll be some of they young tearaways from one of the

78

council estates,' stated her friend, firmly. 'No discipline, do as they like, what do you expect?'

'Very well, you can start cleaning up,' Johns told them, 'and you'd better start listing what's broken or missing. I'll just nip outside and let DI Anderson know the score.' He reappeared some minutes later, looking grim.

'I take it he was pretty annoyed,' commented Latymer on seeing his face.

'He went flaming ballistic!' Johns concurred. 'He's back in Bodmin and wants to see you there, *now*, Mr Turner.'

'But I can't,' wailed Turner. 'You heard what our chairman's said. I've got to list everything that's been broken and see if there really is anything missing.'

'Well, that'll have to wait. I'm sure these ladies are capable of putting any broken objects all together in one place. As to what's missing, since you don't think anything is, then that shouldn't take very long when you get back. Apart from anything else, we now have a computer graphic simulation which gives some idea of what the murdered man probably looked like. He wants to see if you can identify him.' He turned to Latymer. 'I think he might be coming round to your way of thinking, that it was Smith's body in there.'

'Very well,' said Turner, dismally, 'but I'd like to go back to the flat and change first. It'll only take ten minutes.'

'I'll wait here then, but don't be too long about it, and prepare yourself for trouble,' he warned.

'What do you think, Mr Latymer?' he enquired as soon as Turner had left.

'That either the person who rang him up the other night, or someone sent on his behalf, was looking for those photographs. Anderson made any breakthrough yet at Keeper's Tump?'

'The brief answer's no.' He gave Latymer a meaningful look. 'I'd better leave it at that. Let's just say I don't know what the hell he did in Milton Keynes.'

'Dr Evans told me you'd another murder near here back in April,' commented Latymer.

'That's right. We never did get that one sorted. Mind you, it was nothing like this. The most likely explanation was the old "when thieves fall out" killing, and that it had to do with drugs. The victim was a petty crook from an area in London notorious as a den of dealers.'

Latymer decided to let it rest there for the time being. 'Well, there doesn't seem much point in my hanging about here. I'd like to get back home. That young man was banging on my door at seven o'clock this morning.'

'Why the hell didn't he tell us the truth straight off?'

'That's what I asked him.'

As he returned to his car, it struck him that he should have contacted Maynard. At the very least it was only courteous to let him know what had happened. So far, the story had only made the local radio news, not the national, but it was only a matter of time before the press latched on to a murder in a bronze-age tomb. He dialled Maynard's London number but there was no reply and no answerphone on which to leave a message. Next he rang Berry to bring him up to date with events so far.

Berry heard him out then laughed. 'Good grief, you must take it with you, John, you really must! Ah, say the fates, John Latymer's off on holiday, let's drop a couple of corpses in his path. You say you've got a photograph of these priceless items? Then I think I might be able to help. Could you possibly get back for a couple of days? I know someone at the Ashmolean in Oxford who's really into this kind of thing and it would be interesting to see what he makes of them. Does this local DI know you've got it?'

'No,' admitted Latymer. 'I'm afraid I've bent the rules a little.'

'Which, of course, you *never* do! Mind you, he should be grateful for your help so far, not least getting that foolish young man to own up.'

Latymer looked at his watch. 'Look, I don't know what else Turner's told the police, but he told me that he had a feeling Smith was based in a village near here called St Day. I don't suppose I'll come across anything useful, but I'd like to take a look. Then I'll set off back straight away.' He paused. 'Oh, by the way, have you any idea where Maynard is? I mean, whether he's in London or has gone away? I thought I'd tell him what's happened before he reads it somewhere, but there's no reply.'

'Not a clue. He's not been in the shop now for some time.

I'll try and get hold of him myself. If I do, I'll tell him you'll fill him in yourself when you get back.'

Latymer pulled out the map of Cornwall he'd brought with him and looked for St Day. He'd assumed, given that, like so many of the moorland villages, it was called after an unknown saint, that it must be somewhere nearby on Bodmin Moor. It turned out, however, to be a good thirty miles further west, in what appeared to be a desolate area, pockmarked with old mine buildings. He sighed. Oh well, if he intended getting back to Bristol that night, he'd better get on with it.

Meanwhile, in Bodmin police station, a miserable Turner was being put through the wringer by Anderson. He told and retold his story and even to him it sounded lamer at each repetition. Yes, he knew he should have done everything possible to get Smith to contact the coroner's office; yes, he himself should have done so anyway, if he'd any doubts as to the origins of the artefacts; no, of course he shouldn't have set up some kind of scam to persuade a television company that they'd make a spectacular find if they were prepared to come down and film at Keeper's Tump; no, his only motivation had been to ensure the maximum publicity for the television dig and further his own career, not make money out of it. Eventually he and Anderson reached an impasse, since the DI refused to believe he'd confessed all he knew, while Turner simply didn't know what else to tell him.

After a while, an officer came in to inform Anderson that two people from Crayford Productions were outside, wanting to know if they could finally get off back to London. Anderson looked at Turner and scowled. 'Wait there,' he told him. 'I've by no means finished with you yet.'

Outside, Crayford argued the case for getting his people back to London. 'The students have already been allowed to go and there's plenty of witnesses to the fact that the rest of us didn't arrive until Sunday and were in each other's company almost every minute of every day, except when we went to bed. We've given very full statements to your people. None of us are going to disappear into thin air, but hanging around down here like this is driving me mad. I need to get back and see what, if anything, can be salvaged. As it stands, it looks as if it might well put us out of business.' He didn't mention that added to this very real fear was the fact that his relationship with Adrian had reached rock bottom and that they were all sick to the back teeth of Rosie's whining and phone calls from her agent demanding that she be allowed to return at once.

Anderson reluctantly agreed, after extracting a firm promise that both Pete and Dave would return if called as witnesses at the inquest. 'You may not be at this stage,' he told them, 'since it will almost certainly be opened then adjourned. But you'll definitely be needed later.'

He then strode back into the interview room, this time bringing with him the computerized reconstruction of the victim's face. Recognition didn't take long. Turner looked at it then nodded. 'Yes, that could be Smith.' He looked across at Anderson. 'But I don't understand. He'd arranged to meet us last Monday. What was he doing there over a week earlier? Why did someone want to kill him?'

Anderson smiled evilly. 'That's what I hope you'll be able to help us with,' he said. 'Prepare yourself for a long day. Now, let's start again . . .'

Sergeant Johns had also made a discovery. While waiting to take Turner to Bodmin, he'd retreated into the office, since the cleaners were now busily at work in the museum proper. It was somewhat odd that the thief or thieves had left the computer behind, another reason against the break-in being down to hooligans, who would surely have taken it away and tried to sell it. He went over to the machine and switched it on. A whirring noise came from within and the screen flickered into life but nothing appeared on it. The desktop was empty. Johns drew up the chair and started hitting various keys. Still nothing happened. Then he examined the machine more closely. 'Shit!' he exclaimed. 'It looks as if someone's nicked the hard disk.'

Nine

Latymer soon discovered that getting to St Day took longer and was more complicated than he'd assumed from looking at the map. At one time he found himself on what appeared to be one of two parallel bypasses, the road signs signalling exits to places with crazy names he'd never heard of such as Ventongimps, only to realize, after finally taking one of the turnoffs, that he was heading rapidly away in the opposite direction to where he wanted to go. Finally, after pulling in and referring to the map yet again, he found himself on a narrow, winding road, allegedly leading to St Day as well as somewhere or something called 'United Downs'. He ran into a sudden heavy shower and it wasn't until he'd passed through what must have been the outskirts of St Day that he realized he'd missed the centre of the village altogether and was now on his way to Crofthandy. Aware that he had to go back, he was looking for somewhere to turn safely when he found himself at a crossroads. On his right was a sign saying 'United Downs Industrial Estate' and on his left another pointing simply to 'United Downs'. Very well, since he'd got this far, he might as well explore a little, and to this end he turned left.

Almost immediately he realized he was now in old mining country, the signs of the county's industrial past were all around him. Finding a small car park at the side of the road, he pulled in, left the car and walked to the top of it to get a better view. He found himself looking out across a desolate landscape, dotted with the remains of old workings. Close by were the remains of two engine houses, the mine 'castles' of the eighteenth and nineteenth centuries, and, on the skyline, a whole cluster of them, their ruined chimneys pointing like fingers towards the sky. A notice board informed him that he was looking at what was left of the Great Consolidated Mines and the United Mines, the Wheal Virgin, Cusvey, Andrew, Clifford, Cupboard, Poldory, Squire and 'Cakes and Ale'. Presumably 'wheal' stood for mine and the names were those of major investors or local landowners, though why 'Cupboard', let alone 'Cakes and Ale'? Was there a mine owner who remembered the phrase from *Twelfth Night*?

As he stepped back, a car pulled into the car park and a young man, obviously well equipped for walking, emerged from it, pulling on a woolly hat as he did so. 'You'll need more substantial shoes than those if you're planning to do any of the walks,' he called out, cheerily. 'And something water-proof. This is only a break between showers, I reckon it's going to pour down later.'

Latymer explained he wasn't planning on a walk, he was just touring round and had turned off to find out what 'United Downs' meant. His informant was obviously an enthusiast. 'It'd be worth your while coming back, then. You can walk the disused tramways round the ruins of the mines now – there's an old arsenic processing plant, remains of roads and settling beds, more engine houses, it's absolutely fascinating. And if you're really feeling energetic you can walk down to the sea at Portreath one way, or to the River Fal the other. You won't get lost, they sell booklets and maps in the villages around here.'

'Unfortunately I have to go back to Bristol,' said Latymer. 'Some other time perhaps. Though, to be perfectly honest, I find the look of it rather off-putting. It's probably quite different in better weather.'

'It does affect people in different ways,' the young man agreed. 'Some just see an industrial wasteland, others find it creepy, and people like me become addicted to it. For me its greyness on a day like today is part of its charm. I admit it does have its odd side though. A couple of miles over there,' he indicated, vaguely, 'there's the grave of a gypsy child who was burned to death in an accident years ago. Travellers do still camp out there from time to time, but, even when they don't, somehow there's always fresh flowers on it, sometimes

84

even children's toys. Who puts them there? Nobody seems to know.' He looked up at the sky. 'Right, I must be on my way if I'm going to get a decent walk in before the rain.' And with a cheery wave, he was gone.

Latymer returned to the main road and this time did see the sign to St Day and made his way towards its centre. He'd already decided his trip was a complete waste of time even before he realized that the town or village was substantially larger than he'd imagined and that he was unlikely to get anywhere asking passers-by in the street if they knew of a Mr Smith who might or might not live locally. But, having got this far, he must at least make some kind of an attempt. He parked his car and made for the post office and shop, queuing up behind an elderly man who wanted a parcel weighed, four different kinds of stamps, and his car licence renewed, followed by a plump woman who felt the urgent need to tell the postmistress about the state of her Dawn's marriage.

By the time it reached his turn, Latymer was feeling quite foolish. However, he explained to the postmistress that an old friend of his, name of Smith, was now living in or near St Day, but that he didn't have his new address. 'I thought I'd call in and enquire on the off chance, seeing that I was so near.'

'You don't know the name of the road or street?' she asked, reasonably enough. Latymer shook his head. 'Not even a house name or that of a terrace? We've a lot of terraces in the town.' Latymer had to admit he did not. 'Len,' she called over to the man on the shop counter. 'Do you know anyone called Smith who's moved in around here recently?'

Len shook his head. 'Trouble is, people do come and go these days. We might know him if he was a pensioner or collected benefit here, but if he doesn't . . .'

Latymer thanked them and went back out into the street. Time was getting on, he'd have a brisk walk around the town to stretch his legs, then find a pub which did food. Opposite the post office was a board painted with a hand bearing the legend 'To the church', so he decided he might as well take a look. He crossed over the road on which he'd come in and saw on his right, as promised, a modest church or chapel. But, on the other side of the street, set well back, was what appeared to be a massive gothic folly, the kind of thing beloved of late-eighteenth-century landowners with more money than they knew what to do with, but in this case of monstrous size.

A series of turrets adorned the front of what appeared to be the top of a three-storey building, in the middle of which was a kind of castellated tower with a turret on the top, reminding him inescapably of Saruman's tower in the Tolkien film he'd recently seen. It was quite, quite extraordinary. He opened the gate to it, marvelling as to what on earth it might be and what kind of self-publicist could have dreamed it up, when he suddenly realized he was in a graveyard. The 'folly' was, in fact, a derelict, roofless church. He walked all the way round, noting that all its doors were securely boarded up. Shaking his head in disbelief, he returned to the gate to discover yet another helpful notice, this time detailing sites of interest in St Day. He was just searching for a heading marked 'church', when an elderly couple arrived, the woman holding a bunch of chrysanths. They exchanged greetings. 'Mother's buried in there,' she told him. 'I try and keep her grave nice.' She looked over at the church. 'What do you reckon to our church, then?'

Latymer admitted that it had come as something of a surprise.

'It's what's called the *old* church,' she continued, 'not the *really* old church, there's nothing much left of that. This is the one they built in 1828.'

'For four thousand pound,' added her husband, with a laugh. 'Couldn't do much with four thousand today, could you? But it was a lot of money then. We'd some of the richest mines in the country round here in those days. They called St Day the Tin Capital of Cornwall.'

'What happened to it?' enquired Latymer. 'The church, I mean.'

'Oh, the wealth went, it was difficult to keep it going and sometime back in the 1950s they said it was unsafe. Then the roof fell in and that was that. It's a grand old place, though, isn't it?'

Latymer, who thought it one of the most grotesque buildings

he'd ever seen in his life, managed a tactful reply. The couple went on through into the graveyard and he turned his attention again to the notice board, on which was a quotation from one William Beckford, who had visited St Day and the surrounding area back in 1787. He graphically described the barren landscape, the overhanging pall of black smoke mixed with steam, the gaunt children flogging the mules, the 'woeful figures in tattered garments crawling out of the dark fissures . . . This dismal scene of suffering mules and hillocks of cinders extends for miles,' he continued. 'Huge iron engines creaking and groaning . . . tall chimneys smoking and flaming, which seem to belong to Old Nick's abode, diversify the prospect.' Latymer could well believe it.

As he looked again at the derelict gothic ruin, it struck him with a smile that, with his penchant for all things gothic, it would be right up Maynard's street. Would he consider this 'the real Cornwall' too? The thought prompted him to try Maynard's number again, but there was still no reply. Well, when he finally did reach him, he must certainly tell him about St Day's old church, if he didn't know about it already. Suddenly realizing he was hungry, he went in search of a late lunch.

His original plan had been to drive straight back to Bristol, until he realized that he'd left the brief notes he'd made of the events so far back at the cottage. It was a nuisance, but if he was going to give Keith a reasonably accurate rundown of the story he really ought to have them with him. When he reached the cottage he saw that only the SOCO van was now parked outside. There was no one about. Once inside, he thought he'd better tidy up, then laid the stove ready for his return. It was now raining heavily and a few minutes later the police Land Rover came down the track. Three scenes of crime officers got out, and it drove off, leaving them to follow in the van. It might, thought Latymer, be useful to see if they'd found anything, and he called out to ask how they were getting on.

'Not much luck so far,' responded one of them. 'No sign of anything at all really, except for the fact that the entrance had been disturbed. Looks as if he was killed close by, then dragged inside. But whoever did it left precious few clues behind. I understand that there might now be a positive ID, though.' Latymer wished them good luck and they drove away.

The detour and consequent delay resulted in his hitting heavy traffic and it was mid-evening before he arrived at the bookshop, to be met by Kate, who told him she'd a meal ready for him and had made up a bed. 'You don't want to have to go back to the flat and start sorting things out at this time of night. Plenty of time for that tomorrow. Go through, Keith's waiting for you.'

'Sit down, get your breath back and have a drink,' said Berry, as he walked into the big sitting room over the shop. 'I want to know everything that's happened. I'm sure Kate will be interested too. I'll suggest she joins us, it won't harm the casserole to stay in the oven a bit longer.'

Relieved to unburden himself to a sympathetic audience, Latymer brought them up to date so far as he was able. 'The reason I'm late is that I called back at the cottage to pick up my notes, it's all too easy to forget the exact sequence of events when you don't have to record everything.'

As he expected, they grasped the gist of the story very well. Berry heard him out without interrupting, then asked Latymer if he'd had any luck tracing Smith. 'Where did you say you've been?'

'St Day. No, I didn't, and St Day isn't where I thought it was, nearby on Bodmin Moor, it turned out to be a good bit further west. The whole area's very strange, all desolate mining country, with masses of old workings and ruined buildings. I did make enquiries at the local post office, but it's hardly surprising they couldn't think offhand of a particular man called Smith. I'd have been surprised if they had. But I did find a really weird building in the town.' And he told the Berrys about the old church. 'I couldn't help but think of Maynard, with his obsession with the gothic. He'd be in seventh heaven.'

'I wonder they haven't hired it out to a film company,' commented Kate, 'though you say the structure's not safe. Otherwise I'd have thought whoever owns it would make a fortune. Now, we really must eat.'

After the meal Latymer showed them the photograph of the gold cup and the torque and told them what he'd learned from Turner and from Truro Museum. Both Berry and Kate marvelled at the objects. 'But they're quite beautiful,' said Kate. 'Do you really think this man found them just by metal detecting? I find it hard to believe.'

'My contact at the Ashmolean is going to go mad when he sees these,' declared Berry. 'I've made arrangements for us to meet up with him tomorrow at half past eleven, John, if that's OK by you. But, to get back to the victim, do you think it is this man Smith?'

'I do. According to the SOCO I spoke to just before I left, the police have now got a positive ID. Presumably from young Turner, who I imagine has been given a hard time at Bodmin police station.'

'I can't say I feel much sympathy,' commented Berry.

Latymer yawned and agreed. He was having difficulty keeping his eyes open. 'I think I'll go to bed if that's all right,' he told them. 'It's been a crazy few days. I'm beginning to think there are two Cornwalls, the one I thought I knew, with harbours and beaches and blue skies, and another one of bleak moors and the ruins of its industrial past. Just where Keeper's Tump fits in, I'm not at all sure, or which one Maynard considers to be "the real Cornwall".'

'Harking back to Maynard,' said Berry, 'I still haven't managed to contact him. We'll have to try again in the morning.'

Latymer fell asleep almost as soon as he got into bed, only to wake in the night wishing he hadn't, after a dream in which he was running through a desolate landscape, pursued by some unknown horror, desperately trying to reach a church in which to seek sanctuary, only to discover, when he finally reached the gate, that it was St Day's old church, lit with a lurid glow. At which point he stumbled over the grave of the gypsy child who'd been burned to death, his face smothered in half-dead flowers. He sat up in a cold sweat, after which he lay dozing uneasily until daybreak.

There was no need to telephone Maynard the next morning, because he called in himself, explaining that he'd only just returned from a week in Paris. 'Can't *imagine* why I'm in so much demand,' he trilled. 'Two calls from John and three from you, Keith. You must have found something really special for me. By the way, how's John enjoying my little place?'

'Actually, I wasn't trying to contact you about a rare book. As for how John's been getting on, he's here, so you can ask him yourself. That's why we've been trying to get hold of you. I'll pass you over to him.'

Latymer gave Maynard a brief précis of events, his narrative interrupted from time to time by squeaks and 'oohs'. 'How *dreadful*!' he exclaimed, when Latymer had finished. 'Good *heavens*! To think of a real murder taking place so close to my little country retreat! Do they know who it is? And who did it?'

'There was no definite ID when I left yesterday afternoon,' Latymer informed him, truthfully, 'and I don't think they've a clue as to who did it.'

'But you could have been murdered in your bed!' declared Maynard, dramatically.

'Hardly. Whoever it was they found inside Keeper's Tump, he'd been dead well over a week before I even arrived.'

'And the television too! I'd no idea a television company would be making a programme down there. I'd have been fascinated. I know quite a lot of people in TV, you know. If only I'd known, I could have come rushing down to see for myself, and we could have been cosy in the cottage together.'

'I had no idea it was going to happen until I got there,' said Latymer, firmly pushing so grisly a prospect to the back of his mind.

'Is that why you're back in Bristol, then? Will you be going back?' enquired Maynard.

'I came back because something's cropped up to do with the shop.' Well, it's nearly true, thought Latymer. 'I'm planning to return tomorrow morning if our business has been settled here. I thought I'd spend a few more days in the cottage, if that's all right.'

'Oh yes. I simply don't have time to get down just now. I trust you found everything in order?'

Latymer hesitated. 'To be honest, it was rather damp. In

fact, it was very damp. It looked as if nobody had been there for some time, and I'm afraid all the plants in your conservatory are well and truly dead. Perhaps you should try and get someone from the village to pop in from time to time to air the place, water the plants and so on.'

'Oh, do you think so?' Maynard sounded miffed. 'Perhaps you're right. I suppose it is quite a while since I managed a weekend on the moor.' He sighed. 'I really must make the effort soon, I do love it so.'

'The real Cornwall?' suggested Latymer.

'Oh, quite definitely the real Cornwall.'

Latymer was just about to ring off when he remembered the old church in St Day. 'By the way, knowing your love of all things gothic, have you seen the ruined church in St Day?'

'St Day? Where's that? Somewhere on the moor, I take it?'

'No,' said Latymer, 'it's further west. I suppose the nearest town is Redruth. You obviously don't know the ruin they call "the old church". You must pay it a visit next time you're down in Cornwall. It's just your kind of thing.'

Maynard thanked him. 'I'll bear it in mind next time I "go west". But *do* keep me posted of any new developments, won't you? Promise?'

Latymer did.

He and Berry presented themselves at the Ashmolean a little before the time arranged, to find that Berry's contact, Dr Roger Alan, was already waiting for them. 'I must admit to being very intrigued,' he told them. 'It's not every day I'm offered the prospect of being shown a photograph of the kind of objects you described, Keith.'

'I hoped you might be interested,' said Berry. 'We both feel we're out of our depth with this one.'

'Well, let's go up to my office.'

On the way, Alan to explained to Latymer how he had been one of Berry's earliest customers. 'My interest is in first or unusual editions of the great crime novels of the thirties and forties, especially Chandler and Hammett. Does that period interest you, John?' Latymer confessed to liking Chandler but admitted that, even after having seen the film twice, and reading the book, he'd never been able to get to grips with the plot of *The Big Sleep*.

Dr Alan swept several heaps of papers off two chairs, then invited them to take a seat. 'Right. Now, what have you got for me?' Latymer handed over the photograph. Alan looked at it, then peered closer. 'Good God! What have you got here?' He stood up and went over to the window to look at it again in a better light, then returned and, taking a magnifying glass out of a drawer, went over it carefully, inch by inch. Then he looked across at them. 'I am, to use the vulgar expression, gobsmacked. But I can't think of any other word to describe how I feel. Have you *any* idea what these might be?'

'Well, from what I was told in the museum in Truro, the cup would appear to be very much like the Rillaton Cup, which they told me was found on Bodmin Moor back in the 1830s. All I know about the other is that it's called a torque. Oh, and what the curator of the local museum near where I was staying told me, that the cup was much older than the torque. It was him who took the photograph.'

'Are you saying that he came across these himself, or that someone showed them to him? And that he's done nothing about it? I think you'd better tell me more.'

So Latymer told his story yet again, including the discovery of the corpse in the barrow. 'From your reaction, I imagine this stuff might be said to be worth killing for? That is, if somebody wanted it enough.'

'I don't want to sound overly dramatic, but yes,' Alan concurred. Your local man was right, the cup is early bronze age, possibly as early as 1500 BC, while I'd put the torque somewhere around 800 to 600 BC, though I'd have to see the actual object myself to give you a more accurate date.' He peered at the photograph again. 'In appearance it's not unlike the two found near Towednack in West Cornwall in 1932. They also had a twisted design. It's generally thought they either came from Ireland or that an Irish goldsmith was working in Penwith at the time.' He stopped. 'Now, that does ring a bell. Would you mind if I went and fetched one of my colleagues?' He got up and left the office.

'If it's OK, I'd rather like to come back with you,' said Berry, as they waited for Alan to return.

'I'd be delighted. But what about Kate?'

'She knows I've been dying to get down there ever since you told me about the body. Or rather, both bodies and both victims killed in the same peculiar way.'

Alan returned, bringing with him an elderly colleague whom he introduced as Dr Rutson. 'I've asked Dr Rutson to take a look, because he's fully conversant with Irish gold-working techniques, and also because it's just possible he might know where this came from.'

Rutson carefully examined the photograph, looked at Alan, then nodded. 'Yes, I think you could be right, Alan.' He turned to Latymer and Berry. 'The design of this, so far as it's possible to see from the picture, definitely suggests late-bronze-age Irish gold-working. but it also looks to me like a piece I've actually seen myself. I'm almost certain that it's a torque which was stolen from a museum in County Cork about eighteen months ago. It was usually kept in the national collection in Dublin, but it was out on loan as part of a special exhibition of local artefacts found in and around the area in which the exhibition was taking place, and was by far the most valuable. It was the only thing stolen. My advice to you is that you alert the police without any further delay, they have their own specialists in the field of stolen antiquities.'

Alan smiled. 'Perhaps I should have told you that, although Mr Berry and Mr Latymer now run a bookshop, they are themselves ex-police officers.'

Rutson nodded. 'Well, you'll know the score, then. In the meantime, I'll try and find out all I can about the theft and the origins of that particular piece.'

'He's right, of course,' agreed Latymer as Rutson left them. 'But I think, out of courtesy, I ought to pass all this on to the investigating officer when we get back to Cornwall tomorrow. Mind you, if he doesn't act on it . . .'

Alan looked thoughtful. 'This really is serious, you know. It really does look as if the torque is the one which was stolen in Ireland the year before last. As for the cup . . . Certainly, so far as we know, nothing like it has been reported as having been stolen. Hardly surprising in view of the fact that, so far as is known, there are only two in the whole country, that found at Rillaton and a damaged one which turned up not long ago in Kent.'

'The Truro people told me about that too,' Latymer informed him.

'But this one looks quite perfect. I wonder where the hell it came from! For what it's worth, I'd say that both pieces were marked down for an illegal private collector and that, somewhere along the way, the exercise went wrong, hence their turning up in the possession of this metal-detecting enthusiast. That is, if he was telling the truth.'

'I wouldn't bet on it,' said Latymer. 'So far as I can see, everyone seems to have been lying to everyone else.'

'I was planning on our going out to lunch,' declared Alan. 'But before we do, I've got something to show you. It is Keeper's Tump we're talking about, isn't it? Funny name for Cornwall, the word "tump" meaning "barrow" is more often used in Gloucestershire and Herefordshire. Perhaps it's a corruption of something else . . . However, I was chatting to a friend of mine at the Bodleian and he lent me this.' He lifted a large, leather-bound volume off a shelf. 'It's not the original, to see that you'd need to apply for a reader's ticket and practically be chained to the desk while you looked at it, since it dates from the early sixteenth century. This is a nineteenth-century printed edition with coloured engravings.'

It was a book of stories and legends of the West Country, divided into 'The Counties of Cornwall, Devonshire and Somersetshire'. Alan opened the book. 'There you are.' It was a picture of Keeper's Tump, set against a highly romanticized background. The barrow was both higher and wider than in real life, but the entrance could clearly be seen. Beside it stood an artist's interpretation of the Keeper, a towering figure in a grey-green robe, holding a great two-handed sword, his overall appearance suggestive of King Arthur and Tintagel. But the golden mask covering the face, with its blank eyeholes and fixed mouth, was from an era more reminiscent of Mycenae than legendary Cornwall.

'Right,' said Alan. 'Who's for lunch?'

Ten

Latymer and Berry were back in St Mellick by midday the following day, Latymer feeling somewhat low, since he had been disappointed to discover, when he'd called in at his flat to make sure all was well and collect his post, that there was still no word from Fiona. He'd emailed her personally and via her 'fisherking' website several times from his laptop while he'd been away, but without success. Perhaps, he told himself, it would be better anyway if he left well alone until this present business was resolved one way or the other. They drove through the village, noticing that the incident room was still operating in the village hall, then turned off to the cottage. If police investigations were still going on at the murder scene, then presumably they'd been scaled down, since there were no longer any vehicles parked outside. 'We'd better get all the heating going,' observed Latymer as he let them in. 'We'll need to air the bedding from your room. At least there's been some warmth and fresh air in the place since I've been here.' But, even so, the place still felt and smelled of damp, a fact remarked on by Berry as he stared at the stained paintwork, tacky furniture and unsafe-looking electrical wiring.

'I see what you meant when you said it'd been neglected. It doesn't look as if it's ever been any different, it's as if Maynard simply bought the place then left it exactly as he found it. I was pretty amazed when you described what it was like the other night, and I admit I thought you were exaggerating the state it was in, but it's even worse than you led me to believe.'

Latymer grimaced. 'Perhaps Maynard considers it to be a part of his "real Cornwall": a real Cornish cottage complete with real squalor.'

Berry shook his head in disbelief. 'You should *see* his London flat! Thick white carpet everywhere, in which you sink up to your knees, really expensive brocade curtains, swagged up and dripping with tassels, all kinds of *objets d'art* artistically lit on fancy shelves or in expensive glass-fronted cabinets, a state-of-the-art kitchen straight out of the expensive lifestyle magazines, gold taps on the washbowl in the downstairs loo. You name it, he's got it. Whereas this . . . What's the matter?'

Latymer was standing in the middle of the small sitting room frowning and looking puzzled. 'Just a minute,' he replied. He went through into the kitchen, looked in the conservatory, then ran up the stairs to the upper floor. 'Sorry about that,' he said as he came down again. 'I know it sounds daft, but it feels as if someone has been here while I've been away. Yet, so far as I can see, everything is as it was when I left, though, given the state of the place, it might not be all that obvious even if it wasn't.' He continued looking round. 'No, everything seems OK. All my stuff is still either here or up in the bedroom, including my laptop and the books on the table, and yet . . .'

'I'll go and check on the doors and windows from outside,' said Berry, and went out through the front door.

Perhaps this whole thing is just getting to me, thought Latymer: the ropey cottage, the bronze-age grave, the corpse, the bleak moor outside. Berry reappeared a few minutes later. 'Well, nothing seems to have been forced or broken, so far as I can see,' he declared, reassuringly. 'There's no sign anyone's tried to break in through either the back or conservatory doors, or attempted to force any of the windows, and you'd have noticed if anything had been tried at the front, wouldn't you?'

'It seemed perfectly all right when I let us in. The lock's a Yale with an older type of lock underneath it. I don't know if that one works but, if it does, Maynard never gave me the key for it, just those for the front, back and conservatory doors. The conservatory's such a rundown and flimsy structure, a burglar or intruder could get in there pretty easily, but he'd then be faced with the kitchen door, which has two bolts as well as a lock. Not to mention the fact that the police have been camped out here most of the time.' He paused, then made up his mind. 'I'll have one more look around, just to satisfy myself.' He went back upstairs, came down again, went through the kitchen into the conservatory, then returned to the sitting room. 'No, I must be getting paranoid. Bring the bedding down from the other bedroom, will you, while I get the stove going. Then we'll open one of those cans of soup.' He went out to the shed to fetch in the logs. The routine tasks helped, but his feeling of unease persisted.

On the way down from Bristol they'd agreed that one of their first tasks must be to visit Bodmin police station, see DI Anderson and tell him what the Ashmolean experts had said about the cup and the torque, not least that their existence should be reported to the special investigation unit dealing with such matters. 'Of course, he might well have already done so,' suggested Berry.

'He probably has,' agreed Latymer. 'Either way, he won't thank us for making the suggestion, he'll see it as me sticking my oar in again. But we'd be failing in our duty if we didn't and, whatever he thinks, it doesn't prevent our making further enquiries and passing the info on.'

They called first at the incident room in the village to see if Anderson was there. The scene, if not exactly a hive of activity, was busy enough. There was no sign of the DI, and Sergeant Johns, who seemed to be more or less in charge, informed them that he was presently at the police station in Bodmin and was likely to be there for some time if they wanted to drive over.

'How are things?' enquired Latymer.

Johns shrugged. 'We put out the usual stuff on TV and local radio, asking anyone who had any information that might be useful to contact us, if any unusual activity had been noticed around Keeper's Tump at the relevant time. We had the usual kind of response. The odd nutter, those wanting to help but with very little to say that's of any real use, a few with theories of their own, and a couple of people warning us that it's all down to the Curse of the Keeper and that he should never have been disturbed. The SOCOs have more or less finished at the site itself.'

'And Turner? Presumably Anderson found what he finally had to say useful?'

Johns gave him an odd look. 'I think you'd better ask the DI yourself.' He paused as if considering saying more, then decided against it. 'I'll be interested to know what you make of it. I'll be going back to Bodmin myself shortly. Perhaps I'll see you over there.' And with that they had to be content, as he was then called to the phone.

The desk sergeant at Bodmin police headquarters noted their request to speak to DI Anderson and said he'd see what he could do. Detective Inspector Anderson, he informed them, was very tied up at present. Latymer explained that he had been at Keeper's Tump when the body was found, had persuaded the curator of Lanwithen Museum to talk to the police, and that he and his colleague, Keith Berry, had information which might assist the police with their enquiries. The sergeant disappeared briefly, then returned to inform them that DI Anderson would see them shortly. A further half hour passed without any word and Latymer was just about to suggest they came back some other time, when Anderson erupted through a door behind the desk.

He looked at Latymer and Berry without a smile or a greeting. 'If you'd like to come through,' he grunted. He led the way into his office, dropped into his seat behind the desk and motioned them to sit down. 'So, Mr Latymer, what brings you in here?' he enquired, without further preamble.

Latymer, after introducing Berry, then explained how his business partner had arranged for them to see Dr Roger Alan, an expert on bronze-age artefacts, at the Ashmolean Museum, and mentioned the astonishment he'd expressed at the sight of the objects displayed in the photograph.

'What photograph?' queried Anderson.

'The one young Turner gave me,' replied Latymer. 'One of those he took himself.'

'He'd no business to do that,' snapped Anderson.

'I don't see any reason why he shouldn't have let me have a single copy, since I'd persuaded him to hand the rest over to you,' commented Latymer. 'After all, I did persuade him to stop messing about and tell you the truth. I'd mentioned the artefacts to Keith over the phone, and it was his idea that we try and find out more about them. The reason we're here now is because Dr Alan confirmed that both objects do indeed date from the bronze age, the cup from around 1500 BC, the torque from about eight hundred years later. He was particularly interested in the torque, and called in a colleague, an expert on Irish bronze-age gold-work, who is virtually certain that it's one that was stolen from an exhibition in Ireland over eighteen months ago. He advised us to contact the relevant police specialists on stolen antiquities straight away, but I felt it was only courteous that we should tell you what we've found out and that you decide who to speak to and when.'

'Thank you, but that won't be necessary.' Anderson settled back in his seat with a superior smile.

'I take it you've already done so, then,' commented Berry.

'It's not necessary, because it's not true,' Anderson responded, triumphantly.

Latymer frowned. 'What's not true?'

'In fact,' continued Anderson, ignoring the question, 'you've saved me some time, Mr Latymer. I was about to try and contact you myself and ask you to come in and see me.'

'Have you actually charged Turner? If so, may I ask with what?'

'If I do, it will be with wasting police time. The story you persuaded him to tell me was a complete fabrication from first to last. A farrago of lies. There never was a man called Smith who walked into the Lanwithen Museum bringing a couple of priceless objects with him.'

Latymer stared at him. 'Sorry, I don't understand.'

'Then let me enlighten you.' Anderson was obviously enjoying himself. 'After Turner was brought in here following the break-in at the museum, he did indeed tell us the same story. Over and over again. That a man called Smith had brought two ancient gold objects into the museum, which he claimed to have found with the aid of a metal detector, and that together they'd planned how Turner would try and attract a television company to excavate at Keeper's Tump and, if successful, how they would then arrange for the objects to be "found". He even signed a statement to that effect. It all took some time, but eventually he was released on police bail, after I'd warned him that he might possibly face charges under the new act regarding such finds. He finally left here about seven o'clock in the evening, but then, just before ten o'clock, I was called at home and told Turner had come back and wanted to retract his statement.'

Latymer sat bolt upright. *'What?'*

'You see, Mr Latymer, there never was a man called Smith, there never was any treasure. It was all part of an elaborate con to get a film unit interested in making a programme down here.'

Latymer looked at Berry, then back at Anderson. 'Come on, what about the photographs?'

'Fakes.'

'They can't be.'

'Oh, but they can. Apparently Turner got some mate of his in London to mock them up, using computer graphics and a digital camera, because at one stage he'd thought about sending copies out to the various programme makers, claiming that they'd been found close to Keeper's Tump, that there was a strong possibility that there was more inside and that he was keeping quiet about them for the time being in the hope that there'd be sufficient interest to mount a television dig.'

'So, why didn't he do that?' queried Berry.

'He told me it was because he was worried that the TV people might get stroppy when they discovered there was nothing there, and would demand to know how he came by the others.'

'So, where does he allege the objects in the photograph came from?' persisted Latymer.

'Apparently the image of the gold cup was taken from a photograph of one found in Cornwall years ago, and the necklace thing, presumably from somewhere else; a book, I imagine. It's amazing what you can do with computers and digital photography these days.'

'But that can't be true,' Berry broke in. 'As we've just told you, that torque was stolen in Ireland eighteen months ago. It's never been seen since.'

'Then obviously the picture of it was taken some time ago.'

This is getting us nowhere, thought Latymer, and changed the subject. 'So, what is it you wanted to see me about?'

'Turner's original story. Oh yes, he admits that was what he told you, but only because, following the discovery of the body in Keeper's Tump, you went into the museum and pressured him. Lent on him, he said.'

'But that's simply untrue,' protested Latymer. 'I realized something was troubling him when we were waiting for your men to interview us after the body had been discovered at the site.' He broke off. 'I take it you still *have* a body? At least I saw that for myself. Turner gave the strong impression of knowing more than he was saying. So yes, I did go and see him the next day and it was even more apparent to me that he was concealing something which might well be important, but at that stage he wasn't prepared to say anything. Then, on the morning of the break-in at the museum, he knocked me up at seven o'clock in the morning, claiming he'd received threatening phone calls from a man demanding he hand over photographs of certain artefacts he had in his possession. I'm sure Turner's fear was genuine. In fact he was so frightened he'd spent the previous night in a pub in Bodmin. It was then I persuaded him to tell you what he'd told me. He intended to call you from the museum straight away, but then, of course, he had to deal with the results of the break-in.' He paused. 'And what about the break-in? A mere coincidence?'

Anderson smiled again. 'So it would seem. We found fingerprints on a window frame which match those of a young tearaway who lives on an estate near here. He denies it, of course, but there's little doubt that he was there. I expect to charge him any time.'

'So this fellow Turner now claims that he made the whole thing up?' Berry reiterated.

'That's right. He based his imaginary "Mr Smith" on someone he'd seen in the museum during the summer.'

Latymer was determined to persevere. 'And you really believe what he says about faking the photographs?'

'Better than that.' Anderson was positively smug. 'I've spoken with the person who faked them. Apparently, after Turner got back from here, he rang him at his flat in London

101

to tell him what had happened, and he was sufficiently concerned to get straight on the overnight train, then come in and tell us about the deception in person. He explained that he was under the impression it was all to do with a practical joke his friend Matt was going to play on someone. I have to say I believe him. He seems a very sensible young man. He says he'd never have lent himself to such a major deception.'

'And the body?' enquired Latymer. 'I was under the impression you'd had some kind of an ID.'

'That's down to Turner as well. When he was brought in, he claimed to recognize the computer likeness as being very similar to that of Smith, but after he'd retracted his first story he admitted that he'd only done so to lend credence to what he told us. So, we still don't know who it is. But we'll get there in the end, never fret.' Anderson exuded confidence. 'But, whoever it is, I doubt it has anything to do with stolen antiquities.'

'I'm sorry, I simply can't believe any of this,' declared Latymer.

'It hardly matters to me whether you do or not,' retorted Anderson. 'Your meddling with a possible witness has resulted in a great deal of wasted time. You're fortunate I don't intend charging you as well as Turner. From now on, keep out of it. I suggest you both go back where you came from and stick to selling books!'

The interview was obviously at an end. Anderson pointed them in the direction of the exit, then disappeared into the back of the building. As they were making their way back to their car, Johns arrived back. 'I take it the DI has filled you in,' he commented, on seeing their faces.

Latymer shook his head. 'It sounds quite incredible to me.'

Johns glanced up at the building. 'Look, it's difficult to talk here. I'm off duty at six. Is there any chance we could meet up somewhere?'

'We'd be only too pleased,' Latymer assured him.

Johns thought for a moment. 'It might be a good idea to meet somewhere fairly anonymous. How about Jamaica Inn at seven o'clock? It's halfway between here and Launceston and you can't possibly miss it. See you there, then.'

102

'What the hell do you make of all that?' enquired Berry as he drove them away.

'As your Dr Alan so graphically put it, I'm gobsmacked,' said Latymer. 'Absolutely gobsmacked. Did he actually *hear* what he was saying to us? It just doesn't make any sense.'

'So, what do you want to do now?'

'Well, my first instinct is to rush over to Lanwithen Museum, haul Turner out of his office and demand to know what the hell he thinks he's playing at. I'd also like a chat with this helpful and sensible friend who dropped everything to rush down to Cornwall, in order to explain about the photographs. I wonder if he's still down here? But I think Turner would be straight on to Anderson if we did, and where would that leave us? No, the sensible thing is to see what Johns has to say. He obviously isn't convinced by the turn of events either.'

'In view of all this, perhaps we'd better just go back to the cottage and make sure I won't picturesquely catch pneumonia after a night in one of Maynard's damp real Cornish beds,' suggested Berry. 'Also, you can show me this Keeper's Tump of yours before it gets dark.'

They arrived at Jamaica Inn a little before seven and noted that, in spite of the time of year and doubtful weather, the car park was pretty full, suggesting there must be a fair crowd inside. They entered through an area which, a notice informed them, was the 'Peddler's Bar'. Latymer had only the haziest memory of Daphne du Maurier's tale of smuggling and wrecking folk, except that an evil vicar was somehow involved, but Berry had re-read it more recently, since several of the du Maurier novels could loosely be classified as crime fiction and early editions were in great demand. The peddler, he enlightened his friend, was a minor character in the book and 'Joss Merlin', whose supposed demise was commemorated on a brass plaque, the pub's fictional landlord. A number of rooms led out from each other, but they eventually found Johns sitting in a quiet alcove next to a vast fireplace in which was a fire of logs the size of small tree trunks.

Johns looked across at Latymer, as Berry went to get in the drinks. 'I take it you're not convinced?'

'That's putting it mildly. As I told you, I find it incredible. It doesn't make any sense. At least Turner's first story was coherent and, indeed, believable. He really was frightened enough to have spent the night in Bodmin rather than stay in his flat. As for the supposedly faked photographs, I'll get Berry to tell you what we found out about the cup and the torque when we went to see his contact at the Ashmolean Museum in Oxford.'

Berry did so, setting out the information they had gleaned from the two experts. 'Dr Alan and his colleague were absolutely certain that the cup and the torque were genuine objects. The cup was completely new to both of them and, in spite of what your DI said, is, we understand, slightly different to that found down here years ago. As for the torque, it's almost certainly one stolen from an exhibition in Ireland eighteen months ago.' He paused as Johns took this in, then added, 'Do you think the photographs were faked?'

'I simply don't know,' Johns admitted. 'I saw Turner's friend when he arrived but I wasn't present when Anderson interviewed him and asked how he'd done it.'

'I've been thinking about that,' said Latymer. 'There's no doubt that extraordinary things can be done these days using computer and digital technology. I went to see *The Return of the King* a few days ago and saw what appeared to be elephants three times the size of real ones, and with half a dozen tusks apiece, carrying what looked like wooden pagodas on their backs full of fighting men! There must have been a score of them trudging across the screen. I suppose, if it's possible to do that, then it would be a simple matter to take images from elsewhere and place them against another background.' He gave an exasperated sigh. 'But when I think about it, I'm almost certain that when Turner told me about the phone call he had demanding he hand the photographs over, he added that his caller had said, "and the negatives as well". I simply don't know what to make of it. Has Anderson had them examined by experts?'

'Not that I know of,' said Johns. 'I think he's more than happy to accept the explanation as it stands. But, like you, for me it simply doesn't hang together, there are too many coincidences. For a start, you have to accept the body inside Keeper's Tump was there by chance and was unconnected to anything else, not to mention the break-in following on from what Turner had told you about receiving a threatening phone call.'

'Anderson told us you'd a fingerprint match for that. He said they were those of a local yob (presumably a lad who already has a record), but who denies it.'

'Wayne Jenkins. Certainly his fingerprints were on both the window frames at the back of the building, but I'm not entirely convinced. It turns out that the back of the museum is one of the places local lads "hang out" of an evening and, although Lanwithen's several miles from Bodmin, a couple of youngsters drive old bangers. Apparently locals have complained about their activities and the refuse men say it's not unusual to find empty lager cans and fag ends there, especially after the weekend. Wayne's mother claims he was at home all that night. He says he had toothache and didn't want to go out and that his mates will back him up.'

'As they would,' commented Berry.

'As they would,' Johns agreed. 'Except that, in this case, he also has rather more believable back-up: corroboration from his dentist. Apparently Wayne turned up at the surgery in the morning, clutching his face and complaining about the pain. The dentist found an abscess in a tooth, give him a prescription for antibiotics and told him to come back again in a week. It's not enough to convince Anderson, though.'

'And you still don't know the identity of the corpse?'

'No, though I could have sworn Turner was telling the truth when he said the picture looked like his Mr Smith. He went quite pale when he saw it. It wasn't possible to let him see the actual body, the face was too far gone.' Johns sighed. 'This all suits Anderson down to the ground. Nothing complicated, no theft of artefacts, no threatening phone calls in the middle of the night. A worrying story which turns out to be untrue and a simple explanation for what actually did happen. All he's left with is the body of an unidentified man which we can't even ID from dental records, since, most unusually, the chap had perfect teeth. No dental work at all. If it hadn't been for the filming, it's very likely he would never have been found.'

'Which suggests that the killer had no idea that a television programme was about to be made there,' Berry pointed out.

Johns agreed. 'Which in turn begs the question what was he doing up there? Meeting someone? It's a bloody odd place for a rendezvous. Did the murderer plan to stick him inside Keeper's Tump right from the start?'

'Another thing,' said Latymer. 'I understand the cause of death was a stab wound to the heart from a weapon like a stiletto, just like the man you found on the beach last April. It's such an unusual method, do you think they could be linked?'

Johns looked surprised. 'How do you know about that?'

'It just happens that the pathologist's an old mate of mine. He told me, because he had a run-in with Anderson over the other murder and wasn't impressed.'

'Did you see anything of Turner when he came back and changed his story?' enquired Berry.

'Briefly. I was there when Anderson started interviewing him, but then a detective constable arrived and I wasn't needed.'

'How was he? Determined? Upset? After all, he'd spent all afternoon being questioned and repeating one story before suddenly deciding to change it.'

'He was . . . it's difficult to say. It was strange. He'd been all over the place first time round – angry, emotional, upset – but when he came back it was as if he was just going through the motions, speaking by rote. Though he did say he was dead tired.'

'Obviously something pretty drastic must have happened after he got back home,' commented Berry.

Latymer agreed. 'But personally I'd rule out some Damascene conversion, following intervention by the Almighty. What was this friend of his like?'

'Very smart. Trendy dresser. I'd say public-school educated. He told Anderson he'd read English at Oxford. To be honest, he looked an unlikely mate for Turner. Anderson got someone to look into Turner's background: working class lad from up north, took his degree in one of the old polytechnic universities and only just scraped through. He landed the job at Lanwithen because they've no money and he came cheap. It seemed he was gambling everything on television putting the museum on the map.'

'Which I suppose fits either scenario,' commented Latymer. 'But if the second one is true, then Turner was taking more than a gamble, he was shooting himself in the foot if nothing was found. Is there any way you can persuade Anderson to have Turner in again to go through the various discrepancies in his stories?'

'I doubt it.' The young sergeant looked depressed. 'It's a bloody difficult situation. He is the boss. Oh, and there's one more thing. Whoever broke in took away the hard disk from the computer, which makes it even more unlikely the break-in's down to local lads. Anderson says he'll look into it.'

'Have you ever thought of transferring to plainclothes?' enquired Berry.

'I was considering it very seriously until he arrived. But, as things are, I'm leaving it for now. We don't get on particularly well as it is, it would be even worse if we had to work together more closely.' He looked at his watch. 'I'd better go. What are you thinking of doing now?'

'Sticking it out for a few more days,' said Latymer. 'We'll do our best not to cross Anderson's path, but I'd dearly like to talk to Turner again if there's any way of doing it that won't make things worse, though I suppose he's not to know we've already seen Anderson. I could just call in to see what's happened about the museum break-in and I'd be interested to meet this smart friend of his if he's still about, though I imagine he might well have gone straight back to London. I'd also like to find out if there's any way of telling for certain if a photograph has been faked or not. If we do find out anything that's relevant, I promise we'll pass it on to you. We aren't yet ready to throw in the towel and stick to selling books!'

Eleven

The village of St Mellick lies some six miles north-east of the town of Bodmin. Nothing is known about the saint after whom the village takes its name, but that can also be said of many other 'saint' villages on Bodmin Moor and elsewhere in Cornwall. The supposed 'holy wells', often found close to such villages, were originally springs sacred to pagan gods and goddesses who later became confused with little-known Celtic saints. The church, which dates from the late fifteenth century, was comprehensively restored, as were many others in north Cornwall during the early 1860s. It was while working on one such restoration, in the village of St Juliot, that the author, Thomas Hardy, met Emma Gifford, who became his first wife. The village itself has no distinguishing features, but just under a mile outside it, in the direction of Lanwithen, lies a bronze-age barrow, or grave, known locally as 'Keeper's Tump'. There are a number of prehistoric monuments on Bodmin Moor, often given strange names such as 'the Cheesewring' and 'the Hurlers', all with their particular legends, but no other referred to as a 'Tump'. An ancient manuscript states that the Keeper was a bronze-age warrior who was betrayed to his death by treachery and that, as he lay dying, he laid a curse on any person disturbing his rest. It is said that his two most faithful servants refused to leave the place of burial after the funeral rites, and that, during the night, they were turned into the two standing stones nearby, known as the Guardians. Legend has it that the Keeper was buried wearing a gold breastplate and golden mask and surrounded by precious objects

made out of gold. Also, that disaster has always befallen anyone attempting to break into the burial chamber.
A.J. *Green*, Cornish Walks & Legends, *1912.*

Berry came down the next morning brandishing a battered-looking volume, to find Latymer already up and about. 'Look what I found on a shelf up there last night.' He pulled a face. 'It's in pretty grotty condition, hardly the kind of thing Maynard buys from us. But see what it says here.'

Latymer took it from him and ran his eye down the page. 'About the "precious objects made out of gold". Do you think it could be referring to the cup?'

Latymer put the book down and wiped his fingers. 'Ugh, it really is in a dreadful condition, it looks as if every page is stained with damp. As to the treasure, I doubt it's that specific. But disaster certainly fell on somebody, even if he wasn't intending to disturb the Keeper's rest. And my instinct still is that it was Smith in there, whatever Turner might have said since.'

Berry looked at the book again. 'I don't imagine it would be worth much even if it was in good condition. I imagine Maynard picked it up somewhere locally, such as a car-boot sale. Or perhaps it was here when he bought the place. It certainly wouldn't sit comfortably beside his first editions of Mrs Ratcliffe and Edgar Allan Poe. It's interesting though.'

After breakfast they decided to drive into Lanwithen and visit the museum, Latymer pointing out that he had a good excuse for doing so. 'I'm merely dropping in to see if everything's straight now and whether or not the police have found the culprits.' The museum's official opening hours were from ten until five, but when they arrived outside the building at a quarter past ten, the front door was firmly shut and there was no sign of life. They were standing outside considering what to do next when they were hailed by a passer-by.

'Museum's shut,' she told them. 'Vandals broke in a few days back and made a terrible mess, so they closed it, though I've heard it's supposed to open up again today.'

'Do you happen to know where the curator lives?' enquired Latymer. 'I was with him when he discovered what had

109

happened and I'd be interested to know if the police have caught anyone yet.'

'Shouldn't think so!' she responded with a cynical laugh. 'As to the curator, he's got a flat in Kilmar Terrace. Down there and first right. You can't miss it, it's over the Spar shop. There's a door at the side with his name over the bell. Don't know whether you'll find him there, though, haven't seen him around for several days.'

Latymer turned to Berry. 'What do you think?'

'That we should go round and ask him how he is, if the museum will be reopening today and if the police have picked up the perpetrators. I don't imagine Anderson's been on to him warning him against us, at least not yet.'

They left the car where it was and walked the short distance to the Spar shop. Latymer pressed the bell. 'Well, here goes.'

There was a brief pause, then they heard the sound of someone coming down the stairs calling out, 'OK, I'm on my way!' The door was opened to them by a man of about thirty, dressed in what holiday hotels describe as 'smart casual wear'. He looked inquiringly at Latymer and Berry.

'Sorry to disturb you,' Latymer apologized, 'but we were looking for Matt Turner. Is he in?'

The young man shook his head. 'Afraid not. Can I help?'

'Well, actually I was hoping to see him to find out if the police had got anywhere with discovering who broke into the museum the other day. I arrived shortly after the break-in was discovered, you see. Is he likely to be out long?'

'Well, actually he's gone away for a few days. Oh, I'm Marcus Smeaton, by the way, an old friend of Matt's. I had to come down to Cornwall on business and he suggested I use his flat. Obviously I don't know what's been happening up at the museum, though someone came round yesterday and said something about one of the volunteers going in and opening up later on today.'

'So, do you know when your friend is likely to be back?' enquired Berry.

'He said he'd be away for about two or three days and would give me a call and let me know.' Smeaton gave them an easy smile. 'Sorry I can't be any more helpful than that. Can I tell him who called?'

'Don't bother,' said Latymer, 'it's not important. We might try and drop by again before we go back home.'

'OK. Have a nice day, then.' And, with a cheery wave, Smeaton closed the door.

'Now, what do you make of *that*?' enquired Berry, once they were out of earshot.

'I suppose if Turner's got himself into a real state over this, he might well have gone off for a few days, perhaps back to his home, wherever that is. But where does that leave the museum? Also, it might well be that Anderson would want to talk to him again.' He paused. 'Hang about, didn't Anderson say he'd been released on police bail? And who the hell was that?'

'Turner's helpful friend, I imagine. This whole affair may be riddled with coincidences, but the likelihood of two of Turner's old mates turning up within hours of each other beggars belief. Anyway, shall we go and see if the museum's open now?'

A hastily tacked up notice outside now announced that the Lanwithen Museum was open, and they went inside to find Mrs Pengelly firmly ensconced behind the ticket desk looking anything but pleased. 'We called by earlier,' explained Latymer, 'but the museum was still closed. I'm glad to see you've opened again. By the way, is it possible to have a word with Mr Turner?'

This produced a minor explosion. 'Have a word with Mr Turner, is it? You're not the only one who'd like to have a word with him, including Mr Trembath, the chairman of our trustees. Gone off somewhere, he has, without a word of explanation to anybody.' She peered through her glasses at Latymer. 'You were here, of course, when we found someone had broken in, weren't you? I remember now. *And* when the police came and took Mr Turner away to Bodmin.'

'So, you don't know where he is or when he'll be back.'

'Only that some friend of his from London came in here the day after the break-in and said Mr Turner had "gone away for a few days". Well, all I can say is that when he does come

111

back he'll be in some trouble. If he thinks he can just walk back in here, large as life, he has another think coming, especially after being taken away by the police like that. That police sergeant sounded proper cross. So, when he does come back, it's likely he'll be out of a job. Poor Betty, that's his secretary, can't do nothing much because the computer's broke.'

'Are you saying they arrested him?' enquired Berry.

'If they did, then we've not been told nothing. But, if they didn't, what was he over to Bodmin police station for all that time? No smoke without fire, is what I say.' She looked over her glasses at Berry. 'I take it you're with this other gentleman?'

'Yes, we run a bookshop together in Bristol, along with my wife,' Berry informed her. 'Since John was staying down here, I thought I'd join him and see if I can pick up anything interesting for the shop. We mostly deal in second-hand books, you see. I don't suppose you know anyone around here who might have books to sell? No? Well, we'll keep looking. I was sorry to hear you'd had a break-in. Have the police got anywhere with it yet?'

'I've heard they think it's that Wayne Jenkins over to the estate, as I just said to Betty, I could well believe it. That family's rough as rats. Always has been. As for his friends, we've told the police time after time how they come and hang around out the back there since the town's been smartened up, but they don't listen.'

Berry looked sympathetic. 'No wonder you're annoyed. Has there ever been a break-in before?'

Mrs Pengelly shook her head. 'No. But it was only a matter of time, weren't it?' With the excuse of showing Berry the museum, Latymer led the way to the back room containing the farm implements to enable them to discuss what to do next.

'What do you think of my visiting this estate and seeing if I can track down Wayne Jenkins?' suggested Berry, who'd had considerable experience in dealing with young offenders and antisocial behaviour while he was in the force. 'What about you, though?' said Berry. 'This is where we could do with two cars.' In the end it was decided that Berry would drop Latymer back at the cottage, which would at least give him time to assemble all the information they'd gleaned so far and see if it was possible to reach any kind of a conclusion, while Berry went in search of the dreaded Jenkins family.

Although Perranwell Estate was larger than he'd expected in such a rural area, Berry, with his previous experience of massive run-down inner-city estates in Birmingham, with their tower blocks, acres of identical housing and terraces of boarded-up shops, felt that the residents of Perranwell Estate didn't have a great deal to grumble about. True, there were a number of neglected properties with junk in the garden and curtains that looked as if they were rarely drawn, but nothing on the scale he'd seen elsewhere, and it was clear from the carriage lamps and smart new front doors that a number of tenants had bought their properties. An enquiry at the post office and shop elicited the information that the Jenkins family lived at 19 Colwell Crescent, followed by the query, 'What's that little bugger done this time?' Berry mentioned his surprise at the size of the estate and was told it was down to overspill from Plymouth in the 1960s. 'That's when those Jenkinses came here. Should have gone back to Devonport where they belong.'

It wasn't too difficult to guess which house was number nineteen. Rank grass grew all over the front garden and two old bicycles lay rusting at the side of the path. Berry rang the bell Nothing happened. He rang again and, when that produced no result, knocked loudly. A large shape loomed up at the other side of the murky pane in the front door, which was then opened about six inches. 'Who are you?' enquired the occupant.

Berry gave his name. 'I was wondering if I could have a word with Wayne Jenkins.'

The door opened wider. An extremely overweight lady appeared at the entrance. Berry estimated her age as mid-thirties, though it was difficult to tell. She was wearing one of the fashionable cropped tops so popular with the very young and slim and, as Berry later told Latymer, the large roll of flesh hanging over fluorescent pink pedal pushers was not a

113

pretty sight, nor the ring through her naval. A small and dirty child, with a runny nose and a dummy in its mouth, was clutching at her leg. 'What you want our Wayne for?' she demanded. 'You police? Your lot's already been here twice. Or are you from the Education? If so, you know our Wayne's excluded and you've still done nothing about it. What am I supposed to do with him?'

Berry explained, as tactfully as he could, that he was neither. Quickly forming an excuse in his mind, he told her that he represented the company insuring some of the items in the museum and, since he understood that her son sometimes met up with friends behind the building, he'd like to ask him if he'd ever seen anything suspicious or anyone lurking nearby. It was a pretty lame explanation, but since Wayne's mother hardly appeared to be the stuff of *Mastermind* he hoped it would do. 'It might actually help,' he added. 'You know, if Wayne could assist the police in this way.'

The small child tugged at her mother's leg then started to wail. 'And you can belt up, Kylie, while I'm talking to the gentleman.' She frowned as if giving consideration to his request. 'OK, all right then. He'll be down the rec. That's the kids' play area, it's over there. Not that many kids play there, everything's broke.' She picked Kylie up. 'They think our Wayne done it, but he was here all that night yelling with the pain in his tooth. He had to go to the dentist in the morning.' Kylie's dummy dropped out of her mouth and she started wailing again. 'What our Wayne needs,' Mrs Jenkins informed Berry over the racket, 'is a man about the house.'

'Father not here?' enquired Berry, delicately.

'What do you think? Pissed off before he was two. Just like this one's dad.' And with that she shut the door.

Berry drove slowly along to the recreation ground. Even though overall the estate was quite tidy, there was little here to identify its original purpose. Like the Jenkins' garden it was overgrown and litter-strewn. A group of lads, two or three with skateboards, were gathered around what remained of the swings. There were about half a dozen of them altogether, all of whom looked as if they should have been in school. He stopped the car and went over to them. The smallest lad, who'd been handing round cigarettes from a packet, took one out for himself, ostentatiously put the packet back in his pocket, lit it then looked at Berry, waiting for a comment.

Berry ignored him. 'I'm looking for Wayne Jenkins. 'Do you know where I might find him?'

The biggest lad, who was wearing the regulation oversized hooded jacket, grunted, 'Who wants him?'

'I do,' said Berry.

'You fuzz?'

'No. I represent the firm which insures the Lanwithen Museum. All I want is some help.' The lads looked at each other, shrugged and a couple broke away and started skateboarding on a piece of dilapidated tarmac. 'I've spoken to Mrs Jenkins,' Berry continued, 'and explained everything and she said I'd find Wayne down here.'

The hooded boy pushed his hood back an inch or two. 'OK, then. I'm Wayne Jenkins. Is that a problem?'

'I hope not,' said Berry, and went through his explanation once again.

Wayne did, at least, listen. 'OK, then we do sometimes hang out there. It makes a change and there's eff-all to do here. But I never broke in and trashed the place. What'd I want to break into a poxy old museum for and muck about with a lot of old junk?' He gave a triumphant smile. 'Anyway, it couldn't have been me. I'd effing toothache all night. You ask Mr Barnes, he's the dentist. He'll tell you how bad it was. And none of you lot went up Lanwithen that night, did you?' They assured him they had not.

'And you've never seen anything funny going on there when you've been hanging – meeting – up round the back? No strangers?'

'Not that I can think of. Most people keep away when they see us.' To give him his due, Wayne did now seem to be trying. 'But I did tell the bloke in charge – Turner, isn't it? – that he should do something about the state of the back windows. The frames are so rotten you can push your finger in the wood and the putty's all dried up and coming off. Anyone could've broke in.' He stopped as a thought struck him. 'Here, do you reckon the whole thing's one of them insurance jobs? You know, make it look as if stuff's been stolen or broke when it hasn't?'

'That doesn't appear to be the case,' Berry informed him.

'Well, I tell you one thing,' said Wayne, 'they ain't gonna stick this one on me. That DI, or whatever he calls himself, said that, if I didn't tell the truth, at best I'd get hours of community service and at worst be sent to a young offenders institution. I kept on telling him I *was* telling the truth. OK, I've lied plenty of times and I'm excluded from school, but I didn't break into that rotten old museum.' And Berry had to admit that he believed him.

'Look,' he said, 'here's the number of my mobile. If you remember anything you think might be useful, give me a call.'

'Is there a reward in it?' Wayne looked hopeful.

'I don't know,' replied Berry, truthfully. 'But at least it might get you off the hook. At least you'd have the reward of not ending up in a young offenders secure unit!'

He was about to drive back to St Mellick but then he decided to go back again to Lanwithen Museum, since he was now convinced that the break-in had nothing to do with the local youths. He found Mrs Pengelly about to close up. 'There's been hardly anyone in,' she grumbled, 'and I've better things to do with my time. What's brought you here again?'

'I had to come back this way,' he told her, 'and I just wondered if you'd any good postcards of the area, Keeper's Tump and so on?'

'Only what's there and they aren't up to much.' A few sepia postcards of old Lanwithen were displayed in a dusty stand. 'You'll get much better ones in the town.' He thanked her but bought two as a face-saver, hoping he might encourage her to talk. Conversation turned again to the missing curator. 'Mind you,' she said, 'as I was saying to Betty this morning, I think there was something funny after that chap came in here in the summer.'

'Oh yes. What chap was that?'

'I remember him because he was so rude. There's no call for it. Big chap, he was. I told Mr Turner he looked like a farmer but Mr Turner said he'd been abroad and had retired down here. One thing I do know, from the way he talked –

he was Cornish. It was after that we had all this nonsense about television films. Whatever he wanted to talk to Mr Turner about, they kept in touch 'cos I took a couple of phone calls from him when Mr Turner was out.'

'Did he give a name?' enquired Berry.

She shook her head. 'No. He just said Mr Turner would know who he was.'

Berry smiled as he drove away. It just had to be Mr Smith.

After Berry had dropped him off, Latymer walked up to Keeper's Tump. There was no one there and the police tent had disappeared, but plastic tape was still festooned around the entrance and marking a square outside it. He noticed that the crows had settled back on top of the mound and along the remains of the wall, while two were perched on top of the Guardians. No, even without the discovery of the body, it was not a pleasant place. Of course, the Keeper's curse was a story common to many mythologies. Even Shakespeare, four thousand years after the bronze-age warrior had issued his dying curse and been laid to rest, had arranged for the words 'and curst be he who moves my bones' to be carved on the stone above his grave. There were instances too of old tales of buried treasure, long discounted, which had eventually turned out to be partially true. But it was more than the accretion of myth and legend which gave the place its particular atmosphere, it was as if some great wrong or terrible deed had been perpetrated there and left its mark on time.

He shook himself. This wouldn't do, he was getting morbid, too fanciful. He returned to the cottage and switched the kettle on. The old book containing the story of the Keeper was still on the table. He picked it up again. Keith was right. It was not only in a dire condition, it was commonplace enough, one of so many similar local histories published by amateur historians who can't write. He recalled noticing the bookcase in Keith's room, but hadn't taken any particular interest in what might be in it. Now he wondered what else might be up there, though, if there'd been anything really interesting, surely Berry would have found it. Mind you, he wasn't surprised that Maynard had left his decent books in London, given the state

117

of the cottage, but he had been surprised not to find any holiday reading in the sitting room. A couple of shelves had been put across the alcove next to the fireplace, but all that were on them were a few old papers and magazines, circulars, and leaflets advertising local attractions.

However, he decided to see for himself if there was anything his friend had overlooked in the bookcase in Keith's room, after which he really must relight the stove. However, when it got to it there was nothing in the rickety bookcase worth the effort of climbing the stairs, only some dilapidated paperbacks, several battered old hardbacks and half a dozen magazines on antiques dating from the previous year. If this was Maynard's holiday reading, then he didn't think much of it. The paperbacks included Mills & Boon romances, a couple of Agatha Christies and an old copy of Dennis Wheatley's *The Devil Rides Out* with a lurid cover. The hardbacks, with titles like *The Light that Shines,* had obviously been Sunday school prizes. Still, it was worth another look, they'd picked up some real bargains left behind in old houses.

He went downstairs, made some tea, then turned his attention to the stove, cursing that he'd left yesterday's and today's papers in the car. He knelt down in front of the stove. Well, he'd have to make do with some of the stuff on the shelves, Maynard was hardly likely to be saving the junk mail, details of the opening times of Cornish gardens in 1999, or a couple of old newspapers. He leant over and took the newspapers off the shelf. The top one was still damp, in spite of the stove having been lit, but he was surprised to find that the one underneath was quite clean and dry. Intrigued, he looked at the date. It was a copy of the *Daily Mail* dated only three days previously. When he was back in Bristol and there was no one in the cottage. He sat back on his heels and stared at the date. His strange feeling that someone had been in while he was away had been only too right. Someone had. But who? And how had they got in?

Twelve

Berry parked the car outside the cottage and bounded in, eager to tell Latymer the results of his investigations. Not only was he now convinced that the break-in had nothing to do with local tearaways (and even if he hadn't been, it would be hard to believe Wayne Jenkins was capable of stealing a computer hard drive), but he had virtual confirmation of the existence of Mr Smith. He let himself in, then stopped short. There were papers everywhere, drawers pulled out of the dresser, cushions thrown off chairs. From overhead he could hear Latymer moving about and the sound of more drawers being opened. He went to the foot of the stairs and called up. 'What the hell's going on?'

Latymer appeared above him. 'I was right.' He came swiftly down the stairs. 'Someone *was* in here while I was away.'

Berry was genuinely surprised. 'Are you sure? Whatever makes you think so?'

Latymer grabbed the copy of the *Daily Mail* from the table and handed it to him. 'Look at that. Just look at that.'

Berry did so, still mystified. 'So?'

'Look at the *date*. See? That's the day we were in Oxford together. Yet I found it on the shelves over there underneath a paper dated months earlier.'

'You're absolutely sure there's no other way it could have got here?'

'How? I certainly didn't bring it back with me, it's not a paper I ever read. In fact, there were no papers of any kind in the car when we left Bristol, that's why we bought a couple on our way back. Someone was in here that day and was just that bit careless, otherwise we'd never have known. There's no other sign and I've turned the place upside down.'

'I can see that. But however did they get in? We checked the doors and windows and there was no sign of any attempt at forced entry.'

Latymer looked grim. 'Whoever was here must have had a key.'

'What do you suggest we do, then? Call Maynard? See if he's lent a key to someone or lost one? He'll go up the wall at the very idea.'

Latymer shuddered at the thought. 'I'd rather not, at least not for now. We can do without screaming histrionics down the phone, very possibly followed by his dramatic appearance here.' He stopped and grinned. 'Where would he *sleep*? It doesn't bear thinking about . . . No, we'll give it another couple of days before we involve Maynard.' He stopped and surveyed the chaos. 'Sorry about all this. I'll clear up then light the stove.' He paused again. 'What am I thinking of? How did you get on?'

Berry grimaced. 'I thought you'd never ask! Rather well, actually. First I managed to track down "our Wayne", and I truly don't think he had anything to do with the break-in at the museum, let alone the stealing of the hard drive from the computer. All right, so he's the local tearaway, but I believe he was telling me the truth. He's actually quite bright, one of those lads that really could do with a hand up, though I doubt he'll get it. You should have seen his mother!' He launched into a graphic description, then went on to tell Latymer his next piece of news. 'You see,' he concluded, 'it really does look as if someone fitting Turner's original description of Smith did visit him at the library back in the summer; not only that, but he continued to keep in touch with Turner afterwards.'

'I think it's time we had another word with Johns,' said Latymer, unearthing his mobile from under one of the heaps.

'Are you going to mention your suspicions about a break-in here?' asked Berry, as he dialled the number.

'No. At least not yet. It would be hard to prove anyway on the strength of a single newspaper dated when I wasn't here. Who's to say it didn't simply get left in the car and we forgot we'd brought it with us.'

120

Johns was surprised to learn that Turner had disappeared. 'That explains it, then. I rang him at home several times yesterday, as I wasn't able to get a reply from the museum. The DI wants him to come in again to confirm a few things. You say he's likely to be away for a few days?'

'When I called at his flat, the door was answered by a young man claiming to be a friend of his who was using it while he was away. He was pretty vague, but told me he understood he'd be back fairly soon. It struck me he might well be the same friend who so kindly came all this way to volunteer the information that he'd faked the photographs.'

'What was he like?' Latymer gave him a brief description. 'Sounds as if it could be. I'll go over there later on to see for myself, and, whether it is or not, ask him if he knows where Turner's staying and if he has the number of his mobile phone. He might be more forthcoming when the enquiry comes from the police.'

Latymer agreed. 'But what does make it somewhat mysterious is that no one at the museum seems to know where he is either. One of the volunteers is holding the fort and she was furious. She said that Turner hadn't said a word to anyone, not even his employers, about going away. The first they knew of it was when he didn't turn up to open the museum. The part-time secretary can't do much as she can't use the computer because, as the volunteer put it, "it's broke" and they're waiting for permission from the insurers to go ahead and get another. According to her, if and when Turner does get back, he's likely to get the sack. Apparently the chairman didn't go much on his helping you with your enquiries either.'

'It does seem odd.' Johns sounded nonplussed. 'But we can hardly launch a missing-person inquiry when the person hasn't actually been reported missing. I'll have a word with Trembath, he might have heard something by now. By the way, I was going to try and contact you anyway. We think we might finally have got an ID on our corpse.'

'You have?' commented Latymer in some surprise. 'Are you at liberty to tell us about it?'

'Don't see why not. It seems he very likely is (or was) a Brian Simmons from St Erth, that's near Penzance. He was

121

identified by his sister, an elderly lady who must be well into her seventies. She's been away upcountry, staying with her daughter, so she hadn't seen any of the publicity or the picture in the paper, and it was only after she got back a couple of days ago that a neighbour came round with a copy of the local paper, showed her the computerized likeness and pointed out that it looked a lot like her brother. She turned up here this morning with photographs of him. It seems the family came originally from Crofthandy, near St Day, but she married a Penzance man and went to live down there and he went abroad to work like so many Cornishmen do. Apparently he came back about eighteen months ago and has visited her from time to time, which is how the neighbour recognized him.'

'How sure is she that it is him? I don't suppose you were able to show her the body, given the state it's in.' Latymer tried not to sound sceptical. He was only too well aware that it was possible to be mistaken when asked to identify a corpse – worse, that it is possible to do so deliberately. The reason he'd become involved once again in investigating crime was because he'd stumbled over a case where a murder victim had been intentionally wrongly identified by someone determined the victim's true identity should remain unknown.

Johns agreed that it hadn't been possible to let the woman view the remains, but she had been able to give the police a pretty good description of her brother, including his height, build and age – and then there were her photographs. 'She even volunteered to provide a DNA sample and we took her up on her offer. That should settle it one way or another. She couldn't understand why there was nothing with the body, no wallet, no cards, no phone – which apparently he took with him everywhere – and she'd absolutely no idea why he might have ended up dead in Keeper's Tump. She said they'd never been close, her being so much older, and that he was "a mean and grudging sort of man", always out for the main chance and making a bob or two, and wasn't particularly fussy how he did it. But that, when he'd turned up after so many years, she'd done her best to make him welcome. After all, he was her own flesh and blood.

'Did you ask her if he'd been into metal detecting?'

'I did, but she said she didn't know. She said that if he had been, then it would be because he thought he might get something out of it. Anyway, the DI and a constable have gone over to St Erth to take a look in his cottage. If I learn anything about Turner's whereabouts, I'll try and let you know.'

'Before you go, one last thing we think you should know. I'll pass you over to Keith.'

Berry told him what Mrs Pengelly had had to say about Turner's summer visitor.

'I'll definitely get over there in the morning,' replied Johns, 'and get Mrs Pengelly to tell me herself.'

'It does sound as if it might well be Turner's Mr Smith,' commented Berry, after Latymer put the phone down. 'A man who's recently come back after years away, a man who isn't particularly fussy how he makes his money.'

'Then why the hell has Turner changed his story?'

'I can only think someone's got at him, but that still doesn't answer the question – why? It would be interesting to know if they find a metal detector in his cottage. For the record, where's St Erth?'

Latymer went and fetched the map from the car. 'Down there,' he pointed, 'not far from St Ives. That gives me an idea. When I went over to Truro Museum, the finds officer offered to put me in touch with one of the metal-detecting clubs if I was interested in joining one and finding out what they do. He said there was a good one in St Ives. I didn't take up the offer at the time, but now . . .' He looked at the clock. 'He might still be at the museum, I'll give him a call.'

The finds officer was very helpful and willingly parted with the address and telephone number of the secretary of the club. 'He'll be only too pleased to tell you all about it, he's a real enthusiast, and he's in touch with all the other local clubs as well. If you're thinking of taking it up, good hunting!'

Jeff Harding, the St Ives club's secretary, was indeed an enthusiastic advocate of metal detecting and suggested, if they had the time to spare, that they meet up with him the following day so that he could show them how it was done and, yes, he'd be only too happy to talk about finds of all kinds. At this stage Latymer thought it better not to ask if he'd a member from St Erth called Brian Simmons.

Sergeant Johns, as good as his word, drove over to Lanwithen. The information gained from Latymer and Berry had certainly given him a good deal to think about. He started by calling at Turner's flat, not least to see if the friend staying was indeed the same friend that had come into Bodmin police station and allegedly faked the photographs. He rang the bell and waited but there was no reply. He rang again, then, as there was still no result, called in at the shop. The owner, who rented out the flat, was just closing up. No, he hadn't seen anything of his tenant for a few days, and he admitted to being surprised that Matthew Tuner hadn't told him either that he was going away or that he had allowed a friend to stay in the flat in his absence. One of the reasons he let the accommodation, he told Johns, was to have someone living over the shop to deter possible thieves, and he was far from happy at the idea of having a total stranger camped out overhead.

Disappointed, Johns called next on Josiah Trembath. The trust's chairman was very angry indeed. Appointing Turner, he raged, had been little short of a disaster. The man had done precious little for the museum; had involved himself in airy-fairy schemes involving television people without the knowledge of the trustees; the museum had suffered its first ever break-in during the very night he'd chosen to spend somewhere else; he had followed this by being very publicly carted off to Bodmin police station; and now, to cap it all, had gone missing without even the courtesy of asking permission. It was clear Turner would be scanning the situations vacant columns when, or if, he returned.

Johns asked Trembath for Mrs Pengelly's address and went round to see her, only to be told by her husband that she'd gone off on a coach with the local Women's Institute to see a show at Plymouth Theatre Royal. Altogether, it hadn't been a good day.

From a hotel across the county in Fowey, the man who'd given his name as Marcus Smeaton was on the telephone in his

124

room, assuring the recipient of his call that, given some of the unexpected problems, matters were now more or less in hand. 'I trust I've dealt satisfactorily with the first problem you wanted solving, and the police seem happy enough. Hopefully, it'll be some time before there's any comeback. I agree it's annoying about our two friends.'

'What exactly did you say to them?' enquired the recipient of his call.

'That my good friend Matthew was away for a few days and was letting me use his flat while I was down here on business.'

There was a pause. 'And what did they say to that?'

'Nothing much. Only that they might call in again before they went back. I honestly don't think you need worry. From what he said to me, it seems the local DI has no time for them.'

'I still don't like it.'

'Not to worry! What's got into you? As I said, everything's more or less sorted and there's nothing going on to keep them down here.' He laughed and explained what he had in mind. 'See? I think I can guarantee they'll be safely back in Bristol within twenty-four hours, so there's no earthly point in your coming down here yourself. Once I've made sure the plan's worked, I'll be straight back. Trust me, I'm a consultant!'

As Berry drove them over to St Ives the following morning, Latymer actually felt as if he really was on holiday. The weather was good and St Ives and its bay were looking at their very best. Great stretches of pale sand were visible on both sides of the Hayle estuary and, in spite of it being October, gardens and hedges were still bright with flowers. Jeff Harding and his wife lived in a bungalow in one of the estates overlooking the town. He welcomed them in with an offer of coffee and proudly took them through to his lounge to show them the splendid view through his big windows.

'I hope you've plenty of time to spare,' joked his wife as she brought in the coffee. 'Once you get Jeff on his favourite subject, it's almost impossible to get him off!'

'I'm afraid it does become something of an addiction,' he

125

admitted. 'It really is so fascinating. You simply never know beforehand what you're going to turn up and there's always the possibility that you might, just might, be really lucky.'

Latymer smiled. 'How lucky have you been?'

'Nothing spectacular, I'm afraid. When we've had our coffee, I'll show you what there is.'

'The finds officer at the museum explained something of how the act that replaced treasure trove works, and that people are now encouraged to register more or less any find.'

Harding agreed. 'We might all dream of stumbling over a golden hoard but much smaller and far less valuable finds can still add a great deal to the general sum of our knowledge. A Roman copper coin, a denarius, mightn't be worth much in itself, but a number of them found together in one place on the coast helps to confirm that, although the Romans never settled in Cornwall, they most definitely traded here.'

'Would you know if someone had found something spectacular?' enquired Berry.

'If they report it properly, then yes. We might not actually know ourselves exactly what was found, since, not surprisingly, some people who do find real treasure tend to want to keep as much information to themselves as possible, but we'd certainly know that an important find had been made and, of course, rumours abound.'

'What about if they don't do all the right things and try and keep it to themselves?'

'Well, unless they were very careful, rumours would still get around and, if they reached the authorities, then they'd act on them. Also, if such a person wanted to sell on the black antiquities market, they'd need to know how to set about it and who to contact.'

'I understand that there are obsessed collectors with money to burn who aren't particularly worried about the origins of the objects, so long as they can get their hands on them,' said Berry.

Harding agreed that there were, but doubted whether there were all that many of them. 'It's a dodgy business. I wouldn't recommend it, especially as there's every possibility you'll get a pretty good price doing it the proper way. Anyway, let me show you what I've got here.' Harding may have been an enthusiast, but he was not a bore. His favourite objects were displayed in small, glass-fronted cases: a number of coins, including Roman denarii, Elizabethan groats and two silver coins dating from the Civil War, a conflict which, he told them, had been ruthlessly fought in Cornwall. He was particularly proud of two fragments of Anglo-Saxon brooches, along with a complete one he'd been allowed to keep – discovered, he said, while on holiday in Suffolk. He still lived in hopes of an elusive hoard or gold object, but a substantial proportion of valuable finds were, as the finds officer had said, simply turned up by the plough. 'Of course, we find all kinds of relatively modern things. It's surprising what turns up, wedding rings on beaches, for instance, and pocketfuls of loose change.'

After showing them his collection, he took them down to the town and out to the promontory known as The Island to show them how the detector worked. In no time at all it was merrily pinging away, but only to reveal the odd lager can and a single pound coin, while the beach nearby provided only bits and pieces of metal detritus from boats. 'You see,' he said, 'you really do need to be keen, obsessed even. Though as a rule I wouldn't spend much time here.' He then suggested, if they were willing, that he take them to some fields not far away, close to St Erth, where a farmer had given the club permission to see what they might turn up.

'One of our members did find about a dozen Charles I coins. I suppose in those days a good many people hid their wealth while they waited to see who would win, and were then either unable to come back for it or forgot where it was.' He drove them a few miles out of the town and then began methodically sweeping the detector across one of the fields. There was a moment of excitement as the machine picked up a strong signal. Harding knelt down, carefully loosened the earth, extracted something from it, then shook his head and laughed. 'And there was me hoping I'd find something really impressive for you.' He held up a small coil of old wire.

'Are all your members immediately local?' asked Latymer.
'It depends what you mean by "local",' he replied. 'We've

people from Penzance and the Land's End area, a few from Hayle and three or four from St Ives.'

'How about right here?' enquired Berry. 'Anyone living on the spot would have a head start.' But apparently not, the club had no member from St Erth. 'Someone, I can't remember who, told us he thought a chap called Brian Simmons who lived in St Erth was one of your members,' continued Berry. 'He must have got it wrong.' Harding agreed he probably had. 'We've no one of that name in our club. Perhaps he lives in Saint somewhere else.'

There was really little more to say or do. Harding drove them back to collect their car. They thanked him for giving them his time and wished him well for the future. 'I hope we'll see you splashed across one of the colour mags, standing proudly by your gold hoard or holding up the equivalent of the Rillaton Cup!' Latymer told him.

'Well, as I expect you know, some precious objects have turned up at this end of Cornwall from time to time, so you never know. But the Rillaton Cup was found by chance and I doubt very much whether English Heritage or anyone else would encourage people like us to clamber all over their barrows and ancient monuments trying to find another one. Anyway, if you decide you want to join, let me know. We're quite happy to take long-distance members.'

'I imagine most people who go in for metal detecting are like Harding,' commented Berry, as they left St Ives. 'You know, decent, honest, obviously hoping against hope that they'll come across something really valuable, but enjoying the chase as much as anything else.'

Latymer didn't answer. He was beginning to think the whole thing had become a waste of time. Possibly Simmons was 'Mr Smith', but if so, what then? Particularly if Turner stuck to his story or simply vanished without trace. That would suit Anderson very well. He was still convinced there was substance in it, but they had neither the means nor the contacts to enable them to carry on with the investigation. If he'd still been in the force, he'd have sent the photographs away to be checked out, had someone check details of the missing torque

128

from Ireland, got on to all the relevant authorities to inform them someone might be trying to sell two rare items on the antiquities black market. On the other hand, his whole careful construction might be no more than a series of disconnected events; it was all too easy to add up two and two and make five. The gentle euphoria of the morning had evaporated, leaving him even more down. Eventually, aware that he'd said nothing for a considerable time, he told Berry how he felt.

Berry seemed surprised. 'This isn't like you.'

'Put it down to my being under the weather when I came down here, and a general feeling of malaise. We didn't do too badly on the other two cases, but in both we'd a fair bit to go on. I really do believe we've gone as far as we can with this one. Not to mention the fact that the DI in charge of it all obviously hates my guts!'

'What about the intruder in the cottage?'

'Not a pleasant thought, but what did he expect to find? Nothing was stolen. I don't think I'll say anything to Maynard about it, but I might suggest he changes the locks, tell him there have been break-ins in the area – which, after all, is true.'

'So, what do you want to do?'

'Give it another day to tie up any loose ends and pass what information we have on to Johns, then pack it in. The events of the last week have merely pointed up how much at a disadvantage we are in not being able to tap into official records or look at evidence at first hand. I'd like to make the most of the few days holiday I have left, and I'm sure Kate will be only too happy to have you back at the shop.' He looked out of the car window. 'In the meantime, let's make the most of this weather before we go back to St Mellick.'

It was early evening before they got back, and they were relieved to find there were no signs that a covert visitor had been in while they were out. Almost immediately Latymer had a call from Johns to say he'd had no luck in tracking down the missing curator and that there was no sign of his friend either.

'I went to see Josiah Trembath and, when he'd stopped huffing and puffing, he gave me Matthew Turner's home address, so I rang them. His parents say he's not there, nor had they heard from him for several weeks, but that wasn't particularly unusual. I asked them if they knew of any friends he might have gone to, and they came up with a couple of names, which I tried, but they'd neither seen nor heard anything of him either. Obviously they knew nothing about the break-in at the museum or the trouble he's in for disappearing without any warning, and now they're worried he might have had some kind of a breakdown and gone wandering off. His father says, if he doesn't turn up within the next couple of days, he'll formally register him as a missing person.'

'Did you have a word with Mrs Pengelly about the visitor to the museum?' enquired Latymer.

'She was out last night and I simply haven't had a minute to try again today. We're pretty overstretched down here. As for Anderson's visit to Simmons' cottage, the detective constable who went with him told Johns that it looked almost unlived-in, like a holiday cottage. There were a couple of books on local history but no sign of a metal detector – but then he'd not been told to look for one. Among Simmons' papers were catalogues of past Sotheby's and Christie's sales, with various items marked up, and one interesting item: a folder full of bank statements showing that from time to time considerable sums had been paid into his various accounts.'

Latymer heard him out. 'I wish I could have had a look around down there. I'm still convinced Simmons is Smith.'

'Well, you're not going to convince DI Anderson. The inquest will be opened next week and he has his own scenario lined up.'

'Which is?'

'That Turner's supposed scam has nothing to do with the murder. Nor the break-in at the museum. That Simmons was murdered either by a passing nutter, which seems extremely unlikely, or because he fell out with someone over money or a deal. After all, his sister did accuse him of not being too fussy in his business dealings.'

Latymer thanked him then told him that, so far as they were concerned, they'd give it one more day then go back to Bristol, but, before they did so, they'd pass on to him any information they had which might prove helpful.

Johns was silent for a minute, then said, 'Look, I don't know if I'll be able to manage this, but tomorrow is my day off. It wouldn't be too difficult to contact the sister again and ask her permission to have another look round the cottage. One last try wouldn't affect your plans.' So it was arranged that, unless they heard to the contrary, Johns would pick them up the following morning and take them down to St Erth.

Latymer awoke from a deep sleep to hear the sound of a telephone ringing. At first he fumbled around on the chair beside his bed, then realized it wasn't his ring tone. It was very dark outside and, wondering who on earth was calling Berry in the middle of the night, he hunched back under the duvet and tried to go back to sleep. He was just dozing off when he found himself being shaken awake again. 'Hang on!' he grumbled. 'What time do you call this?'

'It's Kate,' said Berry.

'Kate?' Latymer struggled to get himself together. 'What about Kate?'

'She's in intensive care.'

'What? I don't understand. What's happened?'

'I'm not too sure either. The line was very bad. But I've just had a call from Bristol Infirmary. I think they said she'd had a stroke.'

Latymer was fully awake by this time. 'A stroke? Kate? At her age?'

'People can have strokes at any age.'

'What are you going to do?'

'There's a train from Bodmin Parkway at about six o'clock but it takes ages, it wouldn't get me into Bristol until about half past ten. It's five o'clock – if I leave by car now, while the road's clear, I could be there before eight o'clock.'

'Then that's what you must do. It'll take time to clear up here and pack. The last thing we want is to have to come back again. Take my car and go now.'

'What about you?'

'Don't worry about me. They wouldn't let me in to see Kate anyway, if she's as sick as that. I'll see if I can track down one of those car-hire firms where you can pick up a car at one depot and deliver it to another. There must be some down here, with it being a holiday area. One way or another I'll be back in Bristol before the day's out. I'll call you when I'm on my way.'

Berry raced outside and jumped into the car. Five minutes later he was driving through St Mellick on his way to the main road and Bristol.

Thirteen

Dawn was beginning to break as Berry left Cornwall behind and by the time he reached Exeter it was almost light. He knew the motorway from here very well. In spite of his anxiety, as he crossed into Somerset he found himself looking out for familiar landmarks like the fibreglass camel nicknamed 'Humphrey', relic of some past carnival and much beloved by children, which stands in a field gazing out over the traffic; the giant 'wicker man' striding out across the Somerset levels; the iron-age hill fort overshadowing Sedgemoor service station. Several times he considered pulling in and calling Bristol Infirmary, but then decided it was more sensible to press on, as even minutes could make a difference to crossing the city once the morning rush to work began.

As it was, the road remained clear almost until he reached the interchange. He looked at his watch. It was barely half past seven, he'd made good time. He drove to the infirmary, circled round the car park in increasing frustration until he finally found a parking space, then hurtled in through the main door to the reception desk, which was already busy. 'My wife,' he began breathlessly. 'My wife. I've been away. I've had a phone call from you to say she's in intensive care. Kate Berry. Where is she?'

Both receptionists were on the phone. 'Be with you in a minute,' one of them informed him as he drummed his fingers on the desk. Finally she put the phone down and asked how she might help him. He repeated his request. 'What is your wife's name?'

'*Kate Berry*,' he told her.

'And you say she was admitted last night?'

'Didn't you listen to what I said? I've been down in

Cornwall on business and I'd a phone call from here at about five o'clock this morning saying that she'd had a stroke and was in intensive care. I want to know where she is, how she is. I must see her.'

The receptionist nodded. 'Let me see, then.' She tapped into her computer for what seemed to the impatient Berry like half an hour. Then she sat back and frowned. 'Well, she's not on our in-patient list. Bear with me. I'll try intensive care.' In an agony of frustration, he watched her dial the number. 'Have you a Kate Berry there? Kate Berry.' She cupped her hand over the phone. 'How are you spelling it?'

'B–E–R–R–Y!' he bellowed. 'Like in holly berry.'

She gave him a quelling look. 'Well, I've a gentleman here who says she's his wife and that he received a telephone call from us last night informing him that she was in the ICU. No? No, there's no trace of the name here either, that's why I rang you. Yes, it is very strange. Thanks anyway.' She put the phone down. 'They've no one of that name in the ICU,' she told him, firmly.

'But that's what your man said,' he responded desperately. 'Surely you can't think I'm making it up?'

'A stroke, you say?' The receptionist was obviously making an effort. 'I'll try the cardiology and stroke department, but I don't hold out much hope.' With a sinking heart, he watched as she went through an almost identical process only to end up with an identical result. 'I'm sorry,' she said, 'I really am. But she definitely isn't here. Are you absolutely sure your caller said Bristol Infirmary and not Bristol Frenchay Hospital? Though I admit that if she was an emergency then she should have been admitted here.'

'It was definitely the infirmary. But if she isn't here I suppose I'll have to try Frenchay.' He was beginning to feel sick. 'I can't understand it.'

He retrieved his car and drove over to Frenchay, the general hospital, with some difficulty, since the traffic was now building up, and again presented himself in reception. But they were equally adamant that no Kate Berry had been admitted to the hospital the previous night, another receptionist confirming what he'd already been told at the infirmary:

that, from what he'd said about her condition, she would almost certainly have been taken there, since they dealt with all accident and emergency cases. Perhaps there had been a misunderstanding?

He sat in the Frenchay car park and, though there seemed little point, rang the flat. He supposed it might just be that Kate had been able to get their assistant, Greta, to hold the fort before she became incapacitated, but if that was the case then surely Greta would also have rung him? But none of this answered the simple question: where was she? The phone rang and rang but there was no reply, only his own recorded voice informing the caller that neither Kate nor Keith Berry could take their call just now and would they please leave a message after the tone. In desperation he rang the business line in the shop and nearly screamed when yet again he heard his own voice, this time informing customers of the opening hours and a second number if they wished to send a fax. He was about to call Greta when he remembered he'd left his contacts book on the table in the cottage and, as he couldn't remember her address, he couldn't track down her number through directory enquiries.

There didn't seem anywhere else he could try. Obviously the sensible thing was to return home. That was easier said than done, for by this time Bristol was chock-a-block with vehicles, leaving him sitting fuming in lines of standing traffic, but finally he drove into his road, parked the car, unlocked the door to the flat and began taking the stairs two at a time. Then he stopped short. From the kitchen came the familiar sound of the *Today Programme* drawing to its close and the sound of the kettle boiling. He heard Kate call out 'Who's that?' then her head appeared round the door. 'Good heavens! It's you. You gave me quite a fright, I couldn't think who it was.' She stared at him. 'You look *dreadful*, Keith, what's happened? Why are you here?'

He clutched her to him. 'Oh God, Kate, you're all right. You're not seriously ill.'

She broke away and looked at him in bewilderment. 'Seriously ill? What on earth are you talking about? Of course I'm not seriously ill. Look at me.'

135

'But I had a phone call at about five this morning saying you were in intensive care in the infirmary, that you'd had some kind of a stroke. I've just about gone out of my mind with worry. It's John's car out there. He said I must go straight away and he'd pack everything and clear up, then hire a car and follow later. So, I drove like the clappers to the infirmary, and of course they said they'd no one called Kate Berry in intensive care or anywhere else. So, then I went over to Frenchay and, of course, you weren't there either. Then I rang here but there was no reply.'

'I'd run out of milk, that's all. I just slipped out to the little supermarket over the road for a pint, then I ran into Michelle from the library, who told me she'd found a breast lump, and we got talking and . . .' She stopped. 'I don't understand. Was it some kind of a sick joke?'

'I don't know.' He was still shaken. Kate poured him a cup of coffee and he gulped it down. 'I can't believe anyone would play such an appalling trick, at least no one I know and who has my mobile number.'

'Perhaps it's an awful mistake, a wrong number, and even now some poor woman really is in intensive care and can't understand why her husband hasn't reached her.'

Berry began going over the call again in his head. 'No, that can't be it. The phone rang. I admit I wasn't on the ball, I'd been dead asleep. I don't think I gave any number, I just said, "Yes?" I realized later on that the caller's number hadn't been displayed but assumed it was because the call had come from a hospital. Then the voice, a man's voice, said, "Mr Berry?" and I said, "Yes," again, and he said he was calling from Bristol Royal Infirmary and was very sorry to have to tell me that you'd been admitted as an emergency and were now in intensive care. I gibbered something about what could it be and he said a stroke. Perhaps I should have rung back to confirm the call was genuine, but it never even crossed my mind. I didn't stop and ring the hospital on the way back either, as I thought it would only waste more time. So, it couldn't be a mistake, the caller definitely asked if it was me.' He still felt out of breath. 'Look, I'll give John a ring. Tell him not to bother hiring a car. I'll drive down again this evening and we'll come back together tomorrow morning. We had something planned for today, so now he can go ahead and do it.'

He was in luck and caught Latymer just as he was explaining to Johns why he wouldn't be able to go to St Erth with him because of what had happened. On hearing Berry's story, he motioned to Johns to stay where he was.

'And she really is OK, Keith?'

'Absolutely fine. Nothing wrong at all. If I ever find the bastard who set me up, I'll pull his head off! Do you think it's got anything to do with this business?'

'It has to. Presumably whoever did it wanted us out of the way and assumed we'd both go back to Bristol. Anyway, since everything's all right, I'll go over to St Erth with Sergeant Johns as planned. See you later.'

'I don't like the sound of this at all,' commented Johns as they drove away. 'Whatever Anderson says, there are simply too many coincidences. There's still no sign of Turner and no longer anyone in his flat. At least, where the body's concerned, we should get the DNA results shortly, which will prove one way or another if it is Simmons.' He sighed. 'I'm sorry you're going back, you've come up with some really useful stuff, but, given the DI's attitude, I don't blame you.' By the time they reached St Erth, they'd exhausted just about every possible scenario, still without reaching any conclusion. Latymer sat in the car while Johns went round to see Simmons' sister and collect the key. 'This is, of course, strictly against all the rules,' he commented as he reappeared. 'However, she never questioned my asking for it and I'll just have to hope Anderson doesn't find out. Actually we're in luck, he's in Exeter at meetings all day.' And with that he let them in.

The cottage was already beginning to smell damp. It felt unlived-in, even though there were numerous signs of Simmons' occupancy. It was a real bachelor's residence, no frills, no real attempt at making a home. They noted that, in spite of what Turner had said, if indeed Simmons was Smith, then he was on the phone. The sitting room was sparsely furnished, dominated by a large television set with an uncom-fortable-looking oversized winged armchair pulled up facing

137

it. A small bookcase contained a number of popular books on archaeology, two specifically dealing with the south-west of the country. Johns pulled one out. 'It's got to be him, hasn't it? And there's archaeology magazines and journals on antiques as well.'

They searched the room methodically but, finding nothing of interest, turned their attention to the upper floor. Upstairs were two bedrooms and a small shower room. Only one of the two bedrooms was in use. Apart from a single bed, there was a chest of drawers, a wardrobe, a single chair and an alarm clock, nothing else. The drawers yielded only fairly well-worn, but clean, underwear and socks, the wardrobe three expensive but out-of-date suits and a couple of pairs of trousers. 'I expect Anderson or the constable went through the pockets, but I'll check just in case,' said Latymer. In one jacket he found two screwed-up receipts from the local petrol station, in another half a packet of peppermints well past their sell-by date. In the last one he found a torn-off piece of an envelope with a telephone number scrawled on the back. He showed it to Johns. 'It probably doesn't mean anything but we might as well take it away with us.'

The back door opened on to a small, scruffy patch of garden. Obviously Simmons was no gardener, since long, rank grass grew on what had once been a lawn, and the flower beds were overrun by weeds. There was also the ubiquitous shed, so commonplace at the back of most old Cornish homes. Johns peered through the one dirty window. 'I presume they must have looked in here.'

'Well, if they did, they left no trace,' Latymer pointed out. 'Look at the state of the padlock.' The shed door fastened with an old-fashioned hook-and-eye fastening, secured by a padlock locked through the eye. Even with a key, it was so rusty that it would have been impossible to unlock without either the use of oil or by forcing it.

Johns peered through the window again. 'There doesn't seem to be anything much inside. Perhaps that's why they left it, though I'd have wanted to see for myself.' He pulled a face. 'What do we do now? It would be quite easy to force it with a spanner or a wrench.'

Latymer was fully aware of his dilemma. 'So, let me do it. It can't then be laid at your door.' Johns went out to the car and returned with a substantial spanner. After a brief struggle, the loop of the padlock came out of its lock and they were able to open the door. Johns was right. There wasn't much inside. Just a couple of empty boxes, an old oil can, a few logs . . . and a metal detector.

When they got back to St Mellick, Latymer asked Johns to drop him off at the pub for a bite to eat. The discovery of the detector and the now almost certainty that Simmons was indeed Smith had given him a good deal to think about. Leaving it where it was, in the hope that it would eventually be discovered, didn't seem to either of them to be an option, not to mention the fact that it would also provide fingerprint evidence. They'd just have to work out some kind of an explanation for their actions. In the end, they'd wrapped the detector carefully in an old bath towel, then gingerly put it in the boot of Johns' car. The sergeant had then returned the key to Simmons' sister, reassuring her that there weren't any problems, but that he'd noticed the shed behind the house was unlocked, though there didn't seem to be anything of any value in it; which was now true.

Harry was in his usual place at the bar as Latymer entered the pub. He wondered if the village rumour-monger was welded to the stool and possibly even slept there. Harry looked Latymer over and nodded. 'Thought you'd gone, you and your visitor.'

'We're off tomorrow morning. After everything that's happened, I have to say it's not been much of a holiday, let alone a rest. A television company I could accept, a corpse just along the way . . .' Latymer left it there.

'It's a funny old business,' agreed one of Harry's mates, sagely. 'I've heard tell the curator of the museum over to Lanwithen's gone missing too. There's something funny going on, if you ask me, too much that's not right.'

'Too many strangers here, that's what,' continued Harry. 'We didn't have nothing like this here when I were a tacker. Not to mention that there EU and them asylum seekers.'

Latymer tried not to smile. 'You're surely not blaming either the European Union or asylum seekers for the body in the barrow? I've no real idea how the EU affects you down here, and I haven't seen any asylum seekers about anywhere.'

Harry's mate chipped in again. 'I don't think it has anything to do with anything like that. I think it's all down to money. Don't all you lot remember how someone found a gold cup over to Rillaton back in Victorian times? Strikes me that someone found something like that up at Keeper's Tump and someone else tried to take it off him and whopped him one. They say folks can get big money selling things like that on the side.'

Latymer made no reply but had to admit the speaker was pretty close to his own theory. He ate his lunch on his own in a corner, then thanked the landlord, who expressed the hope that he hadn't been too put off to come back again sometime. Latymer made a polite reply. Just as he was about to leave, the man with the theory called him over. 'Here, you were up there, weren't you, when they found the body?'

Latymer admitted that he was.

'What did he look like?'

'You got some gruesome mind, Ivor,' commented the landlord.

'I don't mean I want details of what was done to him, I meant what I said: what did he look like? Big, small, fat, thin, old, young? I've my reasons for asking.'

'Obviously I didn't see the body,' replied Latymer, somewhat economical with the truth, 'but apparently it was in a pretty unpleasant state . . .'

'Ah,' interrupted Harry, 'that'd be the rats and things, probably foxes have ways of getting in there too.'

'But one of the policemen told me that he was a big, well-built chap,' continued Latymer, 'and I think someone said he was Cornish, but not immediately local.'

His questioner looked thoughtful. 'I only ask because about two or three weeks back a chap came in here throwing his weight about.' He turned to the landlord. 'Don't you remember, Sid?' He laughed. 'It must have been the day you went over to Bodmin, Harry, since you weren't here. Anyway, this chap was big and burly, fiftyish, I'd say. Drank bitter with whisky chasers, kept saying how he'd made money abroad while all we stick-in-the-muds back home were still taking folk boat rides and running B & Bs. He got right up my nostrils. Perhaps it was him went up Keeper's Tump and got himself killed.'

'But who by?' queried the landlord.

'Why, the Keeper, of course,' declared Harry. 'He don't hold with no visitors.'

Berry had said that he expected to be back at the cottage about eight o'clock, and it was not yet two o'clock. Latymer had plenty of time to pack everything he didn't actually need and clean and tidy the place up, a courtesy that certainly hadn't been extended to him. He packed everything he'd brought with him into two boxes, then took them upstairs to enable him to clear up the sitting room and vacuum the floor and to make sure he didn't leave anything behind, something he was all too often prone to do when he'd a lot on his mind. He put his coat and anorak upstairs with them. He'd kept his laptop in the bedroom and was about to return it to its case when he realized he hadn't checked his emails for a couple of days.

There was only one mailer but it was the one he most wanted to hear from: *Fiona@fisherking.co.uk*. She was full of apologies for not getting in touch. Her elderly mother, who lived near Norwich, had been taken ill and she'd dropped everything to go and care for her. Happily, her mother was on the mend and, as her sister was now able to hold the fort, she'd returned home. 'On top of everything, I've missed out on your free time,' she wrote. 'Any chance of you coming up here for a few days? It would be so good to see you.' He pushed the 'reply' button and mailed back, 'Can do. Will be in touch tomorrow.'

It was then he heard the key turning in the lock of the front door. Who on earth . . .? It was too early for Keith and anyway he didn't have a key. He froze where he sat. Whoever it was came confidently into the sitting room and Latymer waited, hardly breathing, for him to realize there was someone else in the house and come looking for him. But the intruder had other things on his mind and immediately began talking into his mobile phone.

'Yeah, yeah, yeah – keep your hair on. I just got over here a bit later, that's all. And do you know why? Because our ambitious Dr Davenport insisted that I discuss the final deal with him in person. In Exeter. No problem, he'll meet our price, and bring with him a banker's draft. You could hardly expect that amount in used notes in a plastic carrier! So, that's where I've been and why I haven't got back to you.' There was a pause. '*Of course* I made sure they'd left before I set off. No, I didn't go inside and have a look, but the car had gone and I could see there was no one there. Anyway, our friend will meet us for the handover tomorrow evening as originally arranged . . . For God's sake, don't get so paranoid! No, I haven't yet checked that the stuff's still here, but why the hell shouldn't it be? I rang to reassure you as soon as I got in, because of all your frantic messages . . . Yes, yes, all their gear *has* gone and they're hardly likely to come back, are they? Even if they did, it wouldn't matter a damn now. Look, if you'll let me get off the phone, I'll go and get it and set your mind at rest. You're *what*? You're praying everything will be OK. Say one for me, then, and I'll see you in church!'

At that he went out into the kitchen humming 'We are Sailing' to himself (a song Latymer had never liked), and unlocked the back door. With infinite caution, Latymer went over to the window, stood behind the curtain and peered out as his visitor went over to the shed, unlocked the padlock on the door and disappeared inside. There was the noise of things being shifted, then he reappeared in the doorway carrying a small sacking bundle; and Latymer saw that his unexpected visitor was Marcus Smeaton. He came out into the open, carefully unwrapped the bundle, giving a little skip of pleasure as he did so. Displayed in the sacking were the gold cup and the Irish torque. Then he carefully rewrapped them and went back on his mobile phone again, presumably to reassure whoever he'd been talking to earlier. After which he came back into the house and relocked the kitchen door. Latymer, hardly breathing, looked round for a possible weapon, should he decide to come upstairs. The only possibility was a brass candlestick, presumably to be used if the electricity failed. He grasped it firmly and stood with his back to the wall beside the door, but Smeaton made no effort to climb the stairs. He went straight out of the front door, slamming it closed behind him. Cautiously Latymer crept through into the other bedroom, which gave him a view over the front door, and saw that Smeaton had left his car on the main road. As Latymer watched, he ran swiftly down the path, jumped in, and set off in the direction of Bodmin.

Latymer went straight out to the shed. A number of boxes had been pulled aside, as well as one of the small plastic sacks of logs he'd bought and a few odd ones scattered nearby. The original floor had consisted of old timbers put across rotting concrete and these, in turn, had been covered over with pieces of ancient linoleum, presumably in a vain effort to prevent rising damp. It was easy to see where a piece of lino had been pulled up, uncovering a small rectangular space carefully concealed in the old wooden flooring. My God, thought Latymer, wait until Berry knows these wretched objects have been here all the time, or at least since before I came to stay. He put his hand in his pocket and suddenly felt the scrap of paper with the telephone number that he'd taken from Simmons' jacket pocket. All at once a whole lot of things slotted into place.

Fourteen

He didn't know how long he'd lain there. It must be several days now without food and drink and he was getting noticeably weaker. As well as he was able, bound and gagged as he was, he struggled to lift up his head to look at the night sky. He had no idea where he was, he'd been unconscious when they'd brought him here. He was lying out in the open air, but also somehow inside some kind of structure with high walls. If only he could lose his senses again.

He had no real idea of what it was all about. By the time he'd got back from his first session with the police, he'd already decided that, whatever the outcome of the situation he found himself in, he'd hand in his notice and get the hell out of Cornwall. He'd had enough. All right, so he'd brought some of it on himself with what now seemed to be a crazy idea, but surely he'd never deserved all this? At worst he'd merely suggested to Smith, who needed no persuading, not to inform the coroner of his 'finds', if indeed that's what they were, until they could be legally 'found' during filming.

Weary from answering questions, and with a splitting headache, he'd just opened a can of lager, switched on the television, and slumped down in front of it, when there was a knock on the door. Cursing, he got to his feet, went downstairs and opened it to find himself pushed aside as two men entered. One went ahead up the stairs, the other forced him up behind. The older of the two had well-cut grey hair, was extremely well dressed and spoke with a soft, but deeply unpleasant, voice, and smelled of some kind of expensive aftershave. The other was about his own age, well spoken, but strongly built and tough. It was, however, the older man of whom he'd been most afraid. They'd ignored his demands to know who they were, tied him to a chair and turned the television sound up, although there was no one likely to hear anything, since the property next door was empty. Immediately they began questioning him closely as to what he'd told the police and what he'd done with the photographs. After some prevarication, during which the younger man hit him for the first time, he told them.

After that they went into a corner and muttered to each other, discussing in undertones what to do next, then the older man came over to him. 'You're going to go back now to the police station,' he said, loosening the bonds, 'and tell the police exactly what I tell you to say. If you don't agree, I shall dispose of you now, and if you're thinking of doing anything clever when you get there, forget it. We shall be waiting outside. The last person who tried to do it his way was found in Keeper's Tump. Think about it.' He turned to the younger man. 'You'll be able to sort out the photographs, Marcus?'

'No probs,' he replied. 'Luckily there was still one left in the desk in the library. I played around with it on the computer and it now looks as if the cup and the torque are on top of a bus. If they won't believe the real ones are fakes, I can show them that. I could have done even more if there'd been images on the computer, but there was nothing, not even a shadow on the hard drive. But, even so, digital technology enables you to put anything anywhere.'

The older man smiled. 'What would I do without you, Marcus?'

'Marcus' had then dragged him to his feet and forced him down the stairs and into a large black car. They deposited him outside the police station, reminded him of what would befall him if he didn't do exactly what he was told, and pulled round a corner to wait. He realized now that he should have said something, anything, assaulted one of the policemen if they refused to believe him, so that they'd arrest him and keep him there, but he didn't, and eventually he'd been turned out again on to the street. Immediately the car had pulled up and he was pushed back into it. With hindsight he realized that he was mad not to have grabbed at a chance to save himself, but he'd been naïve enough to think that, having done what he was told, they'd leave him alone. He shivered. He was so cold, so stiff, and he could hardly breathe. But the questioning afterwards had been even worse. Again and again, interspersed with punches in the stomach and arm-wrenching by 'Marcus', he'd been asked if 'Smith' had told him anything else. Tearfully, he'd told them again and again that if he had, he'd tell them, tell them anything if only they'd leave him alone. Eventually he'd passed out. Between them, the two men must have carried him to wherever he was and dumped him. Would they ever come back? Or had they left him there to die slowly? What was this place, where was he? Oh God, he'd never be found.

The recipient of the call from Marcus was feeling a very real sense of satisfaction. After a whole succession of unforeseen and infuriating delays, things were finally going his way. If it hadn't been for Simmons, it would all have been finalized by now. He'd put out feelers about the Irish torque when he first heard it had been stolen. It was obvious to an expert such as himself that the thieves had been amateurs and had no real idea how to dispose of it once they'd got it. Through his excellent contacts he'd tracked its progress from the original robbers to another person, then another, and at that stage had arranged with a small-time villain, whom he'd used before, to make the final arrangements for its purchase and delivery to him. Given his relative inexperience in such negotiations, his envoy hadn't done too badly, but his association with the world of drugs posed a possible future threat, thus making him disposable; with the added benefit that it had saved him a considerable sum of money in paying him off. He smiled to himself. He'd picked up the sixteenth-century Spanish stiletto-like dagger in an antiques market in Malaga. It still gave him a frisson of pleasure that he'd been able to put it to its proper use, not only once but twice.

The cup, of course, he'd acquired quite legitimately, or at least almost so, due to a stunning and totally unexpected piece of luck, and nothing would ever persuade him to part with it, especially as he had so nearly lost it. He pictured it gracing the middle shelf of his secret cabinet, a constant pleasure even if it was only he who ever saw it. As to the unforeseen problems, it had seemed both appropriate and convenient, given the circumstances, to conceal both objects in the same place until such time as he'd made up his mind what to do with the torque and, after all, his chosen hiding place seemed not only appropriate but safe – and anyway he'd assumed it would only be for a few days.

'He would never forget what he'd been through when he discovered they were no longer there. He simply couldn't believe it or what had happened. Still, the dreadful nightmare was nearly over. When he'd first set out to acquire the torque, he'd wanted it for his own collection, but then he'd been approached and offered two rather splendid pieces looted from the Baghdad Museum at the end of the first Iraq war. He'd put out feelers and, as usual, there had soon been a response. So, the torque was to go and he'd have two other rare pieces for his cabinet. What Dr Davenport, loosely attached to the University of Exeter, proposed to do with the torque once he'd got it, he didn't know and didn't care. The man knew its provenance, it was up to him whether he kept it or sold it on yet again.

Now Simmons and his metal detector were finally in the past. Once the torque was handed over and the money changed hands, then that was the end of the whole affair; except for one small inconvenience. He wished now they'd simply disposed of the museum curator straight away but, most unusually, Marcus had suddenly got cold feet, arguing that, although they'd got away with two murders, they shouldn't risk a third. But he'd have to overrule him, not least because Turner might recognize them at some time in the future. Letting him live was too much of a gamble and he'd have to be seen to, if he wasn't dead already. Marcus had also disliked his choice of a venue and they had quite an argument, but on this he'd remained adamant. It had somehow seemed . . . *right*.

As soon as he was sure Smeaton was safely out of the way, Latymer had tried to get hold of Johns, but there was no reply, which was hardly surprising, since, after all, it was his day off and he'd already spent half of it working, even if it was

147

unofficially. Steeling himself, he then rang Bodmin police station and asked if DI Anderson was there, irritated by the fact that something seemed to have gone wrong with his phone, which made it hard to hear, only to be told (so far as he could make out) that Anderson was still in Exeter. Finally he rang Berry to say that since they'd spoken earlier there'd been a major development, too much to tell over the phone, and that he'd been trying unsuccessfully to get hold of Johns and Anderson, since matters had now reached the stage where he felt duty bound to inform the latter, however antagonistic he might be. He ended by asking Berry if everything was now all right and if he was still intending to return to Cornwall.

'So far as I know,' said Berry. 'Kate's out and I'm in the office, there's quite a lot of paperwork piling up.' Latymer's voice had been getting fainter and fainter. 'Here, don't you think it's time you charged up your phone?' he added.

'I always forget,' replied Latymer, sounding as if he were at the bottom of a hole. 'Look, I know this might sound odd, but I'll explain why later, if anyone other than Fiona Garleston calls asking for me, will you say that I'm also back in Bristol? And is there any possibility you could manage another day here? I realize that's asking a lot given the fright you've had over Kate.'

'What? What was that?'

Latymer repeated his request, sounding ever further away.

'I'll have to ask her,' shouted Berry. 'Can you hear me? Can't you give me some idea of what's happened?' he bellowed. 'It must be something pretty drastic.'

'The . . . here.' There was a crackling sound. '. . . cup . . . floor . . . all the . . .' and the connection died.

Feeling guilty at the prospect of leaving her to mind the shop yet again, if only for the night, he'd encouraged Kate to go into town to have her hair done and do some shopping. The devastating feelings he'd experienced when he'd thought she was mortally ill would remain with him for a long time. So, as he'd told Latymer, while Greta was manning the counter, he was in the office struggling to sort out a spate of different orders and chasing up overdue accounts, only to find himself constantly interrupted by a steady stream of telephone calls.

Most were routine, customers either ordering or enquiring after books, but he was continually distracted by others which were just plain irritating, not least because he had to remember to tell the caller that Latymer was back in Bristol but out of the office.

The easiest to deal with was Fiona Garleston. When she rang, he told her the truth, reminding her of his friend's mobile number but pointing out that he'd let the battery run down. Latymer's ex-wife, however, proved rather more difficult. Tess Latymer asked him briskly if she could speak to John, since she hadn't been able to get a reply from his flat for days and when she'd tried him on his mobile this morning, he didn't appear to be answering it. When he said he thought John might have forgotten to charge up his mobile she'd responded, 'Typical!' He'd then explained that John had taken a few days off, at which she'd snapped, 'In Scotland, I suppose,' and rung off before he could say any more. Sometimes he found it hard to understand how someone like John Latymer could have ended up with such a complicated emotional life.

Tess was bad enough, but when Maynard rang in his usual fussy way, Berry's irritation knew no bounds, even though he fully recognized the man's value as a good customer. Maynard wanted to know if there was any chance of getting hold of a couple of first editions of nineteenth-century sensation novels, especially *Lady Audley's Secret*, which he wanted to give to a friend. 'It really is *such* a delightful tale, the pretty little golden-haired creature tripping round the village giving goodies to the poor, who marries the squire but then turns out to be utterly *ruthless*, trying to drown her first husband in a well and then burn her maid to death . . .'

'Yes, I do know the story,' muttered Berry. 'Is there anything else?'

'Are you feeling all right? You sound rather fraught.'

Berry admitted that he was feeling a bit tired and emphasized that he'd a lot of paperwork to get through, hoping that it would encourage Maynard to ring off, but it seemed to have no effect whatsoever. 'You know, Keith,' he complained, 'I must admit I'm a *tad* disappointed that I haven't heard anything from John. I rang him this morning but couldn't get through on his mobile and, of course, there's no phone in the cottage.'

'Well, actually he's back in Bristol,' said Berry, crossing his fingers. 'He's planning to spend the rest of his holiday in Scotland. To be honest, I think he found being so close to a scene of crime was getting him down. No,' he added, hastily, 'I can't put him on to you, he's out looking over some books for me. I'll tell him you called. I know he was going to call you anyway about returning the keys.'

'Have they got anyone for that *awful* murder yet?' Maynard continued, relentlessly. 'Truly it's given me the creeps ever since I heard about it. To think that, if I'd decided to take a trip to Cornwall at the time, I might have actually *been* there when it happened. Worse, it could have been *me* they found in the burial mound, being so close by.' He gave a little squeak of excitement as Berry tried once again to bring the call to an end. 'Though I've been thinking about it, you know. Has John told you about the legend? That the tomb is guarded by the Keeper and that anyone breaking in does so at their peril? Not that I would have *dared* venture into such a place.'

Berry replied that he'd heard something to that effect.

'Well then. Perhaps they shouldn't be looking for an ordinary everyday murderer, but a *supernatural* one. Have they thought of calling in a medium? Or a psychic?'

At which point Keith told him firmly that it was extremely unlikely and thankfully rang off.

There next followed a call from the ex-colleague who had run into Latymer before he went on holiday, to say that he and his wife would be in Bristol again shortly, and perhaps they could all meet up for a drink. 'I'd like to meet John's wife. I'm glad the old boy's found himself a partner in his retirement.' Berry gave him a non-commital answer and tried, yet again, to get on with his work. So, Latymer hadn't told him about his divorce? Well, it was up to him to sort that one out. He considered leaving the receiver off the hook, but then came two calls in rapid succession which he found alarming. In both cases the phone rang, he picked it up, giving his name and that of the bookshop, and in each case there was a brief pause and then the receiver was replaced. He followed up both by ringing 1471 to be told that 'the caller withheld their number'. Was it, he wondered, the hoaxer of the night before, wanting to know if he'd taken the bait and returned home? If so, why? It made him uneasy. He could only speculate as to what it was Latymer had been trying to tell him before the phone died on him. Had it something to do with his wanting to give the impression both of them were now back in Bristol for good?

Somehow he struggled through the rest of the day, setting off from home at about six o'clock, loath to leave Kate alone, although she assured him there was no risk. The shop was firmly shut up and the alarms switched on and anyone calling at the flat would have to phone up from the door first. 'If it's no one I know, then I simply won't let them in,' she assured him. 'Don't worry. Hopefully, you'll be back again by tomorrow lunchtime and, if John does want you to stay another day, I'll ask Greta if she'd mind staying overnight, if it will set your mind at rest. Actually I still think it was just a sick joke. Haven't you thought that it might be someone you put away before you left West Midlands police? Perhaps they've also been down in Cornwall and saw you and somehow got your mobile number.'

He was about halfway to St Mellick when his phone rang. At first he decided to ignore it, but then, in view of the day's strange events, he pulled in to the side of the dual carriageway and took the call. He didn't recognize the caller's number, and his immediate thought was that it was the hoaxer trying again. When he answered, he realized that he was in a poor spot for reception, so the line kept breaking up, but at least he could hear his caller better than he had John that morning. 'Who is that?' he demanded. 'Who are you?'

'Is that Mr Berry?' enquired the caller, nervously.

He certainly didn't sound like the hoaxer. 'Yes,' he answered. 'Who's that?'

'Wayne. Wayne Jenkins. I lost that bit of paper you wrote your mobile number down on, I've only just found it or I'd have rung you before. Hope you don't mind me ringing you, but you said I could if I'd anything to tell you. Well, I have.'

'Go on then.'

'Something happened a couple of nights back I think you should know about The night after you come over to the estate to see me.' His voice took on a conspiratorial tone. 'Look, I think we should have a meet. Now.' Wayne was an addict of television crime series.

'Hardly,' said Berry. 'I'm on the hard shoulder of the A30 about four miles your side of Exeter. Can't it wait? I've had one hell of a day.'

'No. It's really important.'

'Well, can't you tell me now, on the phone?'

'If I did, you'd never believe me. Honest. Look, Mr Berry, something really bad's happened. At least, I think it's something bad.'

Berry sighed. 'Oh, very well. I was reckoning to be back at St Mellick about half past eight. There's not much difference in it. Do you want me to come to your home?'

'No. To Lanwithen. I've a mate there in the town, Kev, he lives six houses down from the Spar shop, number fourteen. He saw what I saw too. Perhaps you'll believe the two of us.'

'Very well,' said Berry, reluctantly. 'Wait there and I'll get to you as soon as I can.'

'Roger and out,' responded Wayne and rang off.

The day was going to be endless. He'd been up since five o'clock and done a day's work in the shop. Better tell John what he was going to do. But Latymer was still not back on the phone. Wearily, he returned to the road and set off again for Cornwall. He felt tired to death as he drove into Lanwithen and made his way to the address Wayne had given him. He knocked on the door, which was opened by Wayne so speedily that it was evident he'd been standing in the hallway waiting. He motioned him to come through. Berry looked around. Unlike Wayne's own home, that of his mate Kev was clean, neat and homely. Kev's mum offered him a cup of tea, then went off to make it.

'OK then,' said Berry, 'let's have it. And it had better be bloody good.'

The two boys looked at each other. 'Wayne was staying over the other night,' said Kev. 'Early on, we saw a copper knocking on the door of the flat over the shop. Then he went

152

into the shop, which was just closing up. We didn't go out to see nor nothing, 'specially not as they think Wayne did the break-in at the museum. We haven't seen nothing of the chap what runs it for days, me mum says he's away and that he'd told no one where he's gone.'

'Is that it?' demanded Berry. 'You've surely not brought me over here to tell me the museum curator's gone missing? Anyway, we knew.'

'No, no,' Wayne assured him. 'That's only the beginning. We stayed up late, talking and that . . . we'd a video we were watching.' A picture formed in Berry's mind of the two lads lying around passing a spliff to each other while making up fantasies in their heads. 'Then we heard a car draw up a bit down the road. They don't get much traffic here night times, so we went to the window and had a look. A fellow got out and let himself into the flat with the key, but it didn't look like Mr Turner. A few minutes later he come down again with another guy and they're helping out some bloke who couldn't walk properly, like he was ill or pissed.'

'Or drugged,' suggested Kev. 'Ere, do you think he was dead?'

'Carry on,' said Berry.

'Well, that's it. They shoved him in the car and drove off.'

'You're absolutely certain of this?'

'Cross me heart and hope to die.'

'Because, if this does turn out to be a wind-up, you'll never hear the last of it. So, if you were that worried, why didn't you tell the police?'

Wayne shook his head in disbelief. 'Do me a favour, Mr Berry. The cops? Believe me? Me they want to stick this one on so it helps their clear-up rate or something? They'd just say we'd made up some fairy tale and blame us for that and all.'

Berry had to admit he had a point. 'I don't suppose you thought to take the number of the car?'

The boys looked at each other again. 'We should've done, I suppose,' Kev admitted, 'but we couldn't see properly from the window and it was dark, the street light hasn't been working for ages. I can tell you one thing, though – it were a dirty great black or dark-blue BMW. A real smart motor.' He frowned. 'Come to think of it, I think it was an S registration.'

'That's right,' said Wayne, obviously trying to visualize the car. 'And I think the first two numbers were one–three, but they could've been one–eight. That's the best I can do.'

'Look,' said Berry, 'if I talk this over with the police and convince them I think you're telling the truth, would you then be willing to talk to them? I'd be quite prepared to be there with you.'

'All right,' Wayne agreed. 'It's a deal.' At this point Kev's mum appeared with mugs of tea which she handed round. Seeing Wayne as the leader of the lads hanging around on the estate, he'd seemed all too true to type: coarse, ill-mannered and very much the swaggering leader of the pack. Yet, in this comfortable domestic setting, with his friend, he seemed altogether different. Surely, thought Berry, there must be some way of getting him back into the education system and encouraging him into something better than a career in petty crime.

The two lads retired to Kev's bedroom to play computer games, leaving Berry alone with Kev's mum. 'It was very good of you to come over, Mr Berry,' she said. 'That Wayne's got a reputation as a tearaway, but he isn't really a bad lad. I blame it all on that mother of his, and the lad's never had no father. It's been one man after the other in that house, it's little wonder he's as he is. When he's here with our Kevin, he always behaves himself. I don't think he'd anything to do with what happened up the museum, whatever the police say. They'd be better spending their time trying to find that Mr Turner. Fancy him just going off like that.' Given the circumstances, Berry felt it unwise to pass on to her his speculation that Wayne and her son might just have seen that Mr Turner being assisted to leave.

After he'd spoken to Berry the second time, Latymer wondered what on earth he should do, given that he'd been unable to contact either Johns or Anderson. If the handover of the torque was to take place the following night, then time was of the essence, but where was the handover to take place? Something

154

flickered at the back of his mind but then went out. He considered what he would have done himself in the same circumstances. The best bet would be to track down the 'bent academic' – Davenport, wasn't it? – then get him to cooperate. He shouldn't be too difficult to find if he was a genuine archaeologist based in Exeter, no doubt a man with an apparently blameless record. Once that was done, then surely it should be possible to use him to devise some means of catching Smeaton and his principal actually making the transaction.

He finished clearing up, after which he felt at a loose end but didn't want to leave the cottage just in case anything happened, though admittedly it seemed highly unlikely that Smeaton would come back. He'd got what he came for. Latymer had been trying to work out just when the cup and the torque were hidden under the floor in the shed. He was almost certain they hadn't been there all that long, certainly not months, a few weeks or days at the most. Before he came down to the cottage? During the day and a half he was away in Bristol? On the whole he thought the former the more likely and, if that was the case, then they'd been out there in the shed throughout his stay. What a thought! Time was getting on, it was dark and he was hungry. Surely Berry would be here soon. He went to see if his phone had charged sufficiently, decided just about, then rang to see if there were any messages. There were three, one from Fiona asking him to call her when he got back to Bristol to make arrangements to see her, another from Maynard wanting to know how the investigation into the murder was going and if the 'beast of Bodmin', as he put it, had been caught yet. 'I know you're back in Bristol now, but you must have heard something. I can't, just can't, go down to St Mellick and stay in the cottage until I know he's been caught. I wouldn't sleep a wink.' The third was from Tess asking why he never answered her phone messages.

It was after nine o'clock by the time Berry knocked on the door. 'I was getting really concerned,' Latymer said as he let him in. 'But, because of what happened, I didn't like to ring Kate, I didn't want to worry her unnecessarily.'

'Sorry,' Berry apologized. 'Couldn't get through to you. I've come via Lanwithen. I've been talking to Wayne Jenkins and his mate.'

'What on earth for?'

'Get me a drink and I'll tell you,' said Berry.

Latymer poured out a malt whisky and handed it to him. 'All right, fire away.'

Berry did so, ending with his conclusion that it had to be Turner the two boys had seen being dragged into the car. 'I don't know what's been going on down here while I've been away, but cap that!'

'I think I probably can.' And Latymer told him of the events of the afternoon. 'I sat up there hardly daring to breathe in case Smeaton came up to check out the bedrooms. I thought that if he or his friend were responsible both for the murder of the man on the beach and Brian Simmons, then they'd hardly baulk at a third and, from what you've just told me, if that was Turner the lads saw, then I'm likely to be the fourth. I wonder what the hell they've done with Turner.'

'Have you any idea who the mystery man behind all this might be?' enquired Berry. Latymer told him. Berry gave a disbelieving laugh. 'You're having me on. Why should a man in his position get involved in something like this?'

'Come on, you know as well as I do that there have always been doctors, lawyers, academics, top-ranking consultants and policemen who've become involved in crime, even to the point of murder, and an obsession for collecting rare objects isn't confined to one profession or one type. The only thing he or she has to have is money.'

'I still can't believe it,' declared Berry.

'Well, we'll see . . . Anyway, somehow he acquires the cup. Suppose he actually found it himself, after all, in the nature of his work he gets around a lot. Perhaps he's a secret metal-detecting freak. Then, at about the same time, he hears about the Irish torque being stolen and somehow gets hold of that too. For some reason he wants to hide them down here for a few days while he decides what to do with them. The cottage would be ideal, the shed even better, and all the locals claim it's hardly ever lived in, but perhaps it just happened to be occupied at the time, which is quite likely, as I'm guessing all this took place back in the middle of the summer. Then it occurs to him: why not use Keeper's Tump? The footpath sign's broken, hardly anyone goes up there any more and, as a further discouragement, there's the legend of the Keeper. He doesn't want to disturb the entrance to the burial chamber, so, presumably at night, he digs a small deep hole somewhere on the mound, puts the stuff inside, then fills it in and pulls the bracken and gorse back over it.

'He'd be taking a risk, but not all that much of one. For some reason we don't know, he decides almost immediately to sell the torque and sets about finding a buyer, but in the meantime along comes our Mr Smith/Simmons, runs his metal detector over the mound and, hey presto, hits gold. So, the whole plan goes hideously wrong. Our man is frantic, he's no idea what's happened or where they've gone. He lets it be known through his clandestine channels that he wants to be told if anything really unusual suddenly appears on the black market. He'll stop at nothing to get them back.

'While Simmons was keeping his cards close to his chest, he was reasonably safe. He might even have got away with it and survived if he'd done exactly as Turner said, kept quiet and done nothing about it until filming began. But presumably he got impatient as time went on and, in spite of Turner's warning, began hinting in certain quarters that he had some stunning artefacts for sale. The news would have got back to our man in no time and he either responded himself or got Smeaton to do it for him, a rendezvous was arranged at Keeper's Tump late at night and the rest, as they say, is history. What the two villains of the piece hadn't taken into account, of course, was the fact that the rarely visited, rather uninteresting, burial mound was about to star in a television archaeology series.' He stood up. 'Anyway, that's what I think. I'll have another try at getting hold of Johns.'

This time Johns was in and Latymer told him, as concisely as possible, about Smeaton's visit to the house and the apparent abduction of Matthew Turner. 'My God,' he exclaimed when he'd heard Latymer out. 'What a can of worms! Look, I know it's late, but I'll have a word with the DI and, if he agrees, we'll be right over.'

157

'I take it Detective Inspector Anderson's back from Exeter, then?'

'No, this is Detective Inspector Bailey. DI Anderson isn't coming back.'

Fifteen

Half an hour later Sergeant Johns arrived, bringing Detective Inspector Bailey with him, by which time Berry had passed beyond almost overwhelming weariness and out the other side into that strange state that precedes exhaustion. Bailey apologized for the lateness of the visit but trusted they'd understand, given the circumstances.

'What's happened to DI Anderson, then?' enquired Berry, innocently. 'We thought he was in charge of the case.'

'He has asked for, and is to be given, a transfer back to Milton Keynes,' said Bailey. 'He's been suffering from stress and is taking some sick leave first. So, I've been asked to take over.'

'He never seemed really to settle here,' Johns pointed out. 'It's such a very different patch from what he'd been used to.'

'Well, I hope he recovers soon and that he'll be very happy back on home ground,' commented Latymer, trying not to smile.

'So,' said Bailey, 'you obviously have a great deal to tell me. But first I must tell you what I know from the paperwork I've seen and from what I've been told. I also need to ask you both some questions. As I see it, the undisputed facts are that a body was discovered in the bronze-age burial mound known as Keeper's Tump a week ago, and that, according to forensics, it had been there for the best part of a fortnight at least; possibly even a little longer. Cause of death was by stabbing, in this case a stiletto-type dagger which actually reached the heart.' He turned to Latymer. 'I understand you drew DI Anderson's attention to the fact that a body found on a beach near Newquay back in April had suffered the same kind of injury. May I ask how you knew this?'

159

'Because it just happened that, when I was a DCI myself, based in the midlands, Dr Michael Evans was our immediately local forensic pathologist. It was totally fortuitous that we met up again at Keeper's Tump after so many years.' He paused, considering the most tactful way to continue. 'He thought it might be useful for me to know. I understood from him that he hadn't got on too well with DI Anderson when he'd been called in to the body-on-the-beach case, and that he felt he might need some support with this one, but apart from Keith I kept it to myself.'

Bailey looked at him. 'I see. No doubt you realize that, strictly speaking, you shouldn't have been told. However . . . you then also took it upon yourself to visit the curator of the museum after the body had been found and question him. Why was that?'

'Because I was sure, from past experience, not only that he was concealing important information from the police, but that he was also frightened stiff. He wouldn't admit to anything then, but, the following morning he knocked me up at the crack of dawn, having spent the night in a pub in Bodmin, following two unpleasant telephone calls. He told me what I imagine he later told DI Anderson – that is, before he changed his story – that a man called Smith had come into the museum back in the summer, bringing with him a gold cup and a torque. He showed me photographs of the objects and I told Keith, my colleague here, about them, and he arranged for us to see an expert in bronze-age archaeology at the Ashmolean Museum in Oxford. He told us that the two objects were at least seven hundred years apart and were of exceptional value. This was then verified by a fellow academic, who told us that he was almost certain that the torque was one that had been stolen from a museum in Ireland about eighteen months ago. I thought that, if that was indeed the case, then Matthew Turner had got himself involved in something very serious indeed, very possibly to do with the black market in antiquities, and that the police art and antiques unit should be told immediately.

'We came back to Cornwall the next day and were so concerned that we immediately went into the police station to

160

tell DI Anderson what we'd discovered, only to find that Turner had returned to the police station after his first interview and completely changed his story. I have to say that I told Anderson I simply didn't believe it. Not, I hasten to add, that I didn't believe what he was telling me, but that I didn't believe what Turner was now claiming: that the whole thing had been a hoax to fool the television company into making a programme down here, and that the photographs both I and the police had been shown were clever fakes. Whereupon he told me that he'd had a definite confirmation that this was the case from a friend of Turner's who, most surprisingly, had rushed down to Cornwall to confess to having produced the photographs using digital technology. It proved impossible to persuade him to consider any alternative, nor was he prepared to link any of this with the break-in at the museum.'

'He told us to go back to Bristol and stick to selling books,' added Berry.

Bailey raised an eyebrow, then referred to his notes. 'I see here that DI Anderson suspected a boy called Wayne Jenkins of having carried out the break-in, a lad with a record.'

'We don't think that's right either,' continued Latymer, 'for reasons Keith will explain. Anyway, it seems unlikely that a boy of that age would have had the skill to remove a hard disk from a computer (which would have been of no possible value to him) rather than making off with the computer itself, something he could get some cash for. And as to his finger-prints being on the window ledge, they may well be there, but along with many others, as it seems it's a popular place for local lads to hang out. Anyway, the wood round the windows is so rotten that anyone could have got in. I imagine the trustees might well have problems with their insurance claim over that. Anyway, I think that brings you more or less up to date with the early stuff,' he concluded.

'Well, before we carry on any further, I'm able to tell you that there is no doubt from the results of the DNA tests that the body found in Keeper's Tump is that of Brian Simmons. This has now also been confirmed by the fingerprints found on the metal detector at his home.' He looked at Johns. 'We'll go into the rights and wrongs of what you did later . . . It shows that he was also into metal detecting, which lends some support to Turner's original story, if Simmons was indeed his Mr Smith. We also now share your concern over Turner's disappearance, and two officers have been sent over to Lanwithen to search his flat.'

'I think we can help there too,' Latymer told him, and turned to Berry. 'Tell them what you've found out.'

So, Berry explained how they'd gone over to Lanwithen to see Turner on their return from Oxford, to be greeted by a young man who gave his name as Marcus Smeaton and who claimed to be a friend of the curator's. 'He told us that Turner had gone away for a few days, that he wasn't sure when he'd be back and that he was using the flat for a few days while in Cornwall on business. We then discovered that no one knew where he was, that he'd apparently gone off without even telling the trustees of the museum. We assume "Smeaton" is the same friend who confessed to faking the photographs, but we don't know. Later that day I went to see Wayne Jenkins and, from what he told me, it's most unlikely he could have done the break-in. He'd been at home all night coping with a bad abscess in a tooth, a virtually cast-iron alibi backed up by his dentist.' Berry then went on to tell Bailey about the hoax phone call, his dash back to Bristol, his subsequent return, and what Jenkins and his friend alleged they'd witnessed.

'If they're telling the truth, things look pretty bleak for Turner being found safe and well,' commented Bailey.

'I really do think they are,' said Berry. 'It really didn't sound like some tale made up to make them feel important. I did a great deal of work with young lads like them in Birmingham, and I believe what they told me was straight up.'

Bailey thanked him, then turned to Latymer. 'And I understand you have an even stranger story to tell, Mr Latymer?'

So, Latymer took him through the events of the day from Berry's early-morning dash to Bristol, through his unofficial visit to Simmons' cottage, to the unexpected arrival of Smeaton, who obviously assumed they'd both left the cottage, and his subsequent phone conversation with whoever was in the business with him. 'I sat up there stunned at what I was

162

hearing, holding my breath in case he realized he wasn't alone in the house. And to think those two wretched bronze-age artefacts that have caused so much trouble – not to mention two, possibly three, murders – were under the floor in the woodshed throughout the time I've been staying here!'

'So, he's called Davenport? The man you say is meeting up with Smeaton and his boss tomorrow night to collect the torque?'

'That's right. I think Smeaton said *Dr* Davenport. I imagine his doctorate's in archaeology or history, not medicine. He's based in Exeter and the inference was that he's attached to the university in some way. I imagine you'll want to get hold of him as soon as possible.'

'I certainly do,' declared Bailey. 'They're meeting up tomorrow night, you say? I suppose he didn't say where?'

Latymer shook his head. 'No, he didn't. But, for what it's worth, I think it might well be somewhere down this end or even further west.' Once again he tried to pin down the vague recollection of something that might be important that had come to him earlier, but without success.

'I must get on to it now, if you'll excuse me.' Bailey took out his phone and rang, not Bodmin, but police headquarters in Exeter, and spoke to one of his colleagues. 'Davenport, Dr Davenport. That's right.' He looked at his watch. 'Yes, I know it's nearly half past ten, but there must be someone in the university who can tell you if they know him and, if so, if they have his address or a general idea of where he lives. There must still be someone on the switchboard, I imagine. They might know. No, so far as I'm aware, he has no form, but check just in case. No, the morning won't do, I need to know right away.' He finished the call and resumed his seat.

'I've also alerted the specialist police who deal with the market in antiquities, and they're seeing what they can find out. I'll tell them about the theft of the torque.'

'We had thought to contact them ourselves,' said Berry, 'but John thought it was only right we told DI Anderson first and left him to do it. Unfortunately, he didn't see the necessity.'

Bailey's phone rang and he picked it up. 'That's quick,' he said, then, 'Oh, it's you, Constable.' He looked across at Johns.

'It's Constable Pender, calling from Turner's flat. No, go on.' There was a long pause. 'I see. No, it doesn't look good, does it? And it fits in only too well with other information I've been given. Very well, lock everything up securely, tell the landlord he mustn't go in and I'll get SOCO organized for first thing in the morning.' He finished the call and turned to the others. 'It seems they've found bloodstains in the flat and signs of a struggle.'

Almost immediately the phone rang again. 'Yes. Very good. I don't suppose DS Charleston's around, is he? No? Then will someone let him know I'll call him at home as soon as I get back to the station? We need to pick up Davenport before he leaves his house in the morning. I'll tell the DS why when I speak to him.' He put down the phone. 'The person on the switchboard had his address and telephone number and they've checked him out and he's not got a record of any kind. Thank you for your time and now I'll leave you in peace. But I'd be grateful if you'd come into the station as soon as possible in the morning.'

His final discussion with Marcus Smeaton had left James Davenport in a state of eager anticipation. He'd finally done it! All his life he seemed to have been lucky, so much so that people had often remarked on it. Lucky to be born an only child into a comfortably off middle-class family in a position to send him to a good school and indulge his hobbies, see him through university without running into debt, then buy him a flat in Bath when he graduated. Lucky also to get a reasonably good lectureship at the first attempt. He hadn't been quite so fortunate in his relationships with women, but then you can't have everything. However, the biggest piece of luck of all was to have won the lottery a couple of years earlier. Two and a half million pounds. He'd signed up to there being no publicity and turned down the organizers' offers of assistance in dealing with his good fortune. He'd managed that quite well himself, at least half of it was safely tucked away in investments offshore. Now he could really indulge a growing passion.

He resigned from his job and bought himself one of the

eminently desirable houses built on top of the city wall in Exeter. He'd always liked Exeter. From his windows he could see over the river to rolling countryside: from his back garden, down the river and out towards the estuary. No one who didn't know would have guessed that he was a lottery winner. He did some part-time lecturing on archaeology at the university, and it was assumed that he must do other things as well, since, although he lived simply, he didn't appear to have any financial worries. Very gradually he'd begun taking soundings and bought his first ever piece.

Following his meeting with Smeaton, he'd been almost too excited to sleep. He'd seen no reason why the transaction couldn't take place in his own home, but apparently the person behind the deal had his own way of doing things. Still, it wasn't too much of a hardship to drive down to Cornwall, given the prize at the end of it. Since his first venture into the market, he had continued buying, most discreetly, some other items on the black market, his most recent buy being a small, but rather splendid, Babylonian carving looted from Iraq. The torque, though, was in an altogether different category and would take up a substantial proportion of that part of the lottery win banked in English banks. But it might well bring him even more luck. For a long time he'd had a fantasy of finding the perfect girl, one who would be totally devoted to him and whom he could trust with his secret, one who would enjoy an endless series of private views of his collection. Yes, he was lucky, very lucky indeed.

He'd woken several times in the night but had fallen quite deeply asleep when the thunderous knocking came at his front door. He woke, blinked, and looked at the clock. It was six o'clock. Who on earth was trying to wake him up at this time? 'Are you there?' shouted a man's voice through the letterbox. 'Come on now, open up.' He pulled on his dressing gown and went downstairs ready to give the caller a piece of his mind. And opened the door to find his luck was about to run out.

Latymer and Berry were at Bodmin police station before nine o'clock in the morning and were shown straight through to Bailey, who was looking pleased and informed them that they'd found Davenport. 'He was pretty amazed when our lads called round at six o'clock this morning. Plenty of money there, lovely house right on the city walls; they don't come cheap. Wonder how he made it? Possibly by wheeling and dealing, I suppose, but somehow I don't think so.'

'What did he have to say?' enquired Latymer.

'Well, at first he just blustered away, threatened to call in a brief, demanded to talk to "someone more senior", and was told a Detective Inspector was as senior as he was likely to get. Eventually, however, as it became apparent that we knew all about the torque and the handover, he calmed down, but even then he didn't seem to realize the seriousness of his position. Not, that is, until he was told that there had already been two murders directly connected with the business, and possibly a third! Anyway, the upshot is that after the gravity of the situation had been spelled out to him, and the likely consequences if he refused to help us, he agreed to cooperate.'

'So, what's the plan?'

'He'll follow all the instructions he's been given, except that he'll have one of our plainclothes men with him. He said he'd been told explicitly that he must come alone and said maybe they wouldn't go through with it if he turned up with someone else, but we'll just have to risk that. We've told him to say that he'd been worried about meeting up in the middle of the night in the middle of nowhere with a banker's draft on him – that's how Smeaton's boss wants the money paid – so he'd brought a friend. Hopefully, by that time, Smeaton and his partner will be so keen to go through with it and get it over with that they won't make a fuss.'

'Where's it to be, then?' asked Berry.

'He's to meet up first with Smeaton at a crossroads near a place called Crofthandy, not far from Redruth, at one o'clock in the morning, and they'll go on from there to the actual meeting place.' Latymer and Berry exchanged glances. 'Do you know something I don't know?'

'It's just that the name cropped up earlier, in connection with Smith,' said Latymer. 'In fact, I went up there myself, as I thought he might live thereabouts. That was before the body was identified as that of Simmons, of course. I went into

166

St Day, which is nearby, and where there's a post office, and asked there. Needless to say, no one had heard of Smith, which was hardly surprising in the circumstances, though it turns out that Simmons and his sister lived in Crofthandy when they were kids. I suppose if you want somewhere out of the way yet not too far from a town and a main road, it's as good a place as any.'

Bailey considered this. 'Any ideas as to a suitable spot?'

'It's pretty desolate up there. On one side of the road there's a rambling industrial estate, on the other old mine workings and ruined engine houses.'

'It all sounds pretty weird to me,' commented Bailey. 'It's almost as if this man is staging some kind of drama.'

Latymer jumped to his feet. *'Of course!'* It's been at the back of my mind ever since I overheard that phone call.' He turned to Bailey. 'Towards the end of it, Smeaton made some kind of joking answer to a remark from the other end. It was something like, "You say you're praying it all goes OK? Well, say one for me. *See you in church.*" Don't you see, Keith?'

'See what?' enquired Berry, mystified.

'The church. I bet the meeting is to be held in that creepy gothic ruin of a church in St Day. If the man behind all this is who I think it is, it makes perfect sense. He is staging his own drama. It all fits.'

While Bailey was certainly a vast improvement on Anderson, he was still somewhat reluctant to agree to Berry and Latymer being present when the torque was handed over. Davenport would have a police minder with him to make sure he didn't defect, he would be there himself with sergeant Johns, who had now officially applied to be transferred to CID, and there would be unobtrusive back-up. He finally agreed, but only on the understanding that they kept well out of the way during the initial stages at least. As to Latymer's belief that he knew the identity of the man behind it all, then they'd soon know if he was right. Meanwhile, a major search was on for Turner, or Turner's body, so far without success.

After having agreed their plans for the evening, Berry had accompanied Bailey and Johns to Lanwithen to interview

Wayne Jenkins and Kev at Kev's home, Wayne rightly being apprehensive as to how his mother might react faced with a visit from the police. He had awful visions of her either being raucous and aggressive, bawling that she knew her rights or, even worse, attempting to be sexy and flirtatious. Once they'd realized that they were likely to be believed, both lads behaved sensibly and told their stories again. Bailey stressed the importance of what they had to say, not least because the state of Turner's flat bore out their accounts. Attempts were already being made to track down the BMW, but there were a good many S-registration BMWs, and the fact that the lads could only recall two numbers, which might or might not be accurate, didn't help much.

'Will you believe me now when I say it wasn't me what broke into that crumby old museum?' demanded Wayne. 'Since we've done all we can to help. And anyway, the dentist knows I couldn't have done it. Ask him.'

'I think you can take it that you won't hear any more about that,' Bailey told him, 'though we may well want both of you to make formal statements later. This is a very serious matter. And if you'll take my advice, for what it's worth, you'll sort yourself out, get back into school, do some work and behave. You're too bright a lad to waste your time messing around getting into needless trouble.'

'What about Anderson, then?' queried Berry as Johns drove them back to St Mellick. 'It was a bit sudden, wasn't it?'

Bailey shrugged. 'The sergeant was right, he never settled. It's one thing coming down on holiday, something entirely different living and working here. He also seemed to have got it into his mind that everyone had a down on him, that no one was cooperating with him properly. I shouldn't say it, but he wasn't good under pressure and, even without your, er . . . intervention, and that of your friend, he was running into criticism for trying to wrap the case up without taking into account all the possible implications.'

Waiting is always the worst part. Berry and Latymer spent the afternoon trying to find things to occupy themselves as they tried to imagine what was likely to happen that night. Berry rang Kate to explain the situation, assuring her that no risk was involved, that there would be plenty of police back-up. 'As soon as the money's changed hands, the police will move in and make the arrests, we won't be involved. However, if you would really prefer that I come back, John says he can manage without me, if that's what you'd prefer.'

She assured him that she did not. 'I think I'll feel happier if the two of you are together and, from what you say, it can't go on much longer, can it? Do you still want me to tell anyone who rings up that you're both in Bristol? If so, where are you supposed to be?'

'At a book sale in . . . oh . . . Bath, Chepstow, somewhere not far away. OK then, see you tomorrow. Hopefully by about lunchtime.'

Gradually the interminable afternoon dragged into the evening. They'd arranged to meet up with Bailey in Redruth at eleven o'clock, meanwhile a watch would be put on the church. 'But suppose it isn't the church,' grumbled Berry, 'we're going to look a right pair of idiots. Not to mention your candidate for Mr Big.'

'I'm convinced the church is the right place, but even if it isn't, then Bailey and Johns will be close by when the initial meeting takes place, and can follow behind. Wherever it is, it won't be far away. I'll ignore your crack about Mr Big. I'm deeply hurt that you have so little faith in me!' Finally, at ten o'clock, they set out for Redruth.

Sixteen

'I think we have everything in place.' Latymer and Berry had met up with Bailey and his constable driver in the car park of a supermarket on the outskirts of Redruth. 'Davenport and the plainclothes sergeant with him are all set and they'll be able to keep in touch right up until the handover.'

'What about back-up?' enquired Berry.

'Should be OK too. Four officers will be waiting in a van parked not far from St Day. With Davenport's minder and us, that should be more than enough, after all, so far as we know, there are only two of them. He turned to Latymer. 'I thought you might be interested to know that I'd a call earlier from DI Anderson.'

Latymer smiled. 'Did you now? Were you surprised?'

'I have to admit I was. He started off by telling me that the case had been preying on his mind. That perhaps, after all, he'd been wrong about some aspects of it, that there were a number of things he should have looked into more carefully and that perhaps, after all, Turner had been telling the truth first time round.'

'Did you tell him Turner's missing?'

'There didn't seem any harm in doing so. Also that we suspected that, at the very least, he'd been abducted and subjected to violence, if not worse. Then he wanted to know where everything was at, had we a suspect in mind and, if so, what we were planning to do.'

'What did you say?'

'I fobbed him off. Said I'd let him know when we got a result and that, in the meantime, he should take advantage of the break he'd been given, so that he'd be on the ball by the time he returned to Milton Keynes. Oh, by the way, they're sending someone down from Scotland Yard tomorrow.'

Latymer blinked. Visions of the grand old days of the 1930s and 40s, when the local bobbies called in 'the Yard', went through his mind. Indeed, his and Berry's last case had involved a replica of a 1945 murder in Warwickshire, when the county police force had called in 'Fabian of the Yard'; to no avail, as it turned out.

Bailey grinned. 'Don't look so stunned! Surely you remember that the Arts and Antiques Unit is based there. They've already been checking up on the torque and they're virtually certain that it is the one stolen in Ireland, though the gold cup is new to them. Nothing like it's either been reported as missing or offered for illicit sale.'

The police van was parked nearby and the four men joined their colleagues in the back of it and prepared for a long wait. At half past eleven Bailey had a call from Davenport's minder to say that they'd left Exeter and were heading down towards Cornwall on the A30 and that, as there was virtually nothing on the road, they expected to arrive at the Crofthandy cross-roads in good time; and yes, Davenport had his banker's draft with him. An hour later, by which time they were becoming increasingly impatient. the minder rang again to say they were about 12 miles from the crossroads leading to Crofthandy and St Day, but that they would wait until shortly before one o'clock before making for the actual meeting place.

'Has Smeaton or anyone else attempted to contact Davenport?' Bailey asked.

'No,' came the response. 'And, to be on the safe side, I've got his phone. It's switched off.'

'Right,' said Bailey, as he concluded the conversation. 'You back-up people can get in position. You know where to wait, the first big car park on the industrial estate. Obviously the sergeant with Davenport will let you know where they're supposed to go after they've met up with Smeaton. We expect it to be the church in St Day, but it might be a good idea to keep an eye out anyway in case anything goes wrong – like the sergeant is unable to call us or they go off somewhere else.'

'You really do think you've got the right place for the handover, sir?' enquired one of the back-up team. 'It seems pretty unlikely on the face of it.'

'Nothing's certain but, given what we know, or think we know, about who's behind all this, then it's a very distinct possibility. But be prepared for anything.'

The van moved off, Bailey and his driver returned to their unmarked car and followed suit, and Latymer and Berry set off behind. 'I hope to God you are right, John,' commented Berry as he took the wheel. 'Otherwise we're really going to be in the shit!'

'From what he said, I think Bailey's quite prepared for any possible change of plan. If it isn't the church, then it must be somewhere equally close. I simply don't believe they've dragged Davenport all the way down here to take him back up the county again.'

When Latymer had first visited the church, he'd noticed that there was room to park a couple of cars on a small piece of wasteground close to the last house on the opposite side of the road. There was one other vehicle there, a somewhat dilapidated van, and Berry reversed into the space, parking a little further back from it. There was no sign of life anywhere. More worryingly, there still wasn't, half an hour later at one o'clock, by which time both men were becoming seriously concerned. 'What's gone wrong?' demanded Latymer, furiously. 'Where the hell are they?'

A few minutes later his own phone rang. It was Bailey. 'You were wrong, Latymer. It seems it isn't the church after all. The meet took place OK. Smeaton's driving some kind of Land Rover or something. Our man said he told them to follow him and that they've turned off on the road down towards the United Downs. We're following behind as cautiously as we can. My driver says there's a little pull-in car park a few yards from where we are and I've told back-up to come down and park there. Will keep—' The phone cut off as he hit a dead spot.

'Now what do we do?' demanded Berry. 'Go after them?' He sighed. 'If you're wrong about this, surely you must be starting to think you might be wrong about our man as well.'

'I don't think we've heard the end of it,' responded Latymer, though he admitted to having doubts, 'but I can't see we'll do any good trailing after them. I think we should stay here a bit longer just in case.' Berry was about to remonstrate, then changed his mind. It wasn't the first time he'd found himself in a similar situation with Latymer and on all but one previous occasion his hunch had finally turned out to be right.

'OK. We'll give it another half hour then we'd better try and contact Bailey again.'

A further twenty minutes passed. Suddenly the phone rang, making them both jump. It was Bailey, roaring with rage. 'They've tricked us!' he exploded. 'We crawled down the road towards United Downs, past the pull-in for cars, without using our lights, until suddenly we saw Davenport's car parked at the side of the road close to where a track goes off towards the mine workings and the old engine houses. It looks as if Smeaton ordered our two to get out of their car and into his so that he could take them on to where the handover's to take place. Given what you've said about your suspect's love for the dramatic, then why not an old engine house? From where we were, we could see the tail lights of their vehicle moving quite slowly, then it stopped by one of the engine houses within what looked like easy walking distance. I called back-up and we set off on foot, we daren't risk taking the car up there. Then, without warning, the lights went out on Smeaton's vehicle and we bloody well lost him!'

'Where are you now?'

'Outside a ruined engine house and they seem to have disap-peared into thin air. There's another, even rougher track, at right angles from this one, going down into a deep dip. He must have led us on then belted down there. Presumably he's tried it before to make sure he could do it. Now we don't know where the hell they are.' His voice came and went, he was obviously running. 'We're making our way back to the road but back-up's spread out all over the place.'

As he spoke, Latymer and Berry saw an unlighted vehicle at the crossroads almost opposite them. It then turned up towards the church, drove slowly past and parked a little way up the road. Latymer spoke softly into the phone. 'Are you still there, Bailey? Can you hear me? I think we can tell you where they are. A four-wheel-drive vehicle, without any lights, just pulled up close to the church and three men are getting out of it. They've been having you on. Whoever's in charge of this must have either got wind of what you proposed to do, or wasn't taking any chances, and so led you round the houses. How long do you reckon it'll take you to get here?'

'Ten minutes, fifteen minutes . . .' The voice was faint. 'Can you hold the fort until then? At least see if you can witness the handover, but for God' sake don't try and do anything else.'

Smeaton and the other two men had now reached the gate of the church. He led them up the path then round the side to the back of the building. 'Come on,' said Latymer, 'this is it. They crossed the road and made their way silently along the side of the church. 'Let's hope they haven't got someone on the look-out,' whispered Berry, as they rounded the corner to find that a door, securely fastened when Latymer had first visited it, had been forced open and was now slightly ajar.

The night was overcast and there was little or no light from the moon. No wonder back-up were floundering about on the United Downs, thought Latymer, that must have been part of the plan. He was now quite certain he was right about the identity of the chief protagonist. Cautiously, they opened the door a little further, hoping against hope that there was no one immediately inside the door, but they had no need to worry, all the activity was at the other end of the building, enabling them to slide in and stand unnoticed against the darkness of the back wall.

'So, where is this man of yours?' quavered Davenport. 'You've dragged us all round the houses and still nothing's happened.'

'You shouldn't have brought your friend with you,' Smeaton told him. 'You know you were told to come alone.'

'I'm glad I did,' retorted Davenport. 'For all I know, you could have murdered me out there in that wasteland and taken my banker's draft with you.'

'If you'd come alone, we'd have come straight here and it would all be over by now,' retorted Smeaton.

'*So, where is he?*' demanded Davenport, his voice high with fright.

'Here,' came the reply and a figure moved out of the shadows.

'Now we'll see who's right,' whispered Latymer. The meeting had indeed been staged for maximum effect. They seemed to have rigged up some kind of makeshift screen from which the figure had emerged into a single beam of light. The light, amid the shadows, made him look exceptionally tall. He was robed from head to foot in a dark garment of some kind, but as to his identity, that remained a mystery, for he was wearing the kind of blank eyeless mask worn by actors in ancient Greek theatre. Except that this one was of gold.

'You disobeyed your orders, Dr Davenport.' The mask gave the voice a strange, unearthly quality.

'I was frightened to come alone.' It was all Davenport could do to speak. 'My . . . my friend won't say anything. I swear it.'

'Very well, it seems I'll have to take the risk. It's time this business was brought to an end, it's gone on too long. You have the banker's draft?' Davenport felt inside his inside breast pocket and took out a long envelope. The masked man produced a small bag from somewhere in his robe; and the handover finally took place. 'You can check it's what you want,' the masked man told him. Davenport put his hand inside the bag and pulled out the torque and held it up, glittering in the light.

His minder immediately made a grab at the masked man, only to be floored by Smeaton. By the time Latymer and Berry reached them, Smeaton was kneeling on the police sergeant's chest, his hands round his throat, while the masked figure struggled to hold on to Davenport. It took both Berry and Latymer to haul Smeaton off Davenport's minder, and they'd just achieved it when they heard Bailey shouting from the doorway down the long length of the ruined nave for everyone to stay where they were, as back-up was close behind. Latymer, panting for breath, turned his attention to the masked figure, catching hold of his robe and forcing him to release Davenport as Bailey and the sergeant raced up towards the group, while

175

from outside came the sound of the back-up vehicle. In the moment of total confusion that followed, the masked man shed his robe and vanished behind the screen.

'Don't worry,' shouted Bailey, 'he can't get away.'

Berry helped the badly shaken police officer, who was retching and gasping for breath, to his feet. Davenport, white-faced and shaking, was standing in the light of the police torches, the torque dangling almost unnoticed from his hand. But where was the masked man? Bailey pushed aside the makeshift screen to discover their quarry had vanished. Behind it was a small opening, little more than a hatchway, which had presumably been opened up in case of just such an eventuality, but it was something else that grabbed his attention. 'My God!' he called out. 'I think there's a body here. Get me some light and get rid of that bloody screen.' The screen was knocked away, revealing a man's body, bound and gagged and apparently comatose.

Latymer, not wanting to waste time seeing the outcome, bent down and crawled out through the opening in an attempt to catch up with the masked man. Once on his feet, he ran down the path and out on to the road. Not only was it a very dark night, but now bands of mist were drifting across in front of him. He looked both ways up the street, but there was no one to be seen, his quarry could have run either way. Then he heard the sound of a vehicle. It might simply be some late-comer on his way home, but it was worth a chance. He shot across the road and climbed into his own car just as a dark BMW, using only side lights, passed his parking space and turned sharp right almost in front of him. He didn't dare start off straight away, as pursuit would be only too obvious, but common sense told him that the man, aware that his accomplice was likely to be arrested, would be making for the main road heading north. The proper thing to do was to return to the church and tell Bailey, who would organize the official pursuit, but that would waste even more time and would be hampered by the fact that he'd been unable to note the car number plate, which appeared to have been obscured in some way. He counted to twenty then set off after the BMW, assuming that Berry, even before he discovered the car was missing, would realize what he'd done, and that the police would give him a lift back to St Mellick.

He drove out of St Day, down the winding B road and on to the bypass and from there to the main road which led out of Cornwall, but between that point and the dual carriageway leading on to the motorway, it was still almost all single carriageway. It was also hilly, with numerous bends, which would make any overtaking difficult. However, he hadn't anticipated that should be much of a problem, given the time of night when there was little or nothing on the road. But, as he almost immediately discovered, it was also the time of night when the owners of huge delivery lorries chose to put their juggernauts on the road, with the result that he found himself having to wait on a side road to let a huge supermarket lorry pass. However, while waiting, he'd been able to see through the mist a number of such vehicles strung out ahead of him that were now grinding their way up a hill; almost certainly the car whose tail lights he could see wedged in between two of them was the BMW. Without the mist the driver would have had some opportunities to pass, but the increasing lack of visibility would make it hazardous, and anyway there'd be no reason as yet for him to think he was being followed. The obvious assumption would be, unless Smeaton said anything to the contrary, that he and Smeaton had originally arrived in St Day in the four-wheel drive.

Everything seemed designed to intensify Latymer's frustration. When the procession of vehicles finally reached the one short length of dual carriageway before Bodmin, he began to pull out to pass the lorry in front, only to discover that one of the lanes had been closed overnight for roadworks, even though, so far as he could see, there was no sign of any activity, and it was his only chance to pass anything before he reached the notorious bottleneck near the oddly named village of Indian Queens. Even as he decided to take a chance, another car appeared out of nowhere and overtook both him and the lorry. Presuming that the roadworks either hadn't started or were over, Latymer followed suit. He caught up with the vehicle, thinking at first that it might be an unmarked police car, but it soon became clear, as he came up close behind, that it was a boy racer in a souped-up Ford Escort. All three cars, having passed all the lorries, were nearly at the end of the supposed roadworks, with the bottleneck coming up, which would delay the lorries further and would also have delayed Latymer had he not taken a chance.

The clock on the dashboard said half past two. He drove as fast as he dared, aware of how tired he was. The mist was now so thick he could hardly make out the car in front. He passed a signpost pointing to Blisland and St Breward and saw, dimly, that the driver was turning off. Only as he passed the turning did he realize that the car which had overtaken him, driven he imagined by a local lad who knew the road, must also have overtaken the BMW in the mist, that it was the BMW that had left the road and that he was now stuck on the dual carriageway with no way of getting off for several miles. He looked behind. It didn't look as if the lorries had yet caught up with him. He screeched to a halt at the first piece of flat ground to his left, reversed into it and started back along the dual carriageway the wrong way. As he reached the turn-off, he saw the lights of one of the lorries coming towards him through the mist, its horn blaring, and pulled off just in time, bathed in a cold sweat.

There was no sign of the BMW. He began to wonder if the chase was worth it, if it had been such a good idea after all. He drove on more slowly now, trying to remember from the map if he was likely to hit a road which would take him to St Mellick. Whether he did or not, if he didn't have any luck soon, then he'd stop, call Berry, and explain what had happened and where he was. The police could take over, as he should have let them do from the first. He drove on for another three or four miles. By now the mist was, if it was possible, even thicker. Suddenly his lights picked up the brake lights of a vehicle and he saw, immediately ahead of him and a few yards to his right, the BMW, parked across an entrance to a gated track. He stopped and went over to investigate. Tyre marks showed that the driver had braked sharply before coming off the road. There was no one in the car, which was unlocked. The gate to the track was swinging open, its hinges making an unpleasant creaking sound reminiscent of the noise made by gibbets. Then, for a brief instant, the mist cleared and, some distance away along the track, he could see a bobbing torch. He parked behind the BMW, blocking it in, and called Berry, only to get a recorded voice asking him to leave a message. He had no alternative but to do so, since he couldn't remember Bailey's number. Doggedly determined, he set off along the track in pursuit.

It was a few minutes before it was noticed that both Latymer and the masked man were missing, as Bailey had other things on his mind. He knelt beside the body, turned it on its back and felt for a pulse. There was barely a flicker. 'Get an ambulance immediately,' he ordered, 'he's just about gone.' He pulled the gag out of the man's mouth and motioned to a police officer to cut the bonds. He looked over to where Berry was standing. 'Come here, will you?' Then, suddenly aware that Latymer must have followed the masked man through the hatchway, he yelled, 'And get out there after that mad idiot in the mask, and see where the hell Latymer's got to.' Then he turned back to Berry. 'Is this Matthew Turner?'

Berry had no idea. 'I'm sorry, I don't know, I never met him. You'd better ask Smeaton.'

'Bring him over,' ordered Bailey. Smeaton, nursing a split lip following the struggle over Davenport's minder, was obviously in no mood to be cooperative. Bailey looked at him with distaste. 'Is this man Matthew Turner?'

Smeaton shrugged. 'Who?'

'Don't play around. You know very well who. Is this Matthew Turner? The curator of Lanwithen Museum.'

'I've nothing to say.'

At this point one of the police officers returned. 'There's no sign of either of them, sir,' he reported. 'It's difficult to see much, though, there's a thick mist out there now.'

Bailey looked at Berry. 'I hope to God your friend hasn't done something stupid. If he has, the fact that he's an ex-copper won't be of any help when I get hold of him.' He turned to his driver. 'Get on to HQ, tell them we're after a highly dangerous man and that we'll need roadblocks on both the A30 and the A390. He's bound to be getting the hell out of Cornwall.'

They heard a vehicle draw up outside, then the sound of feet on the path, along with the rumble of a trolley, and a few minutes later two paramedics appeared in the doorway and carefully manoeuvred the trolley inside. 'Good grief!' exclaimed one, looking round. 'What kind of place is this? It's like Dracula's castle. Where's our man?'

'Down here.'

The paramedic knelt down beside Turner and also felt for a pulse. He straightened up and pulled a face. 'Doesn't look too good.' His partner produced a lamp and shone it down as the first man made a brief examination. 'The obvious injuries look fairly superficial but I'd say there's something badly wrong internally, not to mention that he's also very cold. How long do you reckon he's been out here?'

'We're not sure,' Bailey told him. 'Possibly two or three days.'

'Right, we'll get him into A & E in Truro as quick as we can.' Between them they lifted Turner on to the trolley and then wheeled him away and out of the church, the first paramedic talking to the hospital on his phone as they went. Then the door slammed and the siren wailed as the ambulance raced away.

Throughout, no one had been taking any notice of Davenport. Now he tried to attract Bailey's attention. 'What's your problem?' enquired the DI.

'My banker's draft. He's taken it. That thing in the gold mask's taken it.'

'Then we must hope we can get it back,' snapped Bailey. 'But when we do, we'll have to hold on to it as evidence.'

He then formally arrested Smeaton, cautioned him and ordered him to be taken off to the nearest police station in Camborne to be charged. He then ordered one of the police officers to remain in the church, which had now become a crime scene, until the scenes of crime officers could be called in. In the meantime, he and his driver would follow the van taking Smeaton to Camborne. 'Do you think your friend Latymer had gone chasing off after our masked play actor?' he asked Berry. 'If so, he's no right to have done so. He could find himself in serious trouble. If there was no sign of him, then he should have come back here straight away and left it to us,' a sentiment with which Berry was forced to agree.

They reached the church gate together as Berry looked across the road at where they'd left the car. 'I don't know what the hell he's doing or where he's gone. But, wherever it is, he's taken the bloody car!'

Seventeen

Latymer had been on Bodmin Moor for what seemed liked hours, he'd lost all track of time. At first, as the mist came and went, he'd just about been able to follow the tiny point of torchlight ahead of him, but then it had come down so heavily that he was no longer able to see it and so had nothing to guide him. He had no idea where he was. As for his quarry, it was quite possible that he had a very good idea where he was making for and was confident enough to leave his car by the roadside to confuse any possible pursuers. Latymer doubted if it would be much help to the police, as it was unlikely it was registered in his own name. Unless he was picked up quickly, then he'd every chance of getting clean away: a lift or taxi to a railway station, a train to Bristol, a flight out of Bristol to wherever. He was almost certain to have thought it all through and would have already taken the precaution of obtaining a false passport. Davenport's banker's draft would ensure he had no money worries. I must try Keith's mobile again, he thought, and did so, but whether it was because his own was still insufficiently charged up, or there was no signal within reach, he was unable to get through.

As he struggled on through the coarse, uneven grass and dying bracken, blundering from time to time into unpleasantly prickly clumps of gorse, he recalled having heard how people caught out in unknown territory in fog or heavy mist can become so disorientated that they can no longer tell whether they are walking uphill or down and often discover, when it finally clears, that they've actually been going round and round in circles. The mist was not only cold and clammy but also wet enough to soak into his clothing. He cursed his own stupidity in setting off at night across rough country, notorious for its sudden mists and sea fogs, without a torch, map, or a compass. There were no stars to help him, no horizon to give him a sense of direction, no visible landmark.

It occurred to him to wonder if there were old mine work-ings on the moor. Or other hazards. Keith had told him once, when showing him a first edition of *Jamaica Inn*, that he'd read somewhere that Daphne du Maurier had first come across the inn by chance when she and a friend had become hope-lessly lost for hours in a fog on Bodmin Moor, and that, when they had just about given up hope, they saw faint lights ahead of them shining through the mist, and were taken in for the night. The rider to that was that it was only when daylight came that she realized that, just before they'd reached safety, they'd almost walked over the edge of a small quarry.

Then there were the stories about bogs, all sorts of stories about bogs. He remembered the description of the deeply unpleasant death of the villain, Carver Doone, in Blackmore's novel, *Lorna Doone*, and the way the hero had seen him slowly sink into a treacherous bog and drown. Also how, one night in the pub, Harry, in full narrative mode, had told him a story he'd heard from his grandfather, who'd farmed on Dartmoor, about how, after a snowy and wet winter and when the bogs had finally begun to dry out, a man walking on the moor with his gun and his dog had suddenly come across the spectacle of the head and hands of a dead man rising up out of the mud. 'They never did find out who it was,' Harry had concluded, with relish. 'They buried him in the local graveyard with a headstone saying "In memory of the Unknown Hiker".'

Latymer had found a certain amount of black humour in the tale at the time, but now it no longer seemed very funny. He must pull himself together. Carver Doone was a fictional character in a novel, his fate a mere figment of the writer's romantic imagination. As for the unknown hiker, that might or might not be true: Harry never let the truth stand in the way of a good story. Anyway, that was Dartmoor, four times the size of Bodmin Moor and far more hazardous. At least he hoped it was far more hazardous. He trudged on until he stubbed his foot on the side of a piece of rock and almost tripped. He realized how out of condition he was and sat down on it in an attempt to get his breath back and rest his aching legs. If only the mist would clear.

He pulled his jacket more tightly round himself. What the hell am I doing here? he asked himself. Why on earth have I taken it upon myself to pursue this particular villain instead of leaving it to the police? What would I have felt if the roles had been reversed and I'd been in Bailey's position? Probably furious, outraged even. So, what was so different about this one compared with the other two investigations in which he and Berry had become involved? He mulled it over in his mind. In the first of them he'd been caught up in the affairs of two very different people, a young woman whose man was missing in suspicious circumstances, and Fiona's terminally ill husband, determined justice should be done before his death. In the second, he'd become intrigued, as had many other police officers both past and present, by a sixty-year-old unsolved murder, coupled with sympathy for the unfortunate young man who had been involved in a present-day replica of it. In both cases he'd been able to stand outside it.

But this was different, and now, as he sat and shivered on his rock, he realized why. This time it was personal. There was no bereaved young woman or wrongly suspected student involved in this case, and it had all started at the very time when he'd been forced to take stock of his life while he was off with flu. He had, he hoped, been a good policeman even if Mike Evans had gone somewhat over the top in describing him as 'one of the best', and he still felt his reasons for leaving the force were sound. So, he'd moved on and at first been quite happy to act as a courier for Becketts Literary Tours, but then that had seemed pretty tame after his first freelance case. Now he was enjoying working with Keith and Kate and learning the book trade, but what if that didn't work out either? He didn't even like to contemplate it.

But what had really galled him was the growing realization that whoever was behind this whole affair saw himself as some kind of puppet master capable of making anyone dance to his tune. He now recognized that, right from the start, he'd been made use of, set up to play a part in the man's scheme. The arrogant bastard had seen Keith and himself as nothing more than a pair of ex-plods who now had nothing better to do with their time than sell second-hand books. He must have found them a joke, enjoying the role he'd invented for himself. Looking back on the events of the last few weeks, Latymer was furious with himself for not having seen it earlier.

What had driven the man to become so obsessed with collecting precious objects, so consumed with lust to possess things he could never show to anyone or tell them about, that he would stop at nothing to obtain them? Neither of his two murdered victims, the drug dealer found dead on the beach or the unpleasant Brian Simmons, were particularly sympathetic characters, but they hardly deserved to die in their murderer's desperate drive to obtain ever rarer items to add to his collection. Let alone poor Matthew Turner, whose relatively minor deception had provoked so much trouble and might well have cost him his life.

This wouldn't do, he'd end up getting pneumonia if he sat around much longer. He got to his feet and looked ahead, or at least as far ahead of him as he could see, which was only yards. What had started out as a track was now little more than the remnants of a path, not even that in many places. Still with no sign of the mist lifting, he set out along what he thought was the path. As he walked, thoughts continued to go round and round in his head. He tried to get to grips with what might have happened. Had Simmons somehow managed to steal the objects and, after being warned by Turner of the trouble he'd be in if he tried to sell them, had at first gone along with the television idea but then changed his mind and tried to sell them, unaware of what a risk he was taking, to the very person who'd been their original 'owner'? Or had they truly been hidden in the ground somewhere, where he'd genuinely come across them while metal detecting and had then tried to sell them to the highest bidder? Either way, the collector must have thought he could see a way of acquiring them without it either costing him anything or risking future blackmail. It must have seemed so easy to arrange a meeting at Keeper's Tump (suiting his taste for the dramatic), safely dispose of Simmons inside the burial mound, then hide the items under the floor of a semi-derelict woodshed belonging to a rarely used holiday cottage while he decided what to do next.

But what had thrown his carefully laid plans into disarray was something that he could not possibly have foreseen: Turner's determination to put himself and his museum on the map by persuading a television company not only to come down and make a programme but to make one about Keeper's Tump. It must have given both him and Smeaton a nasty shock. He wondered what his relation with Smeaton was. Minder? Business partner? The other sort of partner? Perhaps all three. He stomped on. Surely, when daylight came, the mist would lift?

Berry'd had ample time to consider what the hell his friend was playing at. He could understand John rushing off in an attempt to prevent the suspect from getting away, but when he'd realized what had happened, why didn't he then come straight back and alert the police? Why go it alone? Without a car and with no way of getting back to St Mellick without a lift from the police, he was still sitting in Camborne police station while the formalities were gone through regarding the arrest of Smeaton and arrangements were made for the SOCOs to get down to St Day first thing in the morning. It had already been a long wait. According to the clock on the wall it was now nearly three o'clock and he was still tired from the previous day. Suddenly he remembered that he'd switched his phone off while they were waiting outside the church. He checked it now and found Latymer's message, then stopped the next officer he saw and told him he had to speak to DI Bailey about a message that had been left on his phone.

A few minutes later, Bailey appeared looking tired. 'Sorry it's taken so long, but we'll have a lift for you any time now.'

'It's not that,' Berry told him. 'There's a message here from John. I don't know what time he sent it but he says that he followed a BMW out of St Day, assuming it was our man, though he couldn't be sure. He kept behind it as well as he could on the main road, was hampered by mist and overnight lorries, but then, he says, it turned off in the direction of . . . Blisland, is it? So, he followed it and later found it abandoned by the road side.' He swallowed. 'You're not going to like this. Apparently he's left his car in front of it, blocking it in, and has set off across the moor in pursuit of the driver.'

'Has he gone off his head?' demanded Bailey. 'I'll get someone down there from Bodmin straight away and, the minute I've finished here, I'll go back myself, then my driver can give you a lift home.'

Finally, after more delay, they set off for Bodmin. Shortly after they left, Bailey took a call from a police officer who had found both cars. 'Have you checked out the ownership of the BMW?' he enquired.

The policeman affirmed that he had. 'But it's not very informative. It's a company car registered as belonging to an outfit called the Seekers Consultancy, with an address in west London. I'm still examining it, but there doesn't seem to be anything in it except for the owner's manual. Nothing in the boot either.'

'Don't look any further then,' said Bailey. At least we might be able to get some decent fingerprints.'

'If I could be dropped off at John's car, now you've checked out the other one,' suggested Berry. 'I've got a second set of keys and I could then take myself home. Actually, it seems sensible to take it back to St Mellick. Presumably John will be in touch again.'

'If he is, then tell him I won't brook any more freelance interference and that I shall need to see him later.' Bailey frowned. 'I wonder if our man realized that we might set up road blocks on the main road and that's why he came off. Hell's teeth, I can see him getting away if we're not careful. He must have a number of options and the mist doesn't help.'

By the time Berry parked the car outside the cottage, he was too tired even to think. There was no further message from John, nor was he answering his phone. Well, there was nothing he could do about it. The police knew he was out there on the moor somewhere and presumably, if there was still no sign of him once it was light, they'd start looking for him. Suppose John had managed to catch up with his man, what then? In normal circumstances he was quite capable of looking after himself, but this was a man who'd already killed twice and had nothing to lose. Perhaps even now he was lurking somewhere, ready to stab him as he had the drug dealer and Simmons. It was touch and go too whether Turner survived. There'd been no more news from the hospital except, according to Bailey, to say that Turner was in a critical condition and was undergoing surgery to remove a badly damaged spleen. On the whole though, thought Berry, he'd put that one down to Smeaton's treatment, rather than a knife in the dark. He made himself some tea then went to bed. He'd think about it all in the morning.

Then, quite suddenly, as quickly as it had come down, the mist began to lift, revealing a watery dawn. Latymer looked around him. There was no sign of his quarry, which was hardly surprising. He also realized, only too well, that when he finally did get in touch with Bailey, he was going to have a lot of explaining to do. The all-consuming rage of the night had passed, leaving him feeling flat and exhausted. The light was now becoming stronger by the minute; it looked as if it was going to be a nice day. Obviously the sensible thing to do was to try and find a road, any road, which would at the very least lead him to a house or farm, if not a village. But in what direction? He wished he'd spent more time studying his maps.

There were a number of hills and ridges, one which he thought might be that known as Kilmar, but even if it was, he couldn't place it in the context of anything else. Well, at least he should now be able to avoid any bogs or quarries. There was still some kind of a broken path ahead of him and he continued on along it. The mist had led him into a world of total silence, blanking out all normal sounds. He'd even been able to hear his own breathing. Now, with the rising sun, he became aware of bird noise, of larks rising into the sky, of a flock of lapwings weaving their extraordinary dance high above him. The best of the heather was over, but there was a good deal still in bloom, as was the gorse, both of which gave off their pungent scents as ground was warmed by the rising sun. If he hadn't been so tired and had known where he was going, it would have been a good day for a walk on the moors.

He climbed up out of yet another dip and suddenly the landscape took on a look of familiarity. He couldn't actually see a road but he was almost certain that the poles carrying the power supply across the horizon were those he was able to see from the cottage. So, where was he now? He quickened his pace as he realized that it all made sense, that he had been following in his quarry's footsteps after all. Was Berry now back at the cottage? Surely he must be. Would he be at risk? He tried to call him but Berry had switched off his phone.

A quarter of a mile or so on, he knew he was right about where he was. He still couldn't see the cottage, but he knew now that it wasn't far away. Then it finally struck him. He was actually on the path which approached Keeper's Tump from the opposite direction to the road and the cottage. He rounded a corner and suddenly the mound was there in front of him. The crows rose at his approach. He could see at once that the entrance to the burial chamber had been disturbed, since, after the police had finished their investigations, they'd roughly filled it in again until it could be dealt with properly. The crows took up position on the wall beside the path, as if waiting for something. The first thing he saw was a torch, which appeared to have been dropped in haste, lying just inside the entrance to the tomb. He picked it up, switched it on and went into the burial chamber proper. Crouched in a corner, the gold cup clasped to his chest, was Jack Maynard. He was quite dead and the look on his face was one of mortal terror.

Berry was woken by Latymer, calling up to him from below. He struggled awake and saw it was nearly nine o'clock. 'Where the hell have you been?' he demanded. 'What were you playing at? Bailey's fit to be tied and I can't blame him.'

'Well, I hope I'll be able to deflect the worst of his wrath,' Latymer assured him. 'The hunt's over.' He yawned and told Berry what he'd found. 'God, I need a bath, a change of clothes and something to eat and drink.'

Berry looked shaken. 'Shouldn't you get on to Bailey straight away? It's the least you can do in the circumstances.'

'It'll wait until I've had a quick bath and got into some dry clothes. Our man's not going anywhere.'

Ten minutes later they called Bodmin police station and told them the news. 'We'll be waiting outside the burial mound until you get someone here,' said Latymer. 'I imagine you'll have to alert everyone likely to be concerned, it looks as if it'll be a repeat of last time.'

'Don't you think you should have made absolutely sure you weren't mistaken before telling the police?' protested Berry, as they set off up the path. 'You said there were no obvious injuries, suppose you just thought he was dead and he's only passed out. You can't risk bringing Bailey here on a wild goose chase. Suppose we find that he's legged it after all,' he continued as they reached the mound.

'See for yourself. It's not likely to do any harm now if I show you.' Latymer went ahead and shone the torch inside. Maynard's body was still exactly as he'd left it.

'Good God!' exclaimed Berry in horror, rooted to the spot at the entrance to the burial chamber. 'What's made him look like that? What do you think he could have died of?'

'Obviously I didn't take a proper look, as you've just reminded me. I merely tried to see if there was any pulse.' He looked at the contorted face. 'Perhaps my night alone on Bodmin Moor in the fog has made me fanciful, but I'd say he died of fright!'

There was a strange kind of déjà vu about what happened next. First, Sergeant Johns and a constable arrived to see that another body, confirmed by both Berry and Latymer to be that of a Jack Maynard, had been found inside Keeper's Tump. 'He's still clutching the missing gold cup,' Johns informed Bailey. 'And no, there's no obvious cause of death that I can see.'

Bailey arrived himself some twenty minutes later, bringing with him another officer and the police doctor, to whom he'd given a lift up from the road. The doctor made a brief examination and confirmed death. He also tried, unsuccessfully, to release Maynard's hands from the cup.

'How long do you reckon?' enquired Bailey.

'Not all that long. I'd say he'd been dead about five hours or so. No obvious cause that I can see. Though the way he's

190

clutching on to that gold beaker, or whatever it is, suggests a massive and sudden heart attack.'

Bailey thanked him. 'In view of everything else that's gone on here, I'm going to have to call in a pathologist. The SOCOs should be here any time now.' He turned to Johns. 'The church in St Day will have to wait, this is somewhat more pressing. Do you want a lift back to your car?' The police doctor declined the offer and set off back along the track on foot. Finally Bailey turned to Latymer. 'You've got some explaining to do, Mr Latymer. You're lucky it looks like he's had a heart attack, or you might well have found yourself arrested on suspicion of murder. After all, we only have your word for it that you didn't catch up with him on the moor.'

'I've no excuse for my behaviour,' Latymer apologized, 'except rage at the way he's been duping us, though I fully realize that's not good enough. I'm not sure what got into me, except a determination that he shouldn't get away with it. Which is why I chased after him across the moors.'

'You were lucky you didn't end up in serious trouble out there,' commented Bailey. 'So, what happened next?'

'After stumbling around in the fog for ages, I had a rest. I think I must have sat there for some time before setting off again along what looked like some kind of path. Finally, thank God, the mist began to clear and the sun came up and a little while later I realized where I was. I recognized the power lines.' He pointed past the mound to the moorland beyond. 'I was about ten minutes walk away, up there. When I got to the burial mound, I could see that the entrance had been disturbed again and saw the torch lying on the ground. So, I shone it inside and there was the body. Then I made my way back to the cottage and rang Bodmin to say what had happened.'

'What time did you reach the mound?'

'I think it must have been just after nine o'clock, I'm not exactly sure. When I first saw Maynard, I wasn't certain he was dead, so I went in to see if I could feel a pulse, because, if he wasn't, then we'd need to send for an ambulance.'

Bailey shook his head. 'It still doesn't excuse what you did, though I admit that you've been right most of the time, from the place for the handover to the identity of the suspect. Well,

that's all for now. I'll talk to you both later.' He turned away.
Will you call the Royal Cornwall, Johns, and see if there's
any news on Turner?' From the road came the steady tramp
of feet. Bailey looked pleased. 'Right, we're getting somewhere. Here are the SOCOs.'

Eighteen

Over a month had passed and Latymer was back in Cornwall once again, this time to attend the inquest on Brian Simmons. Though it would now be little more than a formality, both he and Keith thought it would be interesting to see what might come out of it in view of what had come after. They'd already been informed that the inquest on Jack Maynard, at which they were both expected to give evidence, would take place as soon as the police had finished their final investigations.

Latymer had spent the previous night in Penzance, as Kate Berry had asked him if he could bring some fresh fish back with him. 'I'm told that if you go down to Newlyn, they'll pack it in a special bag or box,' she assured him, 'so your car won't smell of fish!' He'd been quite happy to agree, not least because nothing would have induced him to spend another night anywhere near St Mellick. Newlyn . . . His first visit to Newlyn had proved to be the start of his new career in private investigation, with the chance witnessing of a fight between two fishermen outside a pub and the subsequent discovery of an unidentified young man found floating outside the harbour a few days later. 'You'll be able to share it with us,' Kate had assured him, when he'd enquired what sort of fish she wanted him to buy. 'See what the best bargains are. It's bound to be good when it's so nice and fresh.'

So, he'd breakfasted early, gone down to the port and done as she asked, and a selection of fresh fish was now packed away in ice in a box in the boot of his car. The cheery lady who had advised him what to buy had assured him that they'd be fine in there until the evening. After the melodrama of the old church in St Day and his night in the mist on Bodmin

Moor, not to mention the sight of the body crouched in Keeper's Tump, Cornwall had decided once again to show him its other face. The weather was mild for November, the sun was shining, the sky cloudless and the sea an almost cobalt blue. Across the bay, light glanced off the windows of the houses close to the shore, and, from where he stood on the quay, he could pick out almost every detail of the castle on St Michael's Mount. Which, then, was the real Cornwall? The mere thought of Maynard's coy phrase made him shudder. Was it industrial wasteland around St Day? The barrows and standing stones of Bodmin Moor? Or the picture-postcard scene in front of him? Perhaps all three. Cornwall is a fickle, if not treacherous, county.

He entered the court in Truro just before ten o'clock and noted the presence of both Bailey and Anderson, the latter having presumably come down from Milton Keynes for the occasion. He reckoned ruefully that whatever the two detective inspectors might feel about each other, they'd be at one in condemning him. Also present were Pete and Dave from Crayford Productions, Sergeant Johns (now in plain clothes), with whom he'd kept in touch, and Mike Evans, whom he'd arranged to meet afterwards for lunch. The coroner reopened the adjourned inquest and heard first from Detective Inspector Anderson, who described his own part in the investigation into the murder of the person now identified as Brian Simmons of St Erth. He was followed by Peter Crayford and David Evans of Crayford productions, who described how they had discovered the body in the course of making a television programme, after which Dr Michael Evans gave further details of the injuries sustained by Simmons and confirmed the cause of death. Detective Inspector Bailey then took the stand and explained how he had taken over the investigation from Detective Inspector Anderson.

The coroner listened attentively. 'I understand that investigations are still proceeding,' he asserted, when Bailey had reached the end of what he had to say. Bailey confirmed that they were, and that he would be able to put further information before him at the forthcoming inquest on Jack Maynard, who, he reminded the coroner, had also been found dead in

194

the burial chamber of Keeper's Tump. The coroner nodded. 'And foul play is not suspected in that instance?' Bailey acknowledged that to be the case and trusted that the police would be able to clear up all outstanding matters very shortly. After a brief pause to consult his notes, the coroner returned a verdict of unlawful killing and that, for the time being, was that.

As Latymer came out of the court, he heard someone call out his name. He turned round and saw that it was Peter Crayford. He was obviously in good humour. 'Good to see you again, John.' He smiled broadly. 'Here, rumour has it that you helped catch the murderer. Is it true that he was found dead inside Keeper's whatsit, clutching a golden cup? And that he'd been frightened to death? There was a story in the *Mirror* that people round there in St Mellick were saying he'd brought the Curse of the Keeper down on himself.'

'You shouldn't believe all you read,' commented Latymer, 'but yes, a man called Jack Maynard was found dead inside the burial chamber and everything seems to point to his being Simmons' murderer. But, as to my "catching" him, I'd hardly put it quite like that though I hope both Keith and I were able to help. Anyway, what about you? How's it all going at Crayford Productions?'

A look of satisfaction crossed Pete Crayford's face. 'Well, actually we're very busy. Of course, all this business was an absolute nightmare, we very nearly went bust, but then Dave had this really brilliant new idea. We've got the funding and we'll be starting work on a series of six programmes for Channel Five in the New Year. We're beavering away on the research right now.'

'It's to be hoped you don't come across another body in your next archaeological site, then,' joked Latymer.

'Oh, we're not doing any more archaeology. We've scrapped all that. I mean, everyone's on to it now, aren't they? It's so . . . so *yesterday*. No, this is different. The provisional working title for the series is "Weird and Horrid Murders". I suppose this business here could make one of them, but I have to say that, after what happened last time, I wouldn't like to risk filming there again, however good the story. Anyway, there's plenty more elsewhere, enough for a second series if this one works out, which we're sure it will. People never tire of murder, do they? In fact, I was going to track you down, we're thinking of doing one on the Meon Hill murder, which took place near Stratford-upon-Avon. You know, the one back in 1945 they still call "the witchcraft murder". Someone told us you knew all about it.'

Oh no, thought Latymer, definitely not. 'I think they must have mixed me up with someone else, then,' he lied. 'But, as you must already know, it's a famous case which was never solved. I'm sure you'll easily be able to find all the information you want.' He saw Mike Evans waving to him. 'Sorry, but I have to go. I'm having lunch with Mike then heading back to Bristol. Best of luck. I look forward to seeing the programmes.'

As he crossed the forecourt to meet his friend, he was intercepted by Bailey. 'We'll have an inquest date for Maynard any time now,' he told Latymer, 'and as soon as we do I'll be in touch. The evidence from yourself and Keith Berry will be very useful.' His eyes met Latymer's. 'The least said, the better, I think, about your night on the moors.'

Latymer took the hint. 'I understand Maynard had been involved in the black antiquities market for a long time.'

'The Art and Antiques Unit have traced his activities back almost twenty years. It seems it all began respectably enough. He was a successful interior designer, often called in on a consultancy basis, and, very often, a client, or clients, would ask him if he could find them a suitable piece of antique furniture, a piece of china, or even a picture to complete their decor; which is how he first became involved in the legitimate antiques market. He started travelling abroad, looking for specific pieces, and it was during that time that he became obsessed with rare antiquities and the desire to collect on his own account.

'When the Met took apart that luxury flat of his, they found a cupboard in the wall, hidden away like a priest's hole, full of artefacts from all over the place. Apparently he was negotiating to buy stuff looted in Baghdad, which is why he decided to sell on the torque, which, by the by, is now safely back in

Ireland. You'll be interested to know that they also found a very carefully cleaned seventeenth-century Spanish stiletto, almost certainly the murder weapon used both in the case of Simmons and in the earlier murder of a drugs dealer.'

'What about Smeaton?' enquired Latymer. 'What was his role in the set-up?'

'Partner in the business, minder, negotiator when necessary. Possibly something more intimate, but, if he was Maynard's lover, he's not saying. Once he was told Maynard was dead, he realized he might as well assist us in the hope that it might be taken into account when he comes to his trial. That's not for me to decide, but I imagine they'll throw the book at him. The least serious charge he's facing is handling stolen goods, which, as you know, usually carries a hefty penalty, not to mention aggravated assault and actual bodily harm.' Bailey looked grim. 'He's lucky he isn't being done for Turner's murder. And finally, he's an accessory to the murder of Brian Simmons.'

Latymer suddenly realized how Matthew Turner, whose initial role in what was to follow had been so crucial, had almost dropped out of the picture. 'How is Turner?'

'Back home up north convalescing. His injuries were pretty severe, you know. Smeaton will deserve all he gets. In the circumstances, I don't imagine the CPS will be pressing any charges under the Treasure Act or anything else.'

'And Dr Davenport?'

'He most definitely will. And serve him right.' Bailey smiled, cheerfully. 'Well, no doubt you want to get on. See you at the inquest.'

'So you really didn't have any idea Maynard was involved in anything dodgy?' enquired Mike Evans as he and Latymer sat down for lunch.

'Absolutely none. Why should we? We knew very little about him except that he ran some kind of a consultancy, which Berry assumed must be to do with interior design after seeing the decor of his London flat.'

'What was he like as a person?'

'I think theatrical camp sums it up best, though perhaps the

197

camp was genuine. But, right from the start, it seemed to me to be more the kind of thing put on by some actors. But he was a good customer and always paid very promptly, which is more than can be said of some.'

'What sort of books did he collect?'

'Gothic novels mainly. First editions of Mrs Radcliffe and *The Mysteries of Udolpho*, M.B. Lewis and *The Monk*, and any others in the genre. He also bought early editions of sensation novels like *Lady Audley's Secret* and was prepared to pay a good price for them too, and he was an addict of M.R. James' *Ghost Stories of an Antiquary*, he had several variorum editions of it. Do you know, Mike, what really got me was the way I was set up, kindly offered the use of what, from his description, was a twee little holiday home in "the real Cornwall" where I could recover from the flu. When, all the time, there was the body of one of his victims only a few yards down the lane in Keeper's Tump, and the very objects for which he was murdered were under the floor in the woodshed. Though I did find it very odd when I got down there and saw the state of the place, given his luxurious tastes. It turns out he only ever stayed there when he was doing deals or needed to be out of the way for a few days. It was merely a bolt hole.'

'Surely he must have realized he was taking a risk in letting you stay there?'

'The only risk was the slim one of my inadvertently finding something had been buried under the floor of the shed, which was unlikely. It was more likely he saw me as an insurance, since it was unlikely anyone would break in while I was staying in the cottage. My being there would give him a couple of weeks in which to do a deal with the torque, knowing that the two artefacts would be perfectly safe.'

'Do you know anything more about how he got hold of them in the first place? Did he buy them? If so, he must have been incredibly wealthy.'

'I think I've more or less pieced it together. This is off the record, unofficial information from the police sergeant closely involved with the case who's now been transferred to CID. Probably the most astonishing part of this whole tale is that Maynard not only discovered the gold cup himself, but he found it at Keeper's Tump. He knew all about the Rillaton Cup and how it was found in a cyst, a small chamber outside the burial chamber proper, and, over time, and very discreetly, he carefully examined the top of the mound. According to my informant, Smeaton told the police that Maynard had a hunch, what he described as "a mystical feeling", that there might be something there, in spite of all the assurances that the tomb must have been robbed in antiquity. Very possibly it was, but the cyst had been overlooked, and there it was with the gold cup inside it. He must have been beside himself.

'Of course he recognized that it was incredibly valuable. Then, at about the same time, he acquired the torque for which he'd been negotiating for some time, and which I'm almost certain must have been brought down to him by the man later found dead on the beach. He should have taken both objects back to London, or even put them under the shed floor there and then, but for some reason he didn't. Possibly he felt that the inquiries with regard to the torque were coming too near to home. It would suit his sense of melodrama to hide both pieces away in the cyst for a few days. Then, out of the blue, along comes Simmons with his metal detector and finds them there. In retrospect it turns out that what he told Turner was the truth.'

'It must have been a bloody awful shock for Maynard when he found they'd gone!'

'Devastating. He would have started putting out feelers straight away, to see if they were already being offered on the black market. Weeks, months passed, as at first Simmons wondered what to do with them, after which he held back for a while at Turner's request. But then he got fed up and let it be known that they were for sale. Maynard must have had a quiet laugh when he got Smeaton to get Simmons all the way up to London to negotiate a deal, only to have him then go all the way back to Cornwall for it to take place. And at Keeper's Tump too. So gothic! Maynard must have already planned what he intended to do next. Simmons was oblivious, of course. According to Smeaton, he'd no idea that the

199

mystery man behind the deal was the same person who'd put the objects there in the first place. While they were waiting for Simmons, he and Smeaton had carefully unblocked the entrance to the burial chamber, ready to receive the body. He claims he wasn't actually present when the murder took place, that he waited in the cottage until Maynard came and asked him for help to block up the entrance again. Then, early the next morning, they covered the entrance up with bracken and gorse, so that a casual onlooker wouldn't notice anything was amiss. If it hadn't been for Turner and Crayford Productions, there's every reason to believe Maynard would have got away with it.

'So, while at first it was very useful to have me in the cottage, once the body had been discovered and the police had moved in, he couldn't wait to get me out. You should have heard him on the phone, squeaking about how frightened he was at the very notion of a body being found near his cottage, while, at the same time, as I see now, he was desperate to know how the investigations were going. I'd just put it down to morbid curiosity. Presumably he sent Smeaton down to see if I'd gone for good, only to discover that I was planning to go back, taking Keith with me. After which, he and Smeaton took more drastic measures, such as one of them ringing Keith, pretending to be a doctor, to say Kate was seriously ill in hospital, on the assumption that would force both of us to return home.'

As they reached the coffee stage, Latymer described the carefully staged handover in the church in St Day, so in keeping with Maynard's love of the dramatic, 'Which, it turned out, he not only already knew about when I told him I'd been there, but he was determined to use it as the setting for what he saw as his crowning achievement. He loved all that stuff in the gold mask, of course.' Finally, Latymer admitted how he'd followed Maynard in his car, then pursued him across Bodmin Moor in the mist.

'You were lucky you didn't come to grief yourself,' commented Evans, drily. 'And that Devon and Cornwall police haven't had you drummed out of the county!'

Latymer agreed. 'I must have been mad. I thought I'd lost

him until I saw that the entrance to the burial chamber had been opened up again, though I didn't actually think I'd find him inside it.' He shuddered at the recollection. 'You must admit it was weird the way he was crouched in the corner like that. And the look on his face! It was as if he'd seen something terrible in there that literally frightened the life out of him. I take it you haven't changed your mind about a heart attack?'

Evans shook his head. 'Definitely not. A massive myocardial infarction. It's not all that surprising. He was in his mid-fifties, he'd been suffering a fair amount of stress for weeks and then found himself being hotly pursued across open country. Your description of his lifestyle doesn't suggest he took much exercise and the post-mortem showed he was already heading for problems. He was the type and age for a heart attack, a coronary or a stroke. I agree he did look as if he'd had a fright, but as to what might have caused it, I wouldn't dream of hazarding a guess.' He paused, then smiled. '"Oh whistle and I'll come to you, my lad", perhaps?'

The two men agreed to keep in touch from now on and Latymer set off back to Bristol. He'd had enough of Bodmin Moor to last a lifetime, he told himself as he passed the turn-off to St Mellick. Yet, in spite of everything that had happened, he was feeling considerably happier. In suspecting Maynard, he had, after all, been ahead of the game. He'd also spent a pleasant few days with Fiona Garleston, both agreeing that the relationship was worth pursuing, and he was looking forward to being in charge of the shop for a few days while Keith and Kate took a few days off before the Christmas rush.

No, all in all, things had worked out pretty well. He drove into Somerset, passing Humphrey the camel and the towering wicker man, on up through the Levels and finally out on to the stretch of road near home, with its view of where the Severn opens up, spanned by its elegant bridges. It was now four o'clock and the sun was already setting. He drove into the city to the shop, parked in his parking space and removed the box of fish from the boot. The Berrys looked up as he came in from the back of the shop. 'It's all over,' he told them. 'And here's your fish. Any chance of some chips to go with it?'